here's what subscribers to the **six o'clock scramble** newsletter have to say about the scramble recipes and weekly menus:

I'll take this opportunity to say THANK YOU for the Scramble. It has truly changed my life. It is so nice to know in my mind and in my pantry what is for dinner for an entire week!!! What a mental relief!!! And the recipes have been great.

—Ruth B., Edmonds, WA

The thing that I like best about the Six O'Clock Scramble is that your recipes rarely use processed ingredients. They aren't the typical "family-friendly" recipes that call for a can of cream of mushroom soup and a hunk of processed cheese! Better yet, my kids love most of the dishes!

—Heather F., Vienna, VA

When I first quit work to stay home with the kids, I loved meal planning and was happy to spend a couple of hours every week looking through cookbooks and recipes and making the menus and grocery lists—but after seven years, it's lost its charm! So your newsletter is a huge time and stress relief for me. The meals you suggest are wonderful! It's still important to me to have good family meals, so each newsletter I receive from you feels like a gift.

—Laurie T., Orinda, CA

Your service has given me back about two hours on a Sunday morning! Thank you!!

—Susan C., Scotch Plains, NJ

You are a big hit in this home! Jane and I are using your plan for our meals, shopping, etc. What a timesaver—and some great recipes! Thanks for being in the right place at the right time!

—Rick S., Edmond, OK

My daughter always asks on the way home from school, "Are we having a Six O'Clock Scramble dinner?" And the other night during dinner my husband said, "That Six O'Clock Scramble is the best thing that ever happened to this family."

—Lanelle W., Annapolis, MD

I am a mother of four kids, ages eight, six, six, and four. In my eleven years of marriage and my almost nine years of being a mother, I have never found anything as helpful with dinner as your Web site and recipe subscription. I cannot thank you enough for the time and effort that you put into the recipes. My husband is so happy with the meals that I prepare, and my kids are loving (almost) everything. I have never been a cook, but now I actually enjoy it and look forward to seeing "what's for dinner" this week.

—Laura Lyn D., Franklin, TN

I'm a recent subscriber, and my family has loved every recipe I've tried from your newsletter. Every night they say the meal we are having is now their favorite. It saves me so much time in planning.

—Sharon T., Oklahoma City, OK

I am so thrilled with your newsletter. By the way, so are my husband and children. You have taken all the predinner work out of it for me so that I can prepare wonderful meals that my family loves. For the first time in twelve years of marriage, my husband said, "*Wow*!!!" He said that since I am making five meals Monday through Friday, he will organize something for dinners on the weekends. I get two days off a week because you have organized my shopping and preparing so well!

—Diane S., Dumfries, VA

You save me time; you save me money; and you make me a better cook.

—Ann D., Cedar Rapids, IA

As the mother of an eight-year-old, a six-year-old, and a three-year-old, the "bewitching hour" has always been exactly that!! Your wonderful recipes have made a *huge* difference in the after-school nightmare. I have also found that I have been saving about $200 a month on groceries!

—Lois B., Springfield, VA

I just wanted to let you know how much I'm enjoying the Scramble—my family is, too! It is expanding the horizons of the world's pickiest eaters; I now think that they actually needed some variety. The first night of my Scramble-hood, I made your black-bean burgers, and my seven-year-old said, "Yum" (a word I have not heard in three years) and ate two without blinking. Thought you'd like to know.

—Elizabeth K., Ann Arbor, MI

I wanted to let you know how much I'm enjoying the Scramble. I am doing Weight Watchers and have found so many of the recipes compatible. I may use low-fat cheese or cut down on the oil, but they still come out great.

—Kathy A., Framingham, MA

I still can't believe the amount of stress and distraction that you have removed from my life! I look forward to Wednesday mornings like Christmas. My grocery bill has dropped considerably, and so have the number of trips to the grocery store. My whole family looks forward to dinner.

—Julia B., Cornwall, VT

Your menus have done something wonderful for my family, namely, significantly reduced our dependance on fast-foods.

—Mike R., Albuquerque, New Mexico

My kids look forward to Wednesdays when we get the new menu. I *love* the Scramble!!! It used to take so much time for me to research, plan, make my list, etc. You've simplified our lives and given us the gift of healthy recipes!

—Renee T., Tacoma, WA

Cooking used to be a huge chore. I always dreaded coming up with ideas for dinner and planning out the grocery list. Now I look forward to seeing what you've planned for dinner! For me, it's like opening a menu at a great restaurant and seeing all the tasty things to choose from—and the best part is we get to have them all!

—Susan J., Charlotte, NC

the six o'clock
scramble

also by aviva goldfarb

Peanut Butter and Couscous, Too

(with Lisa Flaxman)

the six o'clock scramble

quick, healthy, and delicious
dinner recipes for busy families

aviva goldfarb

St. Martin's Griffin ❧ New York

www.stmartins.com

Book designed by rlf design

Library of Congress Cataloging-in-Publication Data

Goldfarb, Aviva.
    The six o'clock scramble : quick, healthy and delicious dinner recipes for busy families / Aviva Goldfarb.—1st St. Martin's Griffin ed.
        p.   cm.
    ISBN 0-312-33642-X
    EAN 978-0-312-33642-4
    1. Quick and easy cookery.   2. Dinners and dining.   I. Title.

TX833.5.G67   2006
641.5'55—dc22   2005044674

First Edition: April 2006

10 9 8 7 6 5 4 3 2 1

For Andrew—YTLP
I love you and your appetite

And for our mothers, who cooked for us
And our children, who eat with us

contents

acknowledgments

Many friends and relatives contributed time and recipes to this cookbook, and to them I am deeply indebted. Thank you, first, to my loving, patient, and supportive family: super-tasters Andrew, Solomon, and Celia Goldfarb; my mom, Evely Laser Shlensky, who ensured that our family sat down to a wonderful meal each evening, and my dad, Ronald Shlensky, who kept the dinner-table discussions lively; my sister and brother, Sheba Lux and Lincoln Shlensky, for their moral support and recipes; and my wonderful in-laws, Barbara and Mark Goldfarb and Soozy Miller, for introducing me to so many of their family recipes and helping me test and critique new ones (and thank you, Big Guy, for riding the city bus with Sally R. last winter!). Very special thanks also to my recipe collaborator and cooking muse, Lisa Flaxman, editors extraordinaire Kathryn Spindel and Ruth Robbins, cooking guru Sherry Ettleson, marketing whiz Stephanie Lowet, publicity powerhouse Susan Oliver, dear friends and advisors Jessica Honigberg, Sharon Masling, Nachama Wilker, Jackie Cohen, Kim Tilley, Virginia Maycock, Melissa Murdoch, Robin Thieme, and Christina McHenry, Scramble designers Kieran Daly, Wendy Breakstone, Michael Bleed, and Glenn Hughes, and nutritional consultants Lee Unangst and Susan Mayer and administrative assistant Jeannie Antonetti. My deepest gratitude goes to my St. Martin's editor, Elizabeth Beier, for her contagious energy and sage advice, and Michael Connor for his kindly guidance.

Thank you to the recipe contributors and testers: Claudia Ades, Pearl Barnett, Marta Beresin and Bill Scher, Debbie Boltman, Vicki Botnick, Rhonda Brunnell, Sue Brodsky Burnett, Annie Canby, Elizabeth Cullen, Jolynn Childers Dellinger, Jennifer Doig, Kristen Donoghue, Sara Emley, Debbie Firestone, Cori Flam and Brad Meltzer, Cindy Flaxman, Rhoda Flaxman, Deborah Ford, Jennifer Gross, Leesa Hill, Chris Hoge, Jennifer Jelkin, Gina Jermakowicz, Adina Kanefield, Gina Kaufman, Carolyn Korman, Janet Krolman, Celia Laser, Rachel Laser, Amy Leahy, Debbie Lehrich, Rachel Link, Tamara Lyn, Hilary Lyons, Ruth Marcus, Caryn Martel, Maggie Martin, Margaret Mattocks, Monica Medina, Mary Mitchell, Lizbeth Moses, Sena Murphy, Karen Murray, Lisa Newman, Judith Prebyl, Kelly O'Rourke, Katie Rapp, Diane Ray, Christine Richards, Molly Rubel, Shelley Schonberger, Esther Schrader, Kathryn Schwartz, Karen Shapiro, Evan, Heller An and Miriam Shapiro, Annette Sherman, Jennifer Brown Simon, Linda Singer, Mark Spindel, Nancy Stansbury, Deb Stencel, Vicki Taylor, Kirsten Thistle, Elizabeth Trevor, Robin Wainwright, Judy Warner, David Yang, and Elizabeth Zehner.

Thank you also to the thousands of Six O'Clock Scramble newsletter subscribers for their encouragement, suggestions, and feedback.

A portion of the proceeds from this cookbook and the online newsletter supports the work of the Environmental Working Group and Share Our Strength. I am also grateful to Environmental Defense for the important work they do to keep our sources of food safe and to educate consumers about safe and earth-friendly foods.

the six o'clock scramble

the six o'clock scramble

making it easy to get dinner on the table each night

It's six o'clock in the evening. You have been on the go since dawn. The kids are getting hungry and restless. You want to get a nutritious meal on the table for everyone—fast! So you open the cupboard or refrigerator, hoping for inspiration, and . . . nothing.

A family meal is important to you. You care about nutrition, and you never pictured yourself as the kind of mom or dad who would feed your family something out of a bag, a box, or a can every night. You only have about half an hour until meltdowns begin—for either you or the kids!

How do you feed your family a healthy evening meal they will all enjoy? And how do you do it without having the luxury of being able to spend hours in the kitchen or hire a personal chef?

The Six O'Clock Scramble is my answer to those questions.

Here is the basic plan:

1. The Scramble gives you five quick, healthy, and delicious recipes, including side dish suggestions for each weekday.

2. You shop once a week for ingredients— with the aid of the Scramble's balanced weekly recipes and online grocery lists.

3. With recipes that take thirty minutes or less to prepare, the Scramble promises easy family meals that appeal to both grown-ups and kids.

The Six O'Clock Scramble gives busy cooks a weekly plan to follow. There is no need to think too much at the hectic dinner hour about what to prepare—the menu is ready for you. What's more, there are nutritional analyses for every recipe, so you can tailor the recipes to your nutritional needs.

For each week's menu, there is also a grocery list online to save you even more time. To print out the matching weekly grocery lists for each of the weekly menus in the Six O'Clock Scramble cookbook, visit the Six O'Clock Scramble Web site, www.thescramble.com/cookbook.

Scattered throughout the book are useful tips and suggestions for making dinnertime easier, plus guides to healthy snacks and lunches for your kids.

This cookbook grew out of my online weekly recipe newsletter by the same name. Many thousands of families across the country and worldwide have discovered how much easier weeknight dinners can be if they let someone else plan simple meals for them.

This cookbook is filled with the best recipes from the Six O'Clock Scramble online newsletter, including many subscriber favorites. The menus loosely follow the seasons of the year and the events that shape the year for busy families, such as the beginning of the school year, important holidays, and summer vacation.

All along my favorite recipe testers and cooking assistants have been my husband, Andrew, and our two children, Solomon and Celia. Thousands of subscribers have also given me valuable feedback to improve each family-tested recipe, and many have sent me their favorite recipes to test and include.

These recipes—and the advice and hints sprinkled throughout the book—are tried and true with everyone's families in mind . . . and the loving cooks who want to turn the Six O'Clock Scramble into a successful, even relaxing, time that can bring their family together for a wonderful dinner.

the well-stocked kitchen

staples list

I have found that the key to successful dinners is planning ahead for the week. Having a weekly menu allows me to shop only once a week for ingredients, avoiding last-minute trips to the grocery store. Some people like to grocery shop daily. If you're one of them, read no further—but if you want to avoid going to the grocery store more than necessary, try these tips:

1. Keep a list attached to the fridge (I use a magnetic pad) and update it when you run low on something.

2. Buy lots of milk, fruit, and other essentials each trip—enough to last at least a week.

3. Plan at least five dinners in advance. (I can help with that part!)

4. Keep a well-stocked pantry at home.

Here are the most important items I keep in my pantry, refrigerator, and freezer to make easy, healthy dinners a breeze.

To print out detailed grocery lists for each of the Six O'Clock Scramble's weekly menus, visit http://www.thescramble.com/cookbook.

Pantry Staples

- olive oil
- vegetable or canola oil
- peanut oil
- sesame oil
- nonstick cooking spray
- bread crumbs
- cornmeal
- flour
- white and brown sugar
- honey
- white or brown rice and/or quinoa
- couscous
- wild rice
- 2 (16 ounces each) packages pasta
- 2–4 cans chicken or vegetable broth
- 1 jar (26 ounces) red pasta sauce
- 1 can unsweetened corn kernels
- 1 can (15 ounces) diced tomatoes
- 1 can (15 ounces) tomato sauce
- 1 can (28 ounces) crushed tomatoes
- 1 can (28 ounces) whole tomatoes
- 3 cans black, kidney and/or pinto beans
- tortilla chips
- salsa
- soy sauce
- Worcestershire sauce
- hoisin sauce

rice wine
rice vinegar
balsamic vinegar
white cooking wine
red cooking wine
dry sherry

Spices and Herbs

basil
bay leaves
chili powder
cinnamon
cumin
curry powder
dry mustard powder
kosher salt
oregano
pepper
rosemary
salt
thyme

Refrigerator Staples

Dijon mustard
maple syrup
ketchup
eggs

- butter
- milk
- low-fat plain yogurt or sour cream
- chopped garlic
- shredded Cheddar cheese
- shredded mozzarella cheese
- shredded or grated Parmesan cheese
- feta, Gorgonzola, or goat cheese
- flour or whole wheat tortillas
- mayonnaise
- natural peanut butter
- pine nuts, walnuts, slivered almonds (keep in freezer)

Produce

- minced or fresh garlic
- 1 lemon
- 1 lime
- 2 yellow onions
- carrots
- celery
- fresh ginger (may be kept in freezer)
- lettuce or other salad greens
- frozen chopped broccoli
- frozen chopped spinach
- frozen peas

an explanation of the nutritional information

by Lee Unangst, Six O'Clock Scramble Nutritional Consultant

The Six O'Clock Scramble's Nutritional Information helps you see how the Scramble's recipes compare to other recipes and how they fit into your daily eating habits. They can also be compared directly to Nutrition Facts labels on packaged foods. Here's a quick breakdown of the categories:

Calories
Total Fat
Saturated Fat
Cholesterol
Sodium
Total Carbohydrate
Dietary Fiber
Protein
Sugar

The amount of each nutrient per serving is given in grams (g) or milligrams (mg). The percentages in the Nutritional Information show what percentage of your Recommended Daily Allowance (RDA) one serving of the recipe provides.

Calories are a measure of the amount of energy that we can get from food. Knowing the calorie content of food is important in weight maintenance; extra calories are stored as fat. Calories come from four sources: carbohydrates,

protein, alcohol, and fat. Carbohydrates are your body's preferred fuel and the only source of fuel for your brain under normal conditions. Protein provides the building blocks for muscle and other body structures. Fat is used to make hormones and insulate and pad our bodies. We need all three to be healthy. (Calories from alcohol have no nutritional value.) If you want to know more about your personal caloric needs, go to www.mypyramid.gov and see the new food guide.

Saturated fat, cholesterol, and sodium have all been found to contribute to chronic illnesses. Limiting your intake of these will help reduce your risk. Because of this, it's best to look for foods that have around 20 percent or less of the RDA. The same is true for regular fats.

Saturated fats are solid at room temperature, like butter, shortening, or the fat around the edge of a steak. Cholesterol is found only in animal products; we need cholesterol to make hormones and digest fat, but our bodies make most of the cholesterol we need. Saturated fat and excess cholesterol are key players in heart disease. Sodium is found in food in many forms—most obviously, table salt—but is especially high in processed foods. For many people, salt intake is linked to high blood pressure.

Dietary fiber is a special type of carbohydrate

that your body cannot digest. Dietary fiber keeps our bodies clean, helps us absorb other carbohydrates more slowly, and helps keep cholesterol low. You should try to include in your diet as many foods as possible that have 20 percent or more of the RDA for dietary fiber per serving.

Sugar makes food taste sweet. Foods with a lot of sugar often contain sugar that has been added during processing, and they are typically high in calories and low in other nutrients. Sugar is also linked to dental cavities; the bacteria that damage your teeth like it as much as you do!

It is important to remember that all the nutrients in food are important for our health and that any of them can be problematic in excess. No single nutrient can be blamed for causing weight gain, and no single nutrient will make us healthy and thin. Fads come and go, but we've known for a long time that consuming a variety of foods, and consuming all foods in moderation, is the key to good nutrition.

A note about serving size: On food labels, the serving size is a suggestion for how much of a food should be eaten in one sitting, based upon standards set by the government. For foods in the Scramble, the size of a serving is determined based upon two criteria. The first criterion is that the portion size should be reasonable and satisfying. The second criterion is that the portion size, and especially the number of calories in that portion, should be consistent with a healthy diet. If you consume two portions, you will, of course, consume twice the amount of calories, as well as fat, fiber, and all of the nutrients listed in the Nutritional Information per Serving section that follows each recipe.

fall

week 1

Maple Dijon Baked Chicken

Salmon in a Foil Packet

Farfalle with Mushrooms and Peas

Cheese Quesadillas with Lime Pesto

Greek Pita Pizza

week 2

Spinach Noodle and Cheese Bake

Orange and Lemon Flounder

Cincinnati Chili

Grilled Polenta with Fresh Tomatoes and Basil

VLTs (or BLTs)

week 3

Ginger Chicken

Roasted Halibut with Caramelized Onions

Whole Wheat Turkey-Coleslaw Wraps

Mexican Cornbread Casserole

Thai Noodle Salad with Roast Beef

week 4

Spanish Rice with Ground Beef or Turkey

Tilapia Topped with Warm Cherry Tomatoes and Olives

Crispy Rolled Tortillas with Black Bean Filling

Penne Pesto with Baby Spinach

Roasted Sweet Potato and Apple Soup

week 5

Grilled Teriyaki Chicken Tenderloins

Tortilla Casserole

Sautéed Shrimp with Tomatoes and Lemon

Spinach Manicotti

Broccoli-Leek Soup with Lemon-Chive Cream

week 6

One-Pot Chicken and Vegetable Stew

Red Beans and Rice

Linguine with Shrimp and Feta Cheese

Broccoli, Sausage, and Cheddar Quiche

Salmon Burgers

week 7

Cornmeal-Crusted Catfish

Indian Spiced Lentils with Rice

Chinese Noodles with Greens

Vegetarian Tacos

Goddess Chicken

week 8

Chicken Dijon

Corn and Wild Rice Soup

Pan-Seared Pork Loins with Green Beans

Not-Your-Mother's Tuna Casserole

Southwestern-Style Stuffed Potatoes

This delectable chicken recipe is a snap to prepare, yet it's good enough to serve to company. The sauce is wonderful and keeps the chicken moist and juicy. Serve it with Spaetzle or Gnocchi Parmesan (see p. 299) and steamed green beans.

maple dijon baked chicken

Prep (10 minutes) +
Cook (50 minutes)

8 servings

Nutritional
Information per
serving:

Calories 350, Total
Fat 14g, 22%, Satu-
rated Fat 3.5g, 18%,
Cholesterol 125mg,
42%, Sodium 490mg,
20%, Total Carbohy-
drate 15g, 5%, Di-
etary Fiber 0g, 0%,
Protein 41g, Sugar
13g

1 package split chicken breasts (bone in) and 1 package thighs (bone in), about 8–10 pieces total

⅓ cup apricot jam

⅓ cup Dijon mustard

⅓ cup maple syrup or honey (or any combination of the two)

¼ cup white wine

1 teaspoon dried tarragon or sage

paprika to taste

Preheat the oven to 350 degrees.

Place the chicken pieces in a glass oven-safe dish. In a measuring cup, mix together all the remaining ingredients except the paprika. Pour the sauce over the chicken and turn the chicken pieces in the sauce a couple of times, ending with them skin side up. Sprinkle paprika liberally over the chicken.

Bake the chicken, uncovered, for 45 minutes (some ovens may take a little longer, so check for doneness after 45 minutes), then broil it for an additional 5 minutes to brown the tops.

{ **make healthy popsicles** In plastic popsicle molds, freeze chocolate milk, blended fruit or fruit juice for healthier popsicles.

This baked salmon is a hit with grown-ups and kids. The fish and veggies emerge from the oven moist and sweet. If your market carries them, use preshredded carrots to save chopping time. Serve the salmon with steamed rice and diced pineapple.

salmon in a foil packet

Prep (15 minutes) +
Cook (20 minutes)

4 servings

Nutritional
Information per
serving:

Calories 360, Total
Fat 20g, 30%, Saturated Fat 3.5g, 17%,
Cholesterol 110 mg,
37%, Sodium 660 mg,
28%, Total Carbohydrate 8g, 3%, Dietary
Fiber 2g, 7%, Protein
37g, Sugar 3g

1½ pounds salmon fillet

1 cup slivered carrots (about 2 carrots)

1 cup slivered red or green bell peppers (1 small pepper) or zucchini

2 tablespoons peanut or vegetable oil

2 teaspoons chopped garlic (about 4 cloves)

1 tablespoon minced ginger

2 tablespoons soy sauce

1 tablespoon rice vinegar

1 tablespoon hoisin sauce

Preheat the oven to 450 degrees. Tear off about 2 feet of heavy-duty aluminum foil, and fold it in half to make a double-thick square that measures about 12 inches on each side. Place the foil on a cookie sheet.

Place the fish in the center of the foil. Top the fish with the slivered carrots and peppers.

In a small saucepan, heat the oil over medium heat. Add the garlic and ginger and sauté them until they are fragrant, about 1 minute. Add the soy sauce, vinegar, and hoisin sauce and simmer the mixture for about 2 minutes. Remove the saucepan from the heat.

Pour the sauce carefully over the fish and vegetables. Wrap the foil into an airtight packet around the fish, veggies, and sauce, folding and sealing the edges.

Bake the wrapped fish for 20 minutes. Remove it from the oven and open the package immediately (and carefully) so the fish stops cooking.

This is a simple and delicious weeknight pasta. Serve this dish with whole wheat rolls and additional peas on the side.

farfalle with mushrooms and peas

Prep + Cook =
30 minutes

8 servings

Nutritional
Information per
serving:

Calories 310, Total
Fat 6g, 9%, Saturated
Fat 1.5g, 8%, Choles-
terol 5 mg, 1%,
Sodium 220 mg, 9%,
Total Carbohydrate
48g, 16%, Dietary
Fiber 5g, 20%, Pro-
tein 16g, Sugar 3g

1 package (16 ounces) farfalle or other pasta

2 tablespoons olive oil

1 teaspoon chopped garlic (about 2 cloves)

2 pounds assorted sliced mushrooms (such as shiitakes, buttons, or criminis)

1 teaspoon fresh or dried thyme

½ cup chicken or vegetable broth

½ cup frozen peas

½ teaspoon kosher salt or ¼ teaspoon table salt

½ cup grated Parmesan cheese, plus additional for serving

Heat the water to cook the pasta according to the package directions.

Meanwhile, in a large skillet, heat the oil over medium heat. Add the garlic, mush-rooms, and thyme and sauté them for 1 minute. Add the broth and simmer the mix-ture over medium-low heat, stirring it occasionally.

When you add the pasta to the boiling water. Add the peas and salt to the mush-room mixture. Cook the pasta until it is al dente.

When the pasta is cooked, drain it briefly, allowing some water to cling to the noo-dles, and return it to the warm pot over low heat. Add the mushroom-pea mixture and the Parmesan cheese and stir everything together until it is heated through.

Serve the farfalle immediately, topped with additional Parmesan cheese.

{ **picking up speed** Preparation times for the recipes are estimates, based on my experience making the dishes. If you are overseeing homework, stooping to scoop up blocks, answering the phone, or just taking your time (rather than Scrambling!), they may take you a little longer. I've noticed that recipes usually take longer the first time, so if a recipe becomes a family favorite, it may go more quickly.

These quesadillas have a terrific flavor and are very versatile. You can add cooked chicken or steak, or make some with just cheese for the kids. Serve the quesadillas with corn on the cob.

cheese quesadillas with lime pesto

Prep + Cook =
25 minutes

8 servings

Nutritional
Information per
serving:

Calories 270, Total
Fat 13g, 20%, Satu-
rated Fat 5g, 26%,
Cholesterol 20 mg,
7%, Sodium 390 mg,
16%, Total Carbohy-
drate 28g, 9%, Di-
etary Fiber 0g, 0%,
Protein 11g, Sugar 1g

1 tablespoon olive oil

1 cup finely diced sweet yellow onion

2 tablespoons pesto sauce (store-bought or homemade: see p. 214)

1½ teaspoons fresh lime juice (about ½ lime)

1½ cups shredded Monterey Jack cheese

2 cups sliced or shredded cooked chicken or steak (optional)

8 soft-taco-sized whole wheat or flour tortillas

salsa for serving

In a small nonstick skillet, heat the oil over medium-high heat. Add the onions and sauté them until they are lightly browned, about 10 minutes.

Meanwhile, in a medium-sized bowl, mix together the pesto, lime juice, cheese, and meat (optional). When the onions are ready, add them to this mixture.

Heat a large skillet (or two, to work faster) over medium heat. Add a tortilla to the pan, spread a scoop of the mixture on half of the tortilla, and fold the tortilla in half. Repeat with a second tortilla, so two quesadillas are cooking at once.

When the bottoms of the tortillas are lightly browned, flip them and lightly brown the second sides, about 3 minutes per side. When both sides are browned, remove the tortillas to a plate. Repeat with the remaining tortillas and pesto mixture.

Slice the cooked quesadillas with a sharp knife or pizza cutter and serve them with salsa.

If your kids aren't fond of feta cheese, you can make their mini pizzas with tomato sauce and mozzarella cheese. Serve this dish with a spinach salad with diced strawberries.

greek pita pizza

Prep + Cook Time = 15 minutes

4 servings

Nutritional Information per serving:

Calories 370, Total Fat 18g, 27%, Saturated Fat 9g, 46%, Cholesterol 50 mg, 17%, Sodium 960 mg, 40%, Total Carbohydrate 38g, 13%, Dietary Fiber 2g, 9%, Protein 14g, Sugar 4g

- 6–8 ounces feta cheese, crumbled
- 4 medium-sized pita breads
- 3 ripe plum or Roma tomatoes, diced
- 2 teaspoons dried oregano (or use 1–2 tablespoons fresh oregano or basil)
- 4 teaspoons olive oil

Preheat the broiler. Sprinkle the feta cheese evenly over the pitas. Top each with a quarter of the tomatoes and ½ teaspoon of the oregano. Drizzle 1 teaspoon of the oil on top of each.

Broil the pizzas on a cookie sheet for 5 to 8 minutes until the cheese is bubbly and the pitas start to brown. (You can also cook them easily 2 at a time in the toaster oven at 450 degrees.) Serve them halved or quartered.

grocery bags. paper or plastic?

Environmentalists say it hardly matters which kind you choose. What matters is that you recycle the bags by using them as many times as possible.

This is a great dish for a family dinner, as it's hearty and filling and tastes great. Serve it with baby carrots.

spinach noodle and cheese bake

Prep (25 minutes) +
Cook (30 minutes)

6 servings

Nutritional
Information per
serving:

Calories 380, Total
Fat 11g, 18%, Satu-
rated Fat 7g, 34%,
Cholesterol 30 mg,
10%, Sodium 630 mg,
26% Total Carbohy-
drate 49g, 16%, Di-
etary Fiber 4g, 16%,
Protein 21g, Sugar
11g

1 package (10 ounces) frozen chopped spinach

8 ounces mostaccioli or penne (make the whole 16-ounce box if you want some plain pasta for the kids)

2 tablespoons butter or margarine

1 cup sliced onion (about ½ medium onion)

2 teaspoons minced garlic (about 4 cloves)

¼ cup flour

2½ cups nonfat or low-fat milk

1¼ cups plus 2 tablespoons shredded Parmesan cheese

½ teaspoon dried basil or 1 tablespoon fresh

½ teaspoon dried oregano or 1½ teaspoons fresh

1 can (14.5 ounces) diced tomatoes with Italian seasoning

¼ cup bread crumbs

Preheat the oven to 350 degrees. Spray a 9 × 13-inch baking dish with nonstick cooking spray.

Thaw the spinach in the microwave and drain it thoroughly.

Cook the pasta according to the package directions and drain it.

Meanwhile, in a medium saucepan over medium-high heat, melt 1 tablespoon of the butter or margarine. Add the onions and garlic and sauté them until the onions are softened, about 5 minutes. Add the flour and cook the onions for 30 seconds more, stirring them constantly. Gradually add the milk. Cook the mixture until it is bubbly, about 4 minutes. Remove the saucepan from the heat. Stir in ¼ cup of the cheese, the basil, and the oregano.

In a large bowl, combine the pasta, the onion-cheese sauce, 1 cup of the Parmesan cheese, the tomatoes, and the spinach. Stir the mixture well and spoon it into the baking dish.

On a small plate, using your fingers or a fork, combine the bread crumbs, the remaining 2 tablespoons of the Parmesan cheese, and the remaining 1 tablespoon of the butter or margarine. Sprinkle this topping over the pasta.

Bake the casserole for 30 minutes or until it is thoroughly heated.

This light preparation for fish, suggested by my friend Ruth Robbins, works for any white fish, such as halibut, orange roughy, cod, or tilapia. Adjust the cooking time for the thickness of the fish. Serve this dish with steamed broccolini (baby broccoli) and bulgur wheat cooked in chicken broth and tossed with a handful of chopped seedless purple grapes.

orange and lemon flounder

Prep + Cook =
20 minutes

4 servings

Nutritional
Information per
serving:

Calories 190, Total
Fat 3g, 5%, Saturated
Fat 0g, 0%, Choles-
terol 70 mg, 23%,
Sodium 160 mg, 7%,
Total Carbohydrate
7g, 2%, Dietary Fiber
0g, 0%, Protein 33g,
Sugar 6g

- 1½ pounds flounder fillet
- ¼ teaspoon orange zest (optional)
- ¼ teaspoon lemon zest (optional)
- ¼ cup fresh orange juice (about ½ orange)
- ¼ cup fresh lemon juice (about 1 lemon)
- 1 tablespoon honey
- salt to taste

Preheat the oven to 400 degrees. Place the fillet in a flat baking dish with sides.

Wash and thoroughly dry the orange and lemon. Scrape the zest (optional) from the colorful part of the skin and set it aside before juicing the fruits.

In a measuring cup, whisk together the juices and honey. Pour the mixture over the fish. Sprinkle the top with salt to taste and the zest.

Bake the fish for 15 minutes or until the flesh flakes easily.

meatless mondays Meatless recipes can not only be delicious but can also pay for themselves in lower grocery bills: Meat-free meals are usually less expensive than those with meat. You'll be helping your family stay healthy and protecting the environment by eating less meat, and you will likely be surprised by how little you miss it.

The spices give this simple chili such a rich flavor that it has been a staple in our home for many years. We serve it over egg noodles, topped with shredded Cheddar cheese. Some people prefer it alone or over rice. You can freeze half the chili for a busy night. Serve it with cornbread.

cincinnati chili

Prep (15 minutes) +
Cook (30 minutes)

10 servings

Nutritional
Information per
serving:

Calories 400, Total
Fat 10g, 15%, Saturated Fat 3.5g, 17%,
Cholesterol 75 mg,
25%, Sodium 250 mg,
11%, Total Carbohydrate 52g, 17%, Dietary Fiber 8g, 33%,
Protein 27g, Sugar 6g

- 1½–2 pounds lean ground beef, chicken, or vegetarian ground "meat"
- ½ cup water
- 2 tablespoons chili powder (or more to taste)
- 1 teaspoon cinnamon
- ½ teaspoon ground cloves
- 2 teaspoons sugar
- 1 teaspoon garlic powder
- ½ large onion, coarsely chopped
- 1 can (28 ounces) whole tomatoes with their liquid
- 2 cans (16 ounces each) red kidney beans with their liquid (use a variety without added sugar, if possible)

In a large stockpot over medium heat, sauté the meat in its own juices until it is browned.

Add the other ingredients in the order above. Simmer the chili gently for at least 30 minutes and up to 1 hour.

My friend Nachama Wilker introduced me to this unusual meatless dish that she prepares on the grill. A broiler works almost as well if you don't want to fire up the grill. It's great with a green salad with diced oranges and walnuts, and it also works well as a side dish for grilled steak or chicken.

grilled polenta with fresh tomatoes and basil

Prep + Cook = 15 minutes

6 servings

Nutritional Information per serving:

Calories 160, Total Fat 11g, 17%, Saturated Fat 2g, 10%, Cholesterol <5mg, 2%, Sodium 400mg, 17%, Total Carbohydrate 11g, 4% Dietary Fiber 2g, 8%, Protein 4g, Sugar 2g

1 roll (24 ounces) plain prepared polenta, sliced into ½-inch rounds

¼ cup olive oil

½ teaspoon minced garlic (about 1 clove)

4–5 fresh basil leaves, chopped

½ teaspoon salt

1 medium tomato, diced

grated Parmesan cheese for serving

pepper for serving

Using a vegetable tray (so the slices don't fall through the grates), grill the polenta over medium-high heat until it is lightly browned, about 3 to 4 minutes per side. (Alternatively, broil the slices on a cookie sheet about 4 inches from the heat source until they are browned.)

While the polenta is cooking, in a measuring cup, mix together the oil, garlic, basil, and salt. Put the hot cooked polenta in a single layer on a serving dish. Top it with the diced tomato and the olive oil mixture. Sprinkle Parmesan cheese and pepper on top.

Cruising the aisles of our local health food store, I was intrigued by some of the realistic-looking vegetarian products that have cropped up. I have been impressed by the flavor of many of them, including the Morningstar Farms Veggie Breakfast Bacon Strips. For a quick and light summer meal, here's a recipe for VLTs that are so reminiscent of the real thing that none of our junior and senior testers knew the difference. Of course, these would also be great with real bacon. Serve them with potato chips (see p. 300 to make your own) and a crisp salad.

VLTs (or BLTs)

Prep + Cook =
25 minutes

8 servings

Nutritional
Information per
serving:

Calories 350, Total
Fat 14g, 22%, Saturated Fat 2.5g, 13%,
Cholesterol <5mg,
2%, Sodium 880mg,
37%, Total Carbohydrate 47g, 16%, Dietary Fiber 7g, 28%,
Protein 10g, Sugar 5g

1 box (5.25 ounces) Morningstar Farms Veggie Breakfast
   Bacon Strips (or bacon of your choice)

2–3 tomatoes, thinly sliced

1 head iceberg lettuce

16 slices wheat bread

mayonnaise

colorful toothpicks

Bake the Veggie Breakfast Bacon Strips on a cookie sheet at 350 degrees for 12 to 15 minutes until they are crispy, flipping them once.

Meanwhile, slice the tomatoes and separate enough lettuce leaves for the sandwiches. (Chop additional lettuce to use for the salad.)

Toast the bread and spread one side of each sandwich with mayonnaise to taste.

Assemble the sandwiches with bacon, lettuce, and tomato. Slice each sandwich diagonally and insert a colorful toothpick in each half (skip the sharp toothpick if you are serving the sandwich to a toddler).

cooking to the beat Did you ever notice how much faster cooking and cleaning go when you listen to music? Our kids and I love to play our favorite CDs while we cook, set the table, and clean up.

This dish has an exotic flavor, but we've found that it's not too intense for most kids. Serve it with rice and peas mixed together.

ginger chicken

Prep (20 minutes) +
Cook (50 minutes)

6 servings

Nutritional
Information per
serving:

Calories 330, Total
Fat 16g, 25%, Satu-
rated Fat 4.5g, 22%,
Cholesterol 100mg,
34%, Sodium 710mg,
29%, Total Carbohy-
drate 11g, 4%, Di-
etary Fiber <1g, 3%,
Protein 35g, Sugar 9g

1 whole chicken (plus more pieces, if desired), cut up

1 tablespoon olive oil

4 slices peeled ginger, cut into strips (about 2 tablespoons)

8 ounces sliced mushrooms

4 scallions, chopped

1 can (14 ounces) chicken broth

¼ cup soy sauce

2 tablespoons sherry

2 tablespoons honey

1–2 tablespoons curry powder (to taste)

2 tablespoons mango chutney (or use apricot jam)

Preheat the oven to 400 degrees. Rinse the chicken and put it in a roasting pan, skin side down.

In a medium skillet, heat the oil over medium heat. Add the ginger and sauté it lightly for about 2 minutes. Add the mushrooms and scallions and sauté them for about 3 more minutes until the mushrooms are tender. Spoon the mushroom-ginger mixture over the chicken.

In a medium bowl, combine the chicken broth, soy sauce, sherry, honey, and curry powder. Pour the sauce over the chicken. Cover the pan with foil and cook the chicken for 30 minutes.

Remove the pan from the oven, remove the foil, flip the chicken, and brush the skin with the chutney. Return the chicken to the oven uncovered and cook it for 20 to 25 more minutes until it is cooked through and lightly browned. For extra browning, put the chicken under the broiler for the last few minutes of cooking.

To serve, pour the gravy from the pan over the chicken and rice.

I've been trying to use more halibut, because it's healthy for humans and the environment and is also mild and delicious. Halibut's only drawback is that it can be pricey, so I buy smaller portions and make filling side dishes to go with it. Serve this dish with a baguette and Swiss chard with garlic and Parmesan cheese (see p. 298).

roasted halibut with caramelized onions

Prep + Cook =
30 minutes

4 servings

Nutritional
Information per
serving:

Calories 260, Total
Fat 10g, 15%, Saturated Fat 1.5g, 8%,
Cholesterol 55mg,
18%, Sodium 350mg,
15%, Total Carbohydrate 5g, 2%, Dietary
Fiber 0g, 0%, Protein
37g, Sugar 4g

1 tablespoon olive oil

1 red onion, halved and cut into half rings

1½ pounds halibut fillets

salt to taste

1 tablespoon Dijon mustard

1 tablespoon mayonnaise (or use olive oil)

1 tablespoon balsamic vinegar plus a splash for the onions

1 teaspoon honey

In a medium skillet, heat the oil over medium-high heat. Add the onions, partially cover the skillet, and cook the onions until they start to sizzle and brown, about 10 minutes. Remove the lid and reduce the heat to medium. Continue cooking the onions, stirring them occasionally, until they shrink and turn brown.

While the onions are cooking, preheat the oven to 450 degrees (or preheat the grill to medium-high). Line a baking sheet (or fish-grilling tray) with aluminum foil and spray the foil with nonstick cooking spray.

Put the fish on top of the foil-lined pan (or tray) and season it with salt to taste. In a small bowl, whisk together the mustard, mayonnaise, vinegar, and honey. Brush the mixture liberally over the fish, skipping the skin-covered sides.

Roast the fish in the oven for 10 to 15 minutes (or grill it for 10 to 12 minutes) until a knife slides easily into the thickest part of the fillet and the middle of the fish is white.

A few minutes before the fish is fully cooked, add a splash of balsamic vinegar to the onions and stir them thoroughly.

Remove the fish from the oven to a serving plate. Top it with the onions or serve the onions on the side.

These wraps are a snap to assemble and make a great meal for a warm evening. The dressing is sweet, something like Russian dressing, which may appeal to your kids. If your market carries it, use broccoli slaw instead of coleslaw for a healthy, crunchy zing.

whole wheat turkey-coleslaw wraps

Prep = 10 minutes

6 servings

Nutritional Information per serving:

Calories 410, Total Fat 12g, 18%, Saturated Fat 3g, 15%, Cholesterol 40mg, 13%, Sodium 1440mg, 60%, Total Carbohydrate 50g, 17%, Dietary Fiber 6g, 24%, Protein 22g, Sugar 7g

- 1 bag (12 ounces) dry broccoli slaw or cabbage coleslaw (often sold with produce)
- 2 tablespoons mayonnaise
- 1 tablespoon ketchup
- 1 tablespoon balsamic vinegar
- 1 teaspoon sugar
- 6 whole wheat wraps (or use large flour tortillas)
- 1 pound sliced turkey (or use meatless deli slices)

In a large bowl, mix the slaw with the mayonnaise, ketchup, vinegar, and sugar. Refrigerate the slaw until you're ready to put the wraps together.

Heat the wraps in the microwave on high for about 15 seconds per wrap to soften them. Put 2 or 3 slices of turkey on each wrap and spread a large spoonful of slaw on top of the turkey. Fold one end of the wrap up a couple of inches, so the sauce doesn't drip out of the bottom, and roll the wrap around the turkey and slaw. Cut the wraps in half to serve them.

{ **saving time and money** Far and away, when it comes to getting dinner on the table, the biggest time and money saver I have found is planning ahead. By planning a week's worth of meals and shopping for all the ingredients at once, I invariably manage to have what I need at the ready when time is tight, and I don't waste much food.

This is a taste-bud-tingling, filling, and nutritious baked dish that makes quite a bit of food. For a meatier option, you could add a cup of chopped cooked ham, sausage, or vegetarian ground "meat." This would also be a good meal to bring to a potluck or serve to a casual gathering. Serve it with asparagus, trimmed and broken into thirds, and sautéed with some garlic in a tablespoon of olive oil, and seasoned with salt.

mexican cornbread casserole

Prep (20 minutes) +
Cook (1 hour)

12 servings

Nutritional
Information per
serving:

Calories 310, Total
Fat 16g, 25%, Satu-
rated Fat 9g, 45%,
Cholesterol 115mg,
38%, Sodium 710mg,
30%, Total Carbohy-
drate 28g, 9%, Di-
etary Fiber 4g, 16%,
Protein 14g, Sugar 7g

4 tablespoons butter, melted

4 eggs, beaten

1 cup yellow cornmeal

8 ounces shredded Cheddar cheese

1 can (15 ounces) unsweetened corn kernels
    with ½ cup of their liquid (drain the rest)

1 can (15 ounces) white kidney or cannellini beans, drained

2 cups (16 ounces) low-fat sour cream

1 tablespoon sugar (optional)

½ teaspoon salt

1 cup mild salsa

Preheat the oven to 350 degrees. Spray a 9 × 13-inch baking dish with nonstick cooking spray.

In a large bowl, mix together all the ingredients. Put the mixture in the baking dish.

Bake the casserole, uncovered, until it is firm and lightly browned, about 1 hour. Cut it into squares for serving.

My friend Jessica Honigberg describes this salad as "exquisite," and I couldn't agree more. If your market doesn't carry many Asian specialty foods, you can use sliced red bell peppers in place of the snow peas and substitute angel hair pasta (cooked until al dente and then rinsed in cold water) for the cellophane noodles. Serve the salad with egg rolls on the side.

thai noodle salad with roast beef (or chicken or tofu)

Prep + Cook =
25 minutes

4 servings

Nutritional Information per serving:

Calories 240, Total Fat 6g, 9%, Saturated Fat 1.5g, 8%, Cholesterol 20mg, 7%, Sodium 1040 mg, 43%, Total Carbohydrate 36g, 12%, Dietary Fiber 3g, 12%, Protein 12g, Sugar 5g

- 1 package (3.75 ounces) bean thread or cellophane noodles
- 8 ounces sliced deli roast beef (or use cooked chicken or diced extra-firm tofu)
- 1½ cups snow peas, cut into thin strips
- 1 cup matchstick carrots (you can buy them precut in bags)
- ½ cup high-quality teriyaki sauce, such as Soy Vey (or make your own—see tip below)
- 1 tablespoon fresh lime juice (about ¼ fresh lime)
- 1 tablespoon sesame oil
- ¼ cup chopped fresh cilantro
- 1 small head romaine lettuce, washed and torn

In a medium bowl, cover the noodles with boiling water. (You can use a teakettle for quick boiling.) Let them stand 15 minutes until they are tender. Drain the noodles and chop them coarsely.

Slice the roast beef into thin strips. In a large microwave-safe bowl, combine the beef, snow peas, and carrots.

In a measuring cup, combine the teriyaki sauce, lime juice, and sesame oil. Pour the mixture over the beef and vegetables. Cover the bowl loosely and microwave it on high power for 3 minutes until the mixture is hot.

Add the cooked noodles and the cilantro to the beef and vegetables and toss it well.

Serve the salad on a bed of lettuce.

{ **teriyaki sauce** To make your own teriyaki sauce, combine 3 tablespoons of soy sauce, 3 tablespoons of rice vinegar, 3 tablespoons of rice wine, 1/2 teaspoon each of ground ginger and garlic powder, and 1 tablespoon of brown sugar. Whisk the sauce well until the sugar dissolves.

the halloween question: what's wrong with sugar?

Hardly anything in my life has been able to surpass the joy of being able to knock on almost any neighbor's door on October 31 and get free candy! With my aching sweet tooth, Halloween has always been my favorite holiday. Depending on my age, I would sort, gorge, trade, and savor the bounty of the chilly evening's hunt. Now I subsist on my children's rejects, things that have chunks or nuts or are just too crunchy or gooey for their underdeveloped taste buds.

As a parent, I wonder if I should set any limits on my children's candy consumption on this holiday of sweets. Is there actually anything wrong with kids eating sugar?

To research the issue, I consulted the Web sites of the American Academy of Pediatricians and the American Dietetic Association and spoke to some doctors, including Dr. Christine Richards, a family physician in Richland Center, Wisconsin. It turns out that no direct link has been established between sugar and adverse health effects or even hyperactivity. What nutrition and child health experts do mostly agree on is that too much sugar can lead to obesity, as sugary foods are often high in calories. Sugary foods, particularly sticky ones, can also lead to tooth decay. Finally, sugary snacks too often replace healthier alternatives that have more protein, fiber, and important vitamins. So, although there is nothing inherently bad about sugar, there are important reasons to limit kids' candy consumption.

I asked a pediatric dentist, Dr. Dana Greenwald of Washington, D.C., what approach she recommends to parents of her young patients. Her advice was to let the kids eat whatever they want on Halloween and then throw away the rest or save it for special treats. Since my kids are still young enough to let me confiscate their candy on November 1, I'll probably follow her advice and let my kids have just one night of pure indulgence. I will also try to resist eating the rest of their booty myself.

Healthier Halloween Treats

Since there is no shortage of sweet treats during Halloween week, I've tried to find some spooky afternoon snacks that can balance out all that sugar. Here are a few of the kids' favorites:

Edible Spiders: Let the kids spread peanut butter or cream cheese on a round cracker. Put another round cracker on top without pressing down, so there's a little space between them. Insert eight stick pretzels between the crackers for spider legs. Using a dab of the peanut butter or cream cheese, attach raisins or chocolate chips (the spider's eyes) to the top cracker.

Ghost & Ghoul Sandwiches: Give the kids Halloween-shaped cookie cutters to turn their sandwiches into a scary lunchtime treat.

Broomsticks: Shred pieces of string cheese into long strips. Press them around the end of a pretzel rod and tie a piece of string cheese or string licorice around it to look like a broom.

Pumpkin Faces: Use a few drops of orange (or red and yellow) food coloring to turn cream cheese pumpkin orange. Spread the orange cream cheese on toasted English muffins. Use raisins or chocolate chips to make silly jack-o'-lantern faces.

This one-pot dish from my first cookbook has a hearty, stick-to-your-ribs quality that your family will love. It's a great way to get protein, vegetables, and grains into the meal. If you like, you can wrap it in warm tortillas. For a Cajun flavor, substitute spicy sausage for the ground meat. Serve this dish with steamed artichokes (see p. 298) dipped in melted butter or vinaigrette dressing.

spanish rice with ground beef or turkey

Prep (15 minutes) +
Cook (20–30
minutes)

8 servings

Nutritional
Information per
serving:

Calories 300, Total
Fat 12g, 18%, Saturated Fat 4g, 20%,
Cholesterol 40mg,
13%, Sodium 430mg,
18%, Total Carbohydrate 35g, 12%, Dietary Fiber 4g, 16%,
Protein 15g, Sugar 5g

1 teaspoon olive oil

1 large onion, chopped

1 green bell pepper, chopped

1 pound lean ground beef, turkey, or vegetarian ground "meat"

2 cups water

1½ cups dry white or quick-cooking brown rice

1 can (28 ounces) tomatoes (whole or crushed)

1 tablespoon chili powder

¼ teaspoon salt

¼ teaspoon pepper

In a large stockpot, heat the oil over medium-high heat. Add the onions, bell pepper, and meat and cook them until the meat is browned, about 5 minutes. Add the remaining ingredients and mix everything thoroughly. Bring it to a boil, cover the pot, and simmer it gently over low heat for 20 to 30 minutes, depending on your rice's cooking instructions, until the rice is tender.

This dish takes about ten minutes from start to finish, but you would never know it from the beautiful presentation and delicious flavor. Tilapia is a great fish to use for weeknights, because it is inexpensive, earth friendly, and quick to cook. Our kids also like its mild taste. Serve it with a Cucumber Salad (see p. 297) and a loaf of fresh bread.

tilapia topped with warm cherry tomatoes and olives

Prep + Cook =
10 minutes

4 servings

Nutritional
Information per
serving:

Calories 200, Total
Fat 12g, 18%, Satu-
rated Fat 1g, 5%,
Cholesterol 102mg,
34%, Sodium 180mg,
8%, Total Carbohy-
drate 6g, 2%, Dietary
Fiber <1g, 4%, Pro-
tein 19g, Sugar 2g

2–3 tablespoons olive oil

1–1½ pounds tilapia fillets

salt and pepper to taste

1 pint (about 2 cups) cherry tomatoes, halved

¼ cup fresh chopped parsley

½ cup pitted kalamata olives, halved

1 tablespoon lemon juice (about ¼ lemon)

1 tablespoon Parmesan cheese (optional)

In a large heavy skillet, heat the oil over medium-high heat. Add the fish, season it with salt and pepper, and sauté it, turning it once, until it turns white throughout and flakes easily, about 3 minutes per side. Transfer the fish to a dish or platter with sides.

In the same skillet (without cleaning it), sauté the tomatoes, parsley, and olives for several minutes until the tomatoes are soft. Season the sauce with salt, pepper, and lemon juice. Pour the sauce over the fish, top it with the Parmesan cheese (optional), and serve it immediately.

TIP: When chopping delicate leafy herbs like parsley and cilantro, don't worry if some of the stems get chopped with the leaves as they are also tender and flavorful.

befriend your freezer Frozen fish tend to be less expensive than fresh and never-frozen items, and they help make once-a-week shopping a reality: There is no worrying that frozen fish may spoil before it can be cooked. Defrost it in the refrigerator, under cold running water, or by using the defrost setting on your microwave and cook it immediately. Do not thaw it at room temperature.

This is one of my husband's favorite dinners. We like the flautas baked until they're a little crispy, then smothered with salsa and sour cream. Serve them with tortilla chips, salsa, and corn kernels.

crispy rolled tortillas with black bean filling

Prep (25 minutes) +
Cook (15 minutes)

6 servings

Nutritional
Information per
serving:

Calories 470, Total
Fat 14g, 22%, Saturated Fat 4.5g, 22%,
Cholesterol 25mg,
8%, Sodium 1040mg,
43%, Total Carbohydrate 65g, 22%, Dietary Fiber 10g, 41%,
Protein 23g, Sugar
10g

1 can (16 ounces) black beans, slightly drained

1 can (14 ounces) vegetarian refried beans

2 teaspoons chili powder

½ teaspoon cumin

½ teaspoon minced garlic (about 1 clove)

12 soft-taco-sized flour tortillas

6 scallions, chopped

2 tomatoes, chopped

1 cup shredded Cheddar cheese

salsa for serving

low-fat sour cream for serving

Preheat the oven to 400 degrees. In a medium saucepan, combine the black beans, refried beans, chili powder, cumin, and garlic. Simmer the beans for 5 minutes.

Mash the bean mixture until it is a thick puree (you can use a potato masher right in the pan).

On a clean plate, lay a tortilla flat and place 2 big tablespoons of the bean mixture in the center of the tortilla. Top it with some scallions, tomatoes, and cheese. Roll the tortilla up into a tube shape and place the rolled tortillas in a 9 × 13-inch baking pan, seam side down. Repeat until you've used all the tortillas.

Bake the rolled tortillas until they are lightly browned, about 15 minutes. Use any leftover bean mixture for dipping, and/or dip the rolled tortillas in salsa or sour cream.

My family loves this combination (Celia calls it "green noodles"), but you can always remove some of the noodles before tossing them with the pesto for very picky eaters. Serve the pasta with whole grain bread and chopped cantaloupe.

penne pesto with baby spinach

Prep + Cook = 25 minutes

8 servings

Nutritional Information per serving:

Calories 340, Total Fat 11g, 17%, Saturated Fat 2.5g, 13%, Cholesterol 5mg, 2%, Sodium 320mg, 13%, Total Carbohydrate 47g, 16%, Dietary Fiber 3g, 12%, Protein 11g, Sugar 2g

- ½ teaspoon minced garlic (about 1 clove)
- ½ cup pesto sauce (store-bought or homemade: see p. 214)
- 2 tablespoons olive oil
- 2 tablespoons capers, drained
- 1 package (16 ounces) penne noodles
- 12–18 ounces prewashed baby spinach
- salt and pepper to taste
- shredded Parmesan cheese to taste

In a large stockpot, boil the water for the pasta. Meanwhile, in a large serving bowl, combine the garlic, pesto, olive oil, and capers. Add the pasta to the boiling water and cook it according to the package directions until it is about 1 minute short of being done. Add the spinach to the water for the last minute of cooking.

Drain the pasta and spinach immediately, add it to the bowl, and toss it with the pesto mixture. Season it with salt and pepper, and top it with Parmesan cheese.

to refrigerate or not: who knew?

In general, don't leave perishable food out of the refrigerator for more than two hours.

There is no need to cool heated food before refrigerating it. In fact, to stay ahead of the bacteria that can grow at cooler temperatures, refrigerate food while it's still warm.

You may be surprised by some of the foods whose labels suggest refrigeration after opening. Examples are ketchup, some brands of soy sauce and steak sauce, mustard, jelly, some kinds of chocolate syrup, and salad dressings.

Remember, too, that uncooked ground meat and ground poultry can only be kept in the refrigerator for one or two days before you use or freeze them. Cooked meat and poultry can be stored in the refrigerator for use within three or four days.

This fabulous recipe, created by Lisa Flaxman (coauthor of my first cookbook, *Peanut Butter Stew and Couscous, Too*), is a guaranteed winner—it won second prize in *Parenting* magazine's Recipes 2000 Contest. This pretty soup is easy, delicious, and healthy. Serve it with a crisp salad of diced avocado, cut-up oranges, and grated Parmesan cheese and a loaf of crusty bread.

roasted sweet potato and apple soup

Prep (20 minutes) +
Cook (30 minutes)

6 servings

Nutritional
Information per
serving:

Calories 120, Total
Fat 5g, 8%, Saturated
Fat 0g, 0%, Choles-
terol 0 mg, 0%,
Sodium 310 mg, 13%,
Total Carbohydrate
16g, 5%, Dietary
Fiber 2g, 9%, Protein
2g, Sugar 9g

- 2 medium sweet potatoes, peeled and cubed
- 1 apple, peeled, cored, and quartered
- 1 medium onion, peeled and quartered
- 2 cloves garlic, peeled
- 2 tablespoons vegetable oil
- salt and pepper to taste
- 3–5 cups chicken or vegetable broth
- yogurt, sour cream, or goat cheese to taste (optional)

Preheat the oven to 450 degrees.

Place the sweet potatoes, apple, onions, and garlic in a roasting pan. Toss them with the oil and a few shakes of salt and pepper. Roast the mixture, stirring it every 10 minutes, until the potatoes are soft, about 30 minutes.

Puree the vegetable mixture in a blender or food processor, adding just enough broth to cover it. (You will probably need to puree it in two batches.) Add more broth to the blender until the soup is smooth but not too thick.

Keep the soup warm in a stockpot over low heat.

Stir in yogurt, goat cheese, or sour cream at the table for a creamier taste, if desired.

healthy after-school or anytime snacks

When our kids come home from school, it's been hours since lunch, so the first thing they crave is a snack. I've been thinking about how to resist their entreaties for high-fat foods and sugar-laden goodies and take advantage of this opportunity to sneak some extra nutrition into their diets. I consulted with some creative moms to put together a list of our favorite healthy, easy snacks (beyond the obviously wonderful fresh fruit) to offer our kids after school, or anytime between meals. Here are our suggestions:

Fresh-popped popcorn

Sliced cheese with crackers

Cereal and milk

Celery filled with peanut butter

Sliced apples dipped in honey

Pita or English-muffin pizzas

Cheese sticks dipped in red pasta sauce

Homemade trail mix (pretzels, almonds, Cheerios, dried apricots, and chocolate chips)

Fruit smoothies with yogurt

Low-fat granola or nutrition bars

Quesadillas (melted cheese in a tortilla)

Baby carrots with peanut butter, hummus, or salad dressing

Nachos (melted cheese, beans, and salsa over chips)

Drinkable, spoonable, or squeezable yogurts

saving money by eating leftovers Another great benefit of cooking at home is the delicious leftovers for the next day's lunches. We have a supply of plastic two- or-three-cup serving-sized containers. After dinner, we load up whatever casserole, soup, or pasta we haven't eaten that night into the containers so we have lunches ready to go. My husband usually takes leftovers to work, so he rarely has to buy a meal. I estimate we save nearly $100 per month this way.

There's no need to buy a bottled teriyaki sauce when you can whip this delicious marinade together in ten minutes. You can also use this marinade for fish or tofu, and you can sauté the chicken, fish, or tofu on the stove instead of cooking it on the grill, if you prefer. Serve this dish with rice and grilled asparagus (cooked on a vegetable tray or aluminum foil).

grilled teriyaki chicken tenderloins

Prep + Cook = 20 minutes + Marinate

4 servings

Nutritional Information per serving:

Calories 230, Total Fat 2g, 3%, Saturated Fat .5g, 3%, Cholesterol 100mg, 33%, Sodium 1140mg, 48%, Total Carbohydrate 6g, 2%, Dietary Fiber 0g, 0%, Protein 40g, Sugar 4g

- ¼ cup soy sauce
- ¼ cup rice vinegar
- ¼ cup rice wine
- ½ teaspoon ground ginger or 1 teaspoon minced fresh ginger
- 1 teaspoon minced garlic (about 2 cloves)
- 1 tablespoon sugar
- 1 teaspoon vanilla
- 1½ pounds chicken tenderloins

In a large measuring cup, mix together all the ingredients except the chicken. Put the chicken in a flat plastic or glass container with a lid or a resealable plastic bag and cover it with the marinade. Flip or shake the container several times to distribute the marinade well. Marinate the chicken in the teriyaki sauce for at least 30 minutes (a few hours is ideal).

Preheat the grill. Cook the chicken for 2 to 4 minutes per side, watching carefully, until it is just cooked through (remove a piece to a plate to test occasionally). The tenderloins cook fast, so don't wander away while they're cooking. (Alternatively, broil or sauté the chicken until it is cooked through.)

TIP: To turn the remaining marinade into a dipping sauce, pour it into a small saucepan. Bring the sauce to a boil and simmer it for several minutes. Do not use the marinade as a sauce over cooked chicken without boiling it first, as it may contain harmful bacteria.

This one-dish, meatless alternative to tacos is a snap to prepare and a delicious way to get more healthy beans into your family's diet. For extra fiber, use whole wheat tortillas instead of white. Serve the casserole with roasted green beans (see p. 299).

tortilla casserole

Prep (10 minutes) +
Cook (30 minutes)

6 servings

Nutritional
Information per
serving:

Calories 320, Total
Fat 8g, 12%, Saturated Fat 4.5g, 23%,
Cholesterol 20mg,
7%, Sodium 1230mg,
51%, Total Carbohydrate 50g, 17%, Dietary Fiber 7g, 28%,
Protein 13g, Sugar
10g

- 1 can (15 ounces) pinto or black beans, drained
- 1 can (11 ounces) condensed tomato soup
- 1 can (11 ounces) corn kernels (unsweetened, if possible), drained
- 1 cup mild salsa
- ½ cup low-fat milk
- 6 soft-taco sized flour tortillas, cut into 1-inch pieces (or use 3 cups tortilla chips)
- 1 cup shredded Cheddar cheese

Preheat the oven to 400 degrees. In a large bowl, mix together all the ingredients, reserving half the cheese.

Place the mixture in a 2-quart casserole, cover it with foil, and bake it for 30 minutes. (For a crunchier top, remove the foil and broil the casserole for the final 5 minutes.) Remove it from the oven, uncover it, and sprinkle the remaining cheese on top. Top it with crumbled tortilla chips if you like more crunch.

This dish is surprisingly quick, especially if you buy peeled and de-veined frozen shrimp, and it tastes light and delicious. Serve it with rice or orzo noodles and steamed broccoli.

sautéed shrimp with tomatoes and lemon

Prep + Cook =
10 minutes

4 servings

Nutritional
Information per
serving:
Calories 170, Total
Fat 6g, 9%, Saturated
Fat 1g, 5%, Choles-
terol 170mg, 57%,
Sodium 190mg, 8%,
Total Carbohydrate
5g, 2%, Dietary Fiber
1g, 4%, Protein 24g,
Sugar 2g

- 1 tablespoon olive oil
- 1 pound medium shrimp, peeled and deveined
- 1 teaspoon minced garlic (about 2 cloves)
- pinch of salt
- 1 pint grape or cherry tomatoes, halved
- 2 tablespoons capers, drained
- 2 tablespoons chopped fresh parsley
- 1 teaspoon fresh lemon juice (or try it with a splash of fresh lime juice)

In a large skillet, heat the oil over medium-high heat. Add the shrimp, the garlic, and the salt and cook the shrimp, turning them once, until they just begin to turn opaque but are not cooked through, about 2 minutes. Transfer the shrimp to a bowl and set them aside.

Add the tomatoes to the skillet and cook them, stirring them frequently, until they soften, about 2 minutes.

Return the shrimp to the skillet, add the capers and parsley, and cook the shrimp for 2 more minutes. Add the lemon juice and toss it with the shrimp to coat them.

healthy dessert idea For a light and delicious dessert, layer berries, vanilla yogurt, and granola in clear glass sundae cups to make parfaits. Top them with a dollop of whipped cream.

This noodle casserole, suggested by my friend Ruth Robbins, is great for a buffet or a make-ahead meal, as you can assemble the manicotti and bake it when you're ready to serve it. Our kids liked it so much they didn't even mind the spinach. (We did remind them of the superhuman strength Popeye gets from eating the green stuff.) If you are a true spinach lover, you can use two packages of frozen spinach in the manicotti. Serve it with a fruit salad of diced kiwis and mangoes.

spinach manicotti

Prep (30 minutes) +
Cook (45 minutes)

10 servings

Nutritional
Information per
serving:

Calories 350, Total
Fat 14g, 22%, Saturated Fat 4g, 20%,
Cholesterol 15 mg,
5%, Sodium 240 mg,
10%, Total Carbohydrate 46g, 15%, Dietary Fiber 3g, 12%,
Protein 12g, Sugar 4g

1 package (10 ounces) frozen chopped spinach

1 tablespoon olive oil

1 small onion, diced

1 teaspoon chopped garlic (about 2 cloves)

1 package (8 ounces) sliced mushrooms

1 container (16 ounces) low-fat cottage cheese

1 egg

1 package (12–14 noodles) uncooked manicotti noodles

1 jar (26 ounces) tomato-and-basil flavored pasta sauce

½ cup shredded mozzarella cheese

a few shakes grated Parmesan cheese

Thaw the spinach in a microwave or in a covered pot over low heat. Drain it thoroughly. Preheat the oven to 350 degrees. Spray a 9 × 13-inch baking dish and a piece of foil large enough to cover it with nonstick cooking spray.

In a large skillet, heat the oil over medium heat. Add the onion, garlic, and mushrooms and sauté them until they are soft, about 8 to 10 minutes.

In a medium bowl, combine the cottage cheese and egg. Stir in the thawed spinach and the mushroom-onion mixture. Using your fingers, fill the uncooked manicotti noodles with the mixture. Place the noodles in a single layer in the baking dish. Cover the noodles completely with any leftover cheese mixture and the tomato-basil sauce. Top them with the mozzarella and Parmesan cheeses. (At this point, you can refrigerate the uncooked casserole for up to 24 hours or bake it immediately.)

Bake the casserole, covered tightly, for 40 minutes. Remove the foil for the final 5 minutes of cooking.

Six O'clock Scramble newsletter subscriber and professional event planner Claudia Ades shared her family's favorite soup recipe with me. It looks and sounds so sophisticated, yet it's easy to make. Claudia recommends serving it with baked sweet potatoes (see p. 300) and whole wheat bread.

broccoli-leek soup with lemon-chive cream

Prep (15 minutes) +
Cook (20 minutes)

6 servings

Nutritional
Information per
serving:

Calories 130, Total
Fat 6g, 9%, Saturated
Fat 2.5g, 13%, Choles-
terol 10mg, 3%,
Sodium 180mg, 8%,
Total Carbohydrate
14g, 5%, Dietary
Fiber 2g, 8%, Protein
7g, Sugar 3g

- 2 medium leeks, white and tender green part only
- 1 tablespoon butter
- 1 tablespoon olive oil
- 1½ pounds broccoli, stems peeled, cut into 1-inch pieces
- 3 garlic cloves, thinly sliced
- 5 cups chicken broth
- salt and pepper to taste
- ½ cup sour cream
- finely grated zest of 1 lemon
- 2 tablespoons fresh lemon juice (about ½ lemon)
- ¼ cup snipped chives or scallions, green parts only
- ¼ cup grated Parmesan cheese

Soak the chopped leeks in water for a few minutes to remove all the dirt between the leaves. Remove them from the water, drain them, and finely chop the leeks.

In a medium saucepan, melt the butter in the oil over medium heat. Add the leeks and cook them over medium-high heat, stirring, until they are softened, about 3 minutes. Stir in the broccoli, garlic, and broth, add salt and pepper to taste, and bring the liquid to a boil. Lower the heat, partially cover the pan, and simmer the vegetables until the broccoli is tender, about 20 minutes.

Meanwhile, in a small bowl, mix the sour cream with the lemon zest, lemon juice, chives, and Parmesan cheese. Season it with salt and pepper.

Transfer the soup in batches to a blender and puree it until it is smooth. Stir in half of the lemon-chive cream. Ladle the soup into bowls and top each with a dollop of the remaining lemon-chive cream. Serve it hot.

I made this dish for a big family dinner to rave reviews. Everyone from the grandparents to the kids loved it. Quinoa is a light and delicious whole grain that cooks quickly and is high in protein—it's a great healthy substitute for white rice or couscous. Serve the stew with bread, for soaking up the delicious sauce, and Italian-style cauliflower (see p. 298).

one-pot chicken and vegetable stew

Prep (15 minutes) +
Cook (30 minutes)

8 servings

Nutritional
Information per
serving:

Calories 450, Total
Fat 17g, 27%, Satu-
rated Fat 4.5g, 21%,
Cholesterol 110mg,
36%, Sodium 460 mg,
19%, Total Carbohy-
drate 33g, 11%, Di-
etary Fiber 7g, 30%,
Protein 34g, Sugar 4g

2 tablespoons olive oil

1 package (2–3 pounds) bone-in or boneless chicken thighs

1 medium onion, chopped

2 large carrots, chopped

1 teaspoon chopped garlic (about 2 cloves)

1 tablespoon chili powder

½ cup quinoa (use white rice if you can't find quinoa at your market)

1 can (15 ounces) chicken broth

1 can (28 ounces) crushed tomatoes

1 large white potato, peeled and chopped

1 bag (6–9 ounces) baby spinach

In a large stock pot, heat the oil over medium-high heat. Add the chicken and brown it for about 2 minutes per side.

Add the onion, carrots, garlic, and chili powder and cook the mixture for about 5 more minutes, until the vegetables soften slightly.

In a strainer, rinse the quinoa thoroughly with cold water.

Add the chicken broth, tomatoes, potatoes, and quinoa to the chicken and vegetables. Bring the liquid to a boil, reduce the heat, and simmer the stew for 30 to 40 minutes. Just before serving, stir in the spinach and let it wilt for about 2 minutes.

This recipe from our friend Kristen Donoghue is a favorite weeknight meal of many Six O'Clock Scramble subscribers. It is also wonderful wrapped in warm tortillas. Serve it with chips, guacamole, and salsa.

red beans and rice

Prep + Cook =
25 minutes

6 servings

Nutritional
Information per
serving:

Calories 210, Total
Fat 5g, 8%, Saturated
Fat 0.5g, 3%, Choles-
terol 0mg, 0%,
Sodium 600mg, 25%,
Total Carbohydrate
33g, 11%, Dietary
Fiber 7g, 28%, Pro-
tein 6g, Sugar 5g

- 2 cups cooked rice (about 1 cup dry, but make extra plain rice for picky eaters)
- 2 tablespoons olive oil
- 1 small onion, chopped
- 1 green bell pepper, chopped
- 1 teaspoon fresh minced garlic
- 1 can (15 ounces) kidney beans (preferably without sugar), rinsed and drained
- 1 can (15 ounces) Italian-style stewed tomatoes
- 1-2 tablespoons cumin, to taste
- ¼ teaspoon cayenne pepper (optional)
- salsa for serving
- plain yogurt or sour cream for serving (optional)

Prepare the rice according to the package directions.

While the rice is cooking, in a large skillet, heat the oil over medium-high heat. Add the onion, bell pepper, and garlic and sauté the vegetables until they are soft, about 8 minutes.

Add the beans, tomatoes, and spices and simmer the mixture for a few minutes.

Add the rice and mix the rice and beans together thoroughly.

Top each serving with salsa and yogurt or sour cream (optional).

{ **warm tortillas** To heat tortillas put them in the microwave on high for about 15 seconds per tortilla, or wrap them in foil and heat them in a preheated oven at 350 degrees for 5 minutes.

My friend Melissa Murdoch served this dish to our book club. It was a big hit! (If your family does not eat shellfish, you can substitute chicken or salmon for the shrimp.) Serve it with peeled and sliced cucumbers and baby carrots with dressing.

linguine with shrimp and feta cheese

Prep + Cook =
20 minutes

8 servings

Nutritional
Information per
serving:

Calories 320, Total
Fat 6g, 9%, Saturated
Fat 2.5g, 13%, Choles-
terol 100mg, 33%,
Sodium 320mg, 13%,
Total Carbohydrate
46g, 15%, Dietary
Fiber 2g, 8%, Protein
21g, Sugar 4g

1 package (16 ounces) linguine

1 teaspoon olive oil

¾ teaspoon dried oregano or 1 tablespoon fresh

½ teaspoon salt

¼ teaspoon red pepper flakes (add this at the table if your family doesn't like spicy food)

1 pound medium shrimp, peeled and deveined

2 teaspoons minced garlic (about 4 cloves)

½ cup dry white wine

3 cups diced plum tomatoes (about ¾ pound)

¾ cup finely crumbled feta cheese

Preheat the oven to 350 degrees. Cook the linguine according to the package directions and drain it.

Meanwhile, in a large nonstick skillet, heat the oil over medium-high heat. Add the oregano, salt, red pepper (optional), shrimp, and garlic. Sauté the shrimp until they start to turn pink, about 3 minutes. (Sauté the chicken or fish until it is almost cooked through.) Coat a 9 × 13-inch baking dish with nonstick cooking spray and pour the shrimp into it.

Add the wine to the skillet. Cook it over low heat until it is reduced by half, about 3 minutes. Stir in the tomatoes. Pour the tomatoes and wine over the shrimp. Sprinkle them with the cheese and bake them for 10 minutes. Serve the shrimp over the linguine.

This dinner quiche is as easy as pie, loaded with nutrients, and packed with flavor. It also makes excellent leftovers! Serve it with a fruit salad of oranges, bananas, and grapes (or your favorite fruit) and biscuits for a hearty meal.

broccoli, sausage, and cheddar quiche

Prep (20 minutes) + Cook (40–45 minutes)

8 servings

Nutritional Information per serving:

Calories 260, Total Fat 17g, 26%, Saturated Fat 4.5g, 23%, Cholesterol 115mg, 38%, Sodium 310mg, 13%, Total Carbohydrate 14g, 5%, Dietary Fiber 1g, 4%, Protein 13g, Sugar 2g

1 teaspoon olive oil

½ pound precooked chicken sausage (or use meatless), any variety, cut into bite-sized pieces

1 package (10 ounces) frozen chopped broccoli

1 prepared 9-inch pie crust

4 eggs

1 cup nonfat or low-fat milk

¼ teaspoon mustard powder

¼ teaspoon salt

⅛ teaspoon pepper

½ cup shredded Cheddar cheese

Preheat the oven to 375 degrees.

In a large skillet, heat the oil over medium heat. Add the sausage pieces and cook them for 5 to 7 minutes, tossing them occasionally, until they are lightly browned.

Defrost the broccoli in the microwave or on the stovetop and drain it very well.

Smooth the pie crust into a 9-inch pie dish and trim the edges with a paring knife.

In a medium bowl, beat the eggs with a fork. Whisk in the milk, mustard, salt, and pepper and mix them thoroughly.

Spread the sausage in the bottom of the pie shell. Top it evenly with the broccoli and cheese. Slowly and evenly pour the egg mixture over everything.

Place the quiche on top of a baking sheet to catch any spills. Bake it for 40 to 45 minutes until it is cooked through and very firm. For a browner top, put the quiche under the broiler for 2 to 3 minutes at the end. If time allows, let the quiche cool for 10 minutes before cutting it into wedges.

My friend Nancy Stansbury gave me the recipe for these delightfully easy salmon burgers. Her son Peter devours them, and your family will, too. Serve them as patties with lemon wedges or on a bun or English muffin with tartar sauce. Serve them with steamed peas and rice pilaf.

salmon burgers

Prep + Cook =
15 minutes

6 servings

Nutritional
Information per
serving:

Calories 480, Total Fat 19g, 29%, Saturated Fat 3.5g, 18%, Cholesterol 80mg, 27%, Sodium 1110mg, 46%, Total Carbohydrate 43g, 14%, Dietary Fiber 3g, 12%, Protein 32g, Sugar 2g

- 24–28 ounces boneless, skinless canned salmon
     (or substitute canned chunk light tuna)
- 1¼ cups bread crumbs
- ¼ cup mayonnaise
- 1 egg, beaten
- 1 tablespoon Worcestershire sauce
- 1 tablespoon vegetable oil

In a large bowl, mix together all the ingredients, except the oil. Form the mixture into 6 small patties.

In a large nonstick skillet, heat the oil over medium heat. Sauté the patties for 2 to 3 minutes on each side until they are lightly browned. Remove them from the heat and serve them immediately.

family dinners can nourish bodies and souls

You probably know it instinctively, and there's plenty of scientific proof: Children benefit emotionally and physically from eating dinner with their families. Kids are more likely to make wise food choices when presented with a healthy evening meal. They also gain emotional nourishment from the time spent together with their parents.

Obesity among children is rising at an alarming rate and is increasingly affecting even the youngest children. A recent study from the American Heart Association found that more than 10 percent of preschoolers are overweight, up from 7 percent ten years ago. "Experts blame the prevalence of junk food marketed to children, too much TV, and the *decline in the number of families who sit down together to eat,*" according to the Associated Press (December 23, 2004; my italics).

It's pretty clear that Solomon and Celia, our eight- and six-year-olds, eat better when they eat with us. Few processed foods make it to the table, and the kids are more likely to try new things and eat a balanced meal under our watch. Even most picky eaters get in the habit of eating the family meal if it's presented to them night after night.

Dinner is one of the few times we are all actually in the same room for more than a couple of minutes and we can talk without all the distractions. One night, over our farfalle pasta, Solomon said, "Mom, I haven't looked at your eyes in a long time."

Despite the benefits, few families can arrange to eat together every night. Between athletic practices, dance classes, and late nights at work, many of us lead hectic lives and can barely manage to eat a healthy meal while sitting down, let alone do it simultaneously with other busy people. If your family can't swing dinners together most nights, I'm sure most child experts would agree that eating breakfast together is a great substitute. I'm fine with that, as long as no one touches my coffee!

Catfish is both healthy and easy on the environment. Prepared this way, it's also quite delicious. If your kids' palates are delicate, dip their fish in the egg mixture and coat it in cornmeal only, as Old Bay is a little spicy. Serve the fish with lemon wedges and roasted baby carrots (see p. 299).

cornmeal-crusted catfish

Prep + Cook =
25 minutes

6 servings

Nutritional
Information per
serving:

Calories 180, Total
Fat 6g, 9%, Saturated
Fat 1g, 5%, Choles-
terol 85mg, 28%,
Sodium 55mg, 2%,
Total Carbohydrate
13g, 4%, Dietary
Fiber 0g, 0%, Protein
20g, Sugar 0g

1 egg

2 tablespoons milk

½ cup yellow cornmeal

2 tablespoons Old Bay seasoning

1½–2 pounds catfish fillets (2–3 fillets)

2 tablespoons vegetable oil or butter

In a shallow bowl, beat together the egg and milk. On a plate, using a fork, combine the cornmeal and Old Bay seasoning. Line a countertop, cutting board, or baking pan with waxed paper.

Dip each fillet in the egg-milk mixture, then coat it with the cornmeal mixture. Set it aside on the waxed paper.

In a large nonstick skillet, heat the oil over medium-high heat. Cook the fillets until the cornmeal is browned, about 4 minutes per side. On the second side, check that the catfish is cooked through by cutting into the thickest part with a knife. It should be firm and white throughout.

When I saw this recipe, I wondered how lentils and rice could be as good as Scramble subscriber Sena Murphy suggested. Suspecting that she has good taste, we gave it a try, and it was a big hit. Solomon and Celia both gave it thumbs up, and Andrew and I had several helpings. My more carnivorous friends told me that this dish is also yummy with a little cooked spicy sausage thrown in at the end. It's great topped with plain yogurt and served with a spinach salad with shredded carrots and diced red bell peppers and avocado.

indian spiced lentils with rice

Prep (15 minutes) +
Cook (55 minutes)

8 servings

Nutritional
Information per
serving:

Calories 280, Total
Fat 8g, 12%, Saturated Fat 1.5g, 8%, Cholesterol 0mg, 0%, Sodium 320mg, 13%, Total Carbohydrate 43g, 14%, Dietary Fiber 9g, 36%, Protein 11g, Sugar 10g

¼ cup olive oil

1 large onion, chopped

1 cup uncooked brown rice

2 teaspoons curry powder

2 bay leaves

1 cup dried green lentils

4½ cups water

1 teaspoon salt (or to taste)

½ cup raisins

¼–½ pound cooked spicy sausage (optional)

plain yogurt for serving

In a stockpot with a tight-fitting lid, heat the oil over medium-high heat. Add the onions and sauté them until they start to turn golden, about 5 minutes.

Add the rice, curry powder, and bay leaves and stir the mixture for a minute. Add the lentils, water, salt, and raisins and bring the liquid to a boil. Cover the pot and simmer it until the water is absorbed and the rice is tender, 50 to 55 minutes. Stir in the sausage (optional).

Serve the lentils and rice topped with a dollop of yogurt.

This is an updated version of a recipe by Lisa Flaxman and me that appeared in *Bon Appetit* in 2000. It's still delicious in 2005. Serve the noodles with egg rolls and lime wedges.

chinese noodles with greens

Prep and Cook =
25 minutes

8 servings

Nutritional
Information per
serving:

Calories 270, Total
Fat 4.5g, 7%, Saturated Fat 0g, 0%,
Cholesterol 0mg, 0%,
Sodium 540mg, 23%,
Total Carbohydrate
49g, 16%, Dietary
Fiber 2g, 8%, Protein
8g, Sugar 7g

- 16 ounces lo mein noodles (or substitute linguine)
- ¼ cup soy sauce
- 2 tablespoons rice vinegar
- 2 tablespoons honey
- 2 tablespoons sesame oil
- 2 teaspoons cornstarch
- 4 scallions, chopped
- 1½ teaspoons chopped garlic (about 3 cloves)
- 1 tablespoon minced, peeled fresh ginger
- 9–12 ounces bok choy leaves, chopped, or baby spinach

In a large stockpot, cook the noodles according to the package directions until they are al dente. Rinse them in cold water.

In a measuring cup, whisk together the soy sauce, the vinegar, the honey, 1 tablespoon of the sesame oil, and the cornstarch. Set the sauce aside.

In a large heavy pot, heat the remaining 1 tablespoon of sesame oil over medium heat. Add the scallions, garlic, and ginger and stir-fry them for 30 seconds. Add the bok choy or spinach and sauté the greens until they begin to wilt, about 2 minutes. Add the cooked noodles and the sauce and stir everything together until well blended, about 1 minute.

This recipe from Sherry Ettleson is so versatile—your family may prefer it in a taco shell, wrapped in a tortilla, or inside a pita pocket. Or forget the bread and put the filling on salad greens. A fruit salad on the side will balance the spice and the heat.

vegetarian tacos

Prep + Cook =
30 minutes

8 servings

Nutritional
Information per
taco (Vegetarian
Filling)

Calories 130, Total
Fat 2.5g, 4%, Saturated Fat 0.5g, 3%,
Cholesterol 0mg, 0%,
Sodium 600mg, 25%,
Total Carbohydrate
20g, 8%, Dietary
Fiber 7g, 28%, Protein 11g, Sugar 7g

Nutritional
Information per
taco (Turkey Filling)

Calories 170, Total
Fat 8g, 12%, Saturated Fat 1.5g, 8%,
Cholesterol 45mg,
15%, Sodium 660mg,
28%, Total Carbohydrate 13g, 4%, Dietary Fiber 3g, 12%,
Protein 14g, Sugar 9g

1 bag (12 ounces) vegetarian ground "meat" (or use ground turkey or beef)

1 tablespoon olive oil

1 medium onion, diced

1 medium red bell pepper, diced

1 teaspoon minced garlic (about 2 cloves)

1 small can (6 ounces) tomato paste

1 tablespoon soy sauce

1 tablespoon balsamic vinegar

1 teaspoon sugar

1 teaspoon chili powder

½ teaspoon cumin

1 can (28 ounces) crushed tomatoes with their liquid

8 taco shells, tortillas, or pita pockets

Taco fixings as desired: shredded Cheddar cheese, diced tomatoes, chopped lettuce, salsa, sour cream

Remove the vegetarian ground "meat" from the freezer during the day or as you start to make dinner. (If you are using meat, brown it in the pan first until it is almost cooked through, and then add the other ingredients.)

In a large nonstick skillet, heat the oil over medium heat. Add the onions, red bell pepper, and garlic. Sauté the vegetables for 3 to 4 minutes. Stir in the tomato paste, soy sauce, vinegar, sugar, chili powder, cumin, and crushed tomatoes with their liquid. Bring it to a boil. Lower the heat and simmer for 20 minutes until it is thickened, stirring it occasionally. Stir in the "meat" and cook it for another few minutes.

Assemble the tacos as desired.

meatless meat If you have never tried cooking with vegetarian or meatless ground burger you will be amazed! Once combined with a sauce, it is almost indistinguishable from ground beef, yet it has one-twentieth of the amount of fat and no cholesterol. It's also high in fiber and soy protein.

Anyone who's ever tried Annie's Naturals Goddess Dressing on a salad or as a dip knows how delectable it is. It also makes a delicious sauce for chicken. This one, suggested by our friend Jennifer Brown Simon, is slightly tangy and delectably rich. For a sweeter flavor, add a splash of orange juice or a spoonful of orange marmalade to the dressing and broth before pouring it over the chicken. Serve the chicken with couscous and grapes.

goddess chicken

Prep (10 minutes) +
Cook (30 minutes)

8 servings

Nutritional
Information per
serving:

Calories 360, Total
Fat 6g, 10%, Saturated Fat 2g, 9%,
Cholesterol 145mg,
48%, Sodium 720mg,
30%, Total Carbohydrate 18g, 6%, Dietary Fiber 2g, 8%,
Protein 56g, Sugar 5g

2–2½ pounds boneless, skinless chicken breasts (about 4–6 chicken breasts), cut in half crosswise

1 can (15 ounces) artichoke hearts, drained and cut into ½-inch pieces

1 bag (3 ounces) sundried tomatoes, cut into ½-inch pieces

¾ cup Annie's Naturals Goddess Dressing (or use creamy Italian or Caesar dressing)

½ cup chicken broth

Preheat the oven to 350 degrees.

Place the chicken breasts in a large baking pan with sides. Add the artichoke hearts and sundried tomatoes.

In a measuring cup, whisk together the dressing and the chicken broth. Pour the mixture over the chicken and vegetables. Turn the chicken several times to coat it with the sauce.

Bake the chicken, uncovered, for 25 to 30 minutes until it is cooked through, flipping it once and spooning the sauce over it during baking.

This dish has a succulent, slightly tangy flavor from the mustard. If you suspect that the taste will be too strong for your picky eaters, dredge their chicken in just the flour mixture before baking it. Serve the chicken with mini corn muffins and peas.

chicken dijon

Prep + Cook =
20 minutes

4 servings

Nutritional
Information per
serving:

Calories 350, Total
Fat 6g, 9%, Satu-
rated Fat 3g, 15%,
Cholesterol 145mg,
48%, Sodium 590mg,
25%, Total Carbohy-
drate 13g, 4%, Dietary
Fiber <1g, 4%, Protein
59g, Sugar 0g

- 4 boneless, skinless chicken breast halves
- ¼ cup bread crumbs
- ¼ cup flour
- ½ teaspoon paprika
- 3 tablespoons Dijon mustard
- 1 tablespoon honey
- 1 tablespoon water
- ¼ teaspoon salt
- ⅛ teaspoon pepper
- 1 tablespoon butter

Preheat the oven to 425 degrees. Line a baking sheet with foil and spray it with nonstick cooking spray. Pound the chicken breasts with a mallet to a uniform thickness of about ½ inch. This is important so they cook quickly and evenly.

In a shallow bowl or plate, combine the bread crumbs, flour, and paprika. In another shallow bowl or plate, combine the mustard, honey, water, salt, and pepper. Coat both sides of the chicken breasts with the mustard mixture, then the bread crumb mixture, and place them on the baking sheet.

Melt the butter in the microwave and drizzle it over the chicken breasts. Bake the chicken for 10 minutes or until the thickest part is no longer pink inside.

This hearty soup can be made with sausage or without. It takes a bit longer to make than most Scramble meals, but it's very filling, healthy, and tasty. Plus, it makes enough to serve a crowd or freeze half for another night, so it's like getting two meals in one. Serve it with bread sticks and a green salad with goat cheese, pecans, and sliced pears.

corn and wild rice soup

Prep (25 minutes) +
Cook (40 minutes)

12 servings

Nutritional
Information per
serving:

Calories 260, Total
Fat 9g, 14%, Saturated Fat 3g, 15%,
Cholesterol 20mg,
7%, Sodium 340mg,
14%, Total Carbohydrate 36g, 12%, Dietary Fiber 3g, 12%,
Protein 13g, Sugar 8g

- 12 cups canned chicken broth
- 1¼ cups uncooked wild rice
- 6 cups (about 2½ pounds) frozen corn kernels, thawed
- 2 tablespoons vegetable oil
- 10 ounces precooked smoked turkey or vegetarian sausage, cut into ½-inch pieces (optional)
- 3 carrots, diced
- 2 medium onions, chopped
- ¾ cup half and half

In a heavy saucepan over medium-high heat, bring 5 cups of the broth to a boil. Add the rice, partially cover the pan, and simmer it gently, stirring it occasionally, until all the liquid is absorbed and the rice is almost tender, about 40 minutes. Meanwhile, blend 4 cups of the corn and 1½ cups of the chicken broth in a food processor or blender until a thick, nearly smooth puree forms. Set it aside.

In a large heavy stockpot, heat the oil over medium-high heat. Add the sausage (optional) and sauté it until it starts to brown, about 5 minutes. Add the carrots and onions and cook them, stirring them frequently, for 3 minutes. Add the remaining 5½ cups of the chicken broth and bring the soup to a boil. Reduce the heat to low and simmer the soup for 15 minutes. Add the cooked rice, corn puree, and remaining 2 cups of corn kernels to the soup. Cook it until the rice is very tender and the flavors blend, about 15 minutes. Stir in the half and half. Thin the soup with water, if desired.

This is a simple preparation for a thin cut of meat that can also be used for turkey cutlets. Serve it with rice pilaf.

pan-seared pork loins (or turkey cutlets) with green beans

Prep + Cook =
20 minutes

4 servings

Nutritional
Information per
serving:

Calories 380, Total
Fat 19g, 29%, Satu-
rated Fat 7g, 35%,
Cholesterol 110mg,
37%, Sodium 330mg,
14%, Total Carbohy-
drate 12g, 4%, Di-
etary Fiber 3g, 12%,
Protein 36g, Sugar 3g

- 1 pound frozen cut green beans
- ¼ cup flour
- ¼ teaspoon salt
- 1–1½ pounds boneless pork loins or turkey cutlets
- 1 tablespoon olive oil
- 1 tablespoon plus 1 teaspoon butter
- 1 teaspoon chopped garlic (about 2 cloves)
- 2 tablespoons lemon juice (about ½ lemon)
- 1 tablespoon capers (optional)

Remove the green beans from the freezer and place them in a serving bowl. Put the flour in a shallow dish and mix it with the salt. Dredge the meat in the flour and shake off the excess.

In a large heavy skillet, heat the oil and 1 tablespoon of the butter over medium-high heat. When the butter starts to bubble, add the garlic and cook it for 1 minute until it starts to brown, then add the meat and brown it until it is no longer pink in the middle, about 3 minutes per side. After turning the meat, squeeze the lemon juice on top and sprinkle it with the capers (optional).

With a slotted spatula, remove the meat to a plate and cover it to keep it warm. Add the remaining 1 teaspoon of the butter to the skillet. When it melts, add the green beans. Cover the skillet and cook the beans until they are softened, about 5 minutes.

Return the green beans to their bowl and cut the meat into slices to serve.

This zesty, protein- and fiber-packed tuna casserole is definitely not your mother's tired-out recipe. (Sorry, Mom!) Salsa and black beans give it a Southwestern flavor. It may sound odd, but it's a delicious combination, created by our friend Sara Emley. Serve the casserole with tortilla chips.

not-your-mother's tuna casserole

Prep (30 minutes) + Cook (25–30 minutes)

8 servings

Nutritional Information per serving:

Calories 390, Total Fat 10g, 15%, Saturated Fat 5g, 27%, Cholesterol 60mg, 20%, Sodium 1040mg, 43%, Total Carbohydrate 52g, 17%, Dietary Fiber 6g, 24%, Protein 23g, Sugar 8g

8 ounces egg noodles, penne, or spiral-shaped pasta

1 tablespoon olive oil

½ medium onion, diced

1 medium red or green bell pepper, diced

1 can (6 ounces) chunk light tuna packed in water, drained

veggies (optional): Use about 1 cup (total) of one or more of the following: chopped broccoli (frozen or fresh), corn kernels, chopped tomato, diced zucchini, peas, chopped roasted red peppers

1 can (15 ounces) black beans or kidney beans, drained

1 can (10 ounces) condensed tomato soup

1 soup can of low-fat milk

1 cup mild salsa

1½ cups shredded Cheddar cheese

handful of bread crumbs

Preheat the oven to 450 degrees. Spray a 2- to 3-quart casserole dish with nonstick cooking spray.

Cook the pasta according to the package directions. When the pasta is done, drain it and run cold water over it to cool it.

Meanwhile, in a large skillet, heat the oil over medium-high heat. Add the onions, peppers, and tuna (and optional extra vegetables) and sauté them until they are softened, about 5 minutes. Stir in the beans and remove the skillet from the heat.

In a small saucepan over low heat, stir together the soup, milk, and salsa.

Put half the pasta in the casserole dish. Cover it with half the vegetable-tuna mixture and half the cheese. Make a second layer with the noodles and the rest of the vegetable-tuna mixture. Pour the tomato-milk-salsa sauce over everything. Top it with the bread crumbs and the remaining cheese. If the casserole is very full, set it on a baking sheet before putting in the oven to avoid messy spills. Bake it for 25 to 30 minutes until the top is browned and the sauce is bubbly.

TIP: Chunk light tuna has a lower mercury content than solid white tuna, so it's much safer for kids and adults to eat.

Bon Appetit magazine featured this recipe that I submitted in their "Too Busy to Cook?" column a few years ago. I've updated it to make it lower in fat by substituting nonfat buttermilk for the butter in the original recipe. I've also reduced the preparation time by microwaving the potatoes initially instead of baking them. You can get creative with this recipe by adding bacon bits, sausage, or fresh cilantro. Serve the potatoes with a spinach salad with grated carrots and red onions.

southwestern-style stuffed potatoes

Prep (15 minutes) +
Cook (30 minutes)

4 servings

Nutritional
Information per
serving:

Calories 300, Total
Fat 7g, 11%, Satu-
rated Fat 4g, 20%,
Cholesterol 25mg,
8%, Sodium 410mg,
17%, Total Carbohy-
drate 49g, 16%, Di-
etary Fiber 5g, 20%,
Protein 14g, Sugar 5g

4 large baking potatoes

½ cup nonfat buttermilk

¼ cup mild salsa plus additional for serving

1 cup shredded reduced-fat Cheddar cheese

¼ cup scallions, chopped (optional)

reduced-fat sour cream or plain yogurt for serving

Preheat the oven to 450 degrees.

Prick the potatoes with a fork in several places and cook them in the microwave for about 10 to 20 minutes, rotating them every 5 minutes, until they are soft. NOTE: If you prefer to bake the potatoes, bake them for about 1 hour and 15 minutes at 400 degrees.

When the potatoes are softened, carefully slice them in half lengthwise (use oven mitts!) and scoop out most of the flesh into a large bowl, leaving a ¼-inch thick shell of flesh in the potato skin. Add the buttermilk, ¼ cup of the salsa, the cheese, and the scallions to the potato in the bowl and mash the mixture thoroughly. Fill the shells with the potato mixture, mounding it in the center.

Put the stuffed potatoes on a baking sheet and bake them until they are heated through, about 10 to 15 minutes. For a crispier top, broil them for the final few minutes of cooking. Serve the potatoes with sour cream and salsa.

thanksgiving dinner survival guide
eight suggestions for hosting an easier feast

In our family, we rotate houses for Thanksgiving. When it is our turn to host Thanksgiving dinner, I want to be sure it goes smoothly. Since I don't host big dinner parties often, I have devised some strategies for making the evening easier on us while still indulging our guests.

1. *Involve everybody in the preparations.* Just because I love to cook doesn't mean I have to do it all! I take everybody who volunteers to help up on his or her offer. Last Thanksgiving, Andrew was in charge of the turkey, his mom made sweet potatoes and cranberry sauce, his sister Soozy made zucchini bread, and our friends Lisa and Jonathan brought dessert. The kids made place cards and table decorations, and I made the stuffing and soup.

2. *Make a menu ahead of time.* A few days before the dinner, I make a list of everything—from appetizers to coffee—that will be served, who is making each of them, and when they should be made. I tack the list to the fridge so I can make sure we're on track.

3. *Grocery-shop early.* Just as I do every week, I make a detailed grocery list (consulting my menu) and buy the groceries two days before the feast, so we can start cooking on the day before.

4. *Cook in advance.* The trimmings can all be cooked well in advance of dinner; some will even be done the day before. Everything can be warmed in the oven or the microwave before we sit down. That way, dinner won't depend on timing everything perfectly, and the kitchen won't feel like Grand Central Station at rush hour.

5. *Get the house and table ready the night before.* To avoid exhaustion on the big day, I make sure the house looks nice and the table is set before I go to bed on Wednesday. I even put out the trivets, serving utensils, and water pitchers we'll need.

6. *Keep appetizers easy.* I don't want guests to fill up before the big dinner, and I don't want to add too much to my already long to-do list. Before dinner, I serve easy-to-prepare foods, such as gourmet cheeses, nuts, popcorn, and vegetables and dip. I like to serve this impressively simple appetizer suggested by super-hostess Christina McHenry: Top a layer of goat cheese with a layer of pesto and sprinkle lightly toasted pine nuts on top.

7. *Take the last thirty minutes off.* An experienced hostess once told me that I should try to hold sacred the last half hour before guests arrive. I try to take fifteen minutes to get myself cleaned up and fifteen minutes to turn on some music, read a book with the kids, and relax before the festivities. That way I'm not utterly exhausted before the evening begins.

8. *Finally, make sure the burners are turned off before you set a pie on the stove.* I learned that the hard way a few years ago, when the glass pie dish overheated and shattered, ruining both the sweet potato pie and the nearby soup. But if a mini disaster does strike? More stories for next year!

This popular dish from our 1998 cookbook, *Peanut Butter Stew and Couscous, Too,* is light and tangy. This recipe also works well with extra-firm tofu in place of the chicken. Serve it with couscous and roasted asparagus.

rosemary chicken with artichokes

Prep + Cook =
20 minutes

8 servings

Nutritional
Information per
serving:

Calories 270, Total
Fat 12g, 18%, Saturated Fat 3g, 14%,
Cholesterol 100mg,
34%, Sodium 190mg,
8%, Total Carbohydrate 4g, 1%, Dietary
Fiber <1g, 2%, Protein 34g, Sugar 0g

2 tablespoons olive oil

2–3 pounds boneless, skinless chicken breast halves, cut into 1-inch pieces

1–2 tablespoons fresh or dried rosemary, to taste

2 cans (14 ounces) artichoke hearts, drained and quartered

2 tablespoons lemon juice (about ½ lemon)

In a large nonstick skillet, heat the oil over medium-high heat. Add the chicken and rosemary and sauté the chicken, tossing it frequently, until it is no longer pink, 8 to 10 minutes.

Reduce the heat to medium, add the artichokes and lemon juice, and heat them through. Serve the chicken immediately.

Halibut is a good, firm fish for grilling, and this tasty marinade livens up its mild flavor. Serve it with grilled Italian bread and grilled zucchini (see p. 299) for an entire meal made on the grill.

grilled halibut in soy-ginger marinade

Prep + Cook =
20 minutes +
Marinate

4 servings

Nutritional
Information per
serving:

Calories 200, Total
Fat 4g, 6%, Saturated
Fat 0.5g, 3%, Choles-
terol 55mg, 18%,
Sodium 610mg, 25%,
Total Carbohydrate
2g, 1%, Dietary Fiber
0g, 0%, Protein 36g,
Sugar 1g

- ¼ cup soy sauce
- ¼ teaspoon ground ginger (or ¾ teaspoon minced fresh ginger)
- 1 tablespoon brown sugar
- ½ teaspoon minced garlic (about 1 clove)
- ½ teaspoon dry mustard
- 2 tablespoons lemon juice (about ½ lemon)
- 1½–2 pounds halibut fillets (or use other thick white fish or salmon)

To make the marinade, in a measuring cup, whisk together all the ingredients except the fish.

Put the halibut fillets in a small flat dish with sides, just large enough to hold the fish. Pour the marinade over the fillets and flip them in the liquid several times to coat them. Cover the dish and refrigerate the fish for at least 30 minutes and up to 12 hours.

Clean the grill and spray the grates with nonstick cooking spray. Preheat the grill to medium-high heat. Remove the fish from the marinade, reserving the marinade, and put the fish on a grilling tray, if you have one, or on a folded piece of aluminum foil. Put it on the grill, cover the grill, and cook the fish for 10 to 15 minutes until it flakes easily and is opaque, flipping it once during cooking and basting it with the marinade occasionally. In a small saucepan over medium-high heat, bring the remaining marinade to a boil and simmer it for one minute. Use it as a sauce to spoon over the fish.

TIP: Alternatively, cook the fish in a preheated broiler for about 8 to 10 minutes.

My eight-year-old, Solomon, and I had the exciting experience of making this easy pasta live on the local morning news. While you have to have all your ingredients cooked, measured, and within arm's length to make it in three minutes as we did on live TV, it is very simple to make. This is a great dish for a potluck or picnic, as sesame noodles are kid-friendly and taste great hot, cold, or in between. The chili oil gives the noodles a little spicy bite, but if your family doesn't like their food spicy, substitute toasted sesame oil instead. Serve the noodles alone or with a salad of mixed greens, blue cheese, slivered almonds, and sliced apples.

sesame noodles with peas

Prep + Cook =
20 minutes

8 servings

Nutritional
Information per
serving:

Calories 330, Total
Fat 13g, 20%, Saturated Fat 1.5g, 8%,
Cholesterol 0mg, 0%,
Sodium 570mg, 24%,
Total Carbohydrate
44g, 15%, Dietary
Fiber 4g, 16%, Protein 9g, Sugar 6g

¼ cup sesame oil

2 tablespoons hot chili sesame oil (or use more sesame oil)

⅓ cup soy sauce

2 tablespoons brown sugar

2 tablespoons balsamic vinegar

1 tablespoon minced ginger (optional)

½ cup toasted sesame seeds

1 package (16 ounces) linguine

2 cups frozen peas (or use 1 pound broccoli florets, fresh or frozen)

Bring a large pot of water to a boil.

While the water is heating, whisk together all the ingredients except the linguine and peas in a large serving bowl.

Cook the linguine in the boiling water according to the package directions until it is al dente. For the final minute of cooking, add the peas to the boiling water with the noodles (if you're using broccoli, add it for the final 2 minutes of cooking).

Drain the noodles and peas and toss them thoroughly with the sauce in the serving bowl.

Serve this dish warm, cold, or anywhere in between.

TIP: To toast the sesame seeds, spread them on a baking tray and toast them on a light setting in a toaster oven for about 5 minutes until they are light brown. If you don't have a toaster oven, toast them in a conventional oven on a baking sheet at 325 degrees for about 5 minutes.

This wonderful recipe is great for dinner or brunch. Serve it with corn on the cob for dinner or with salsa and a fruit salad for brunch.

baked huevos rancheros casserole

Prep (15 minutes) + Cook (30 minutes)

8 servings

Nutritional Information per serving:

Calories 260, Total Fat 13g, 20%, Saturated Fat 7g, 35%, Cholesterol 135mg, 45%, Sodium 420mg, 18%, Total Carbohydrate 23g, 8%, Dietary Fiber 3g, 12%, Protein 14g, Sugar 3g

- **12 small corn tortillas**
- **2 cups shredded Monterey Jack cheese**
- **2 cans (4 ounces each) chopped mild green chilies**
- **4 large eggs**
- **2 cups nonfat buttermilk**

Preheat the oven to 350 degrees. Spray a 9 × 13-inch casserole with nonstick cooking spray.

Tear or cut the tortillas into bite-sized pieces and scatter half of them in the bottom of the dish. Top them with half the cheese and half the chilies. Repeat the layers, reserving a handful of cheese for the top of the casserole.

In a large bowl, whisk together the eggs and buttermilk until they are well blended. Pour the mixture over the casserole and top it with the reserved cheese.

Bake the casserole, uncovered, for 30 minutes. Allow it to cool for a few minutes before serving.

Our kids loved eating the chickpeas in this simple stew and declared it "Scramblicious." Serve it topped with sour cream over couscous or rice, passing warm pita bread on the side, or stuff it inside the pitas.

chickpea-tomato stew

Prep + Cook =
25 minutes

6 servings

Nutritional Information per serving:

Calories 180, Total Fat 7g, 11%, Saturated Fat 1g, 5%, Cholesterol 0mg, 0%, Sodium 630mg, 26%, Total Carbohydrate 24g, 8%, Dietary Fiber 5g, 20%, Protein 6g, Sugar 8g

2 tablespoons olive oil

3 shallots, finely chopped (or substitute ½ onion and 2 cloves garlic, finely chopped)

2 teaspoons curry powder

1 teaspoon cumin

1 can (15 ounces) chickpeas (also called garbanzos), drained

1 can (14½ ounces) diced tomatoes

1 cup prepared pasta sauce or tomato sauce

sour cream for serving

handful of fresh mint and/or fresh oregano for garnish (optional)

In a medium to large skillet, heat the oil over medium heat. Add the shallots and sauté them until they start to sizzle. Add the curry powder and cumin and cook the shallots, stirring, for 1 more minute. Add the chickpeas, tomatoes, and pasta sauce or tomato sauce and simmer the stew for about 10 minutes.

Serve it over couscous or rice, topped with a spoonful of sour cream and garnished with a sprinkle of fresh mint and/or oregano.

what you serve and what they eat
the picky eater conundrum

There are a few kids who really seem to enjoy just about everything; our six-year-old friend Eleanor's favorite foods include avocados and tofu. We know some extremely picky eaters, too. We met a four-year-old boy who will *only* eat foods that are brown or white! Most kids fall somewhere in the middle, interspersing simpler foods with some that are more flavorful, in what seems to us a completely random and unpredictable pattern. Almost every family has at least one child they would call a picky eater.

Lots of people ask me how to cope with picky eaters. Some tell me they have to cook more than one dinner for their family because their kids are too picky. Many people assume that because of the variety of foods in The Scramble's menus, my own kids are great eaters. Like most kids, though, their tastes and sense of culinary adventure fluctuate. It turns out that I can't predict what they will and won't like, but I would never have learned that Solomon loves tortellini and Celia adores veggie burgers if I hadn't tried. We encourage the kids to try everything I make, and we give them great feedback for being adventurous.

When Solomon was a toddler, I was really worried about his picky eating. I gained many insights from nutritionist Ellen Satter, who wrote *How to Get Your Kid to Eat (But Not Too Much),* among other books. I've boiled down some of her suggestions here:

Tips for Coping with Picky Eaters

Cut down on (or eliminate) snacks and juice between meals. If kids are not hungry at mealtime, they are unlikely to eat much.

Don't push too hard when it comes to food. You've heard it a million times, but kids won't starve themselves.

Don't get into a food rut. Vary the foods that you serve them, and don't shy away from something just because your children didn't like it in the past.

Offer healthy foods (preferably what the rest of the family is eating) and let your children decide what and how much to eat. Don't bend over backward to find something they love. If your children know you're a short-order cook, they might hold out for something better. (We have modified this by offering cereal with milk as a dinner alternative if the kids really don't like what I've made.)

Try to eat meals together, even if it seems inconvenient. It makes meals a special family time, and your children will be more likely to eat what the rest of the family is eating.

Even if there's only one bite left on the plate, try not to push your children to finish. Let them develop their own sense of when they're full.

For older toddlers and children, you might develop a "one-bite" tasting rule so they will be encouraged to try new things. But keep up your end of the deal—if they don't want more than one bite, try not to push.

Don't be disheartened if you are "blessed" with a picky eater. Most kids gradually grow out of it, especially if their eating habits don't become a source of too much attention.

This recipe from my resourceful friend Lisa Flaxman is a great way to use up that last can of cranberry sauce so it doesn't sit in your pantry until next Thanksgiving. Serve the chicken with couscous, green beans, and leftover stuffing—if you have any!

cranberry chicken

Prep + Cook =
20 minutes

6 servings

Nutritional
Information per
serving:

Calories 330, Total
Fat 8g, 12%, Saturated Fat 1.5g, 7%,
Cholesterol 95mg,
32%, Sodium 290mg,
12%, Total Carbohydrate 25g, 8%, Dietary Fiber 2g, 6%,
Protein 37g, Sugar
23g

- 1 tablespoon olive oil
- 4 boneless, skinless chicken breast halves (1½–2 pounds), cut into 1-inch pieces
- 1 can (15 ounces) whole cranberry sauce
- 2 tablespoons Dijon mustard
- ¼ cup orange juice
- ¼ cup dried cranberries (optional)
- ¼ cup sliced or slivered almonds, toasted (optional)

In a large nonstick skillet, heat the oil over medium heat. Add the chicken and sauté it until it is no longer pink in the center, about 6 to 8 minutes.

In a bowl, mix together the cranberry sauce, mustard, and orange juice. Pour the mixture over the chicken and heat it until it is warmed through. Top the chicken with dried cranberries and toasted almonds, if desired.

My walking buddy Sharon Masling introduced me to this simple and light preparation for salmon. It's a good recipe to serve to company, because the presentation is beautiful with the slivered half moons of lemon fanned across the top of the salmon. Of course, your family is probably worth it, too! Serve the fish with a crisp salad and wild rice tossed with toasted pecans, dried cherries, and a splash of vinaigrette dressing.

salmon topped with slivered lemon

Prep (10 minutes) + Cook (25–30 minutes)

4 servings

Nutritional Information per serving:

Calories 230, Total Fat 14g, 22%, Saturated Fat 3g, 15%, Cholesterol 68mg, 22%, Sodium 230mg, 10%, Total Carbohydrate <1g, 0%, Dietary Fiber 0g, 0%, Protein 23g, Sugar 0g

- 1–1½ pounds salmon fillet
- 1 large lemon
- 1 tablespoon olive oil
- ½ teaspoon kosher salt
- pepper to taste
- 1 tablespoon fresh dill (optional)

Preheat the oven to 350 degrees. Wash the salmon, pat it dry, and place it in a large baking dish. Extract the juice from half the lemon. Cut the other half of the lemon into thin slices, and then cut those slices in half crosswise, so they are now semi-circles.

Brush the salmon with the oil and sprinkle the top of the fillets with the lemon juice, salt, and pepper. Line the lemon slices on top of the fillet so they cover it evenly.

Bake the salmon for 25 to 30 minutes until it is light pink and flakes easily in the thickest part of the fillet. Sprinkle the fresh dill (optional) over the salmon before serving.

I recently smelled the heavenly aroma of this pasta at the home of our friend Elizabeth Zehner, and before I even saw it, I knew I had to have this recipe. When I made it for my family, to my surprise, the kids thought the cannellini beans were the best part. Serve it with chopped cantaloupe and warm rolls.

butterfly pasta with cannellini beans

Prep + Cook =
30 minutes

8 servings

Nutritional
Information per
serving:

Calories 350, Total
Fat 4.5g, 7%, Satu-
rated Fat 0.5g, 3%,
Cholesterol 0mg, 0%,
Sodium 380mg, 16%,
Total Carbohydrate
61g, 20%, Dietary
Fiber 6g, 24%, Pro-
tein 12g, Sugar 4g

2 tablespoons olive oil

2 cloves minced garlic

1 large can (28 ounces) diced tomatoes with their liquid

2 cans (15 ounces each) cannellini beans with their liquid (or use white beans)

1 package (16 ounces) farfalle (butterfly) pasta

1 bunch fresh basil, leaves only, coarsely chopped (about 1 cup loosely packed)

salt and pepper to taste

grated Parmesan cheese for serving

In a large skillet, heat the oil and garlic over medium heat. After a minute or two, when the garlic begins to sizzle, add the tomatoes and the beans. Bring it to a low boil and simmer it for 20 minutes, or until the pasta is ready.

Meanwhile, cook the pasta according to the package directions.

Add the basil to the tomato sauce about a minute before you drain the pasta. Season the sauce with salt and pepper.

Drain the pasta and add it to the sauce or mix the pasta and sauce together in a large metal bowl. Serve the pasta topped with lots of Parmesan cheese.

hot stuff A large metal bowl keeps pasta hot until you're ready to serve it.

My family devoured these mouth-watering sandwiches. For a meatless alternative, triple the amount of mushrooms and follow the rest of the directions. Serve this with Creamy Mashed Potatoes (see p. 300).

grilled steak and portobello mushroom sandwiches

Prep + Cook =
25 minutes

4 servings

Nutritional Information per serving:

Calories 420, Total Fat 21g, 32%, Saturated Fat 6g, 30%, Cholesterol 70mg, 23%, Sodium 300mg, 13%, Total Carbohydrate 33g, 11%, Dietary Fiber 5g, 20%, Protein 30g, Sugar 6g

2–4 portobello mushroom caps (6–8 ounces total)

1–1½ pounds boneless steak

¼ cup olive oil

⅛ cup balsamic vinegar

½ teaspoon chili powder (use 1 teaspoon for a spicier flavor)

1½ teaspoons minced garlic (about 3 cloves)

¼ teaspoon salt

3 tablespoons herbed or plain goat cheese (chèvre)

4 whole wheat buns

Gently scrub the portobello mushroom caps under cold running water with a vegetable brush. Drain and place them with the steaks in a large flat bottom dish with sides.

In a measuring cup, whisk together the oil, vinegar, chili powder, garlic, and salt. Pour the mixture evenly over the mushrooms and steak, and flip them to coat. Refrigerate them for 20 minutes to 12 hours, until ready to cook.

Heat the grill (or the broiler) to medium-high heat. Take the goat cheese out of the refrigerator to soften it.

Cook the mushrooms and steak for 4 to 6 minutes per side until the mushrooms are nicely browned, and the steaks reach the desired doneness. Discard the excess marinade.

For the last minute of cooking, put the buns on the grill to lightly brown the insides of the bread.

Remove the buns, mushrooms, and steak from the grill, and slice the mushrooms and steak into ¼ inch slices. Spread a thin layer of goat cheese evenly over the inside bottoms of the buns, layer them with slices of steak and mushrooms, and eat them immediately.

This is an unusual and surprisingly tasty combination. Use Israeli couscous if you can find it (many markets now carry it), as it has much bigger grains and a great texture, yet still cooks very quickly. Another good option is cooked orzo. Serve the casserole with a fruit salad of diced mangoes, kiwis, and apples alongside a purchased roast chicken.

couscous and savory vegetable casserole with feta

Prep (20 minutes) +
Cook (30 minutes)

8 servings

Nutritional
Information per
serving:

Calories 240, Total
Fat 8g, 12%, Saturated Fat 3.5g, 17%,
Cholesterol 15mg,
6%, Sodium 350mg,
14%, Total Carbohydrate 32g, 11%, Dietary Fiber 3g, 10%,
Protein 10g, Sugar 2g

1 can (15 ounces) artichoke hearts in water

2 tablespoons olive oil

1 teaspoon minced garlic (about 2 cloves)

1 pound sliced mushrooms

8 ounces cherry tomatoes, halved

1 box (8.8 ounces) Israeli couscous (or use 8–10 ounces regular couscous or orzo)

1 cup chicken or vegetable broth

¼ teaspoon pepper

1 cup crumbled feta cheese

Preheat the oven to 350 degrees. Drain the artichokes, reserving the liquid. Slice the artichokes thinly from top to bottom.

In a large skillet, heat the oil over medium heat. Add the garlic and sauté it for 30 seconds. Add the artichokes and mushrooms and cook them for about 5 minutes. Add the tomatoes and cook the mixture for 2 more minutes. Add the couscous, chicken broth, reserved artichoke liquid, and pepper and simmer the mixture for about 2 minutes.

Pour the mixture into a 9 × 13-inch baking dish. Top it with the feta cheese. Cover the dish with foil and bake the casserole for 15 minutes. Remove the foil and bake the casserole uncovered for 15 more minutes.

These chicken strips are a great way to use up leftover stuffing or take advantage of post-Thanksgiving sales. They are also bound to please the kids—and adults—in your family. You can dip them in ketchup, honey mustard, or barbecue sauce. Serve them with steamed green beans.

crunchy chicken fingers

Prep (10 minutes) + Cook (25 minutes)

8 servings

Nutritional Information per serving:

Calories 250, Total Fat 3g, 5%, Saturated Fat .5g, 4%, Cholesterol 70mg, 23%, Sodium 600mg, 25%, Total Carbohydrate 24g, 8%, Dietary Fiber <1g, 4%, Protein 30g, Sugar 3g

- 4 ounces reduced-fat sour cream
- 1 tablespoon Dijon mustard (optional)
- salt and pepper to taste
- 2 cups dry stuffing mix (either herb-seasoned or cornbread)
- 2 packages (about 2 pounds) chicken tenderloins (or use boneless, skinless chicken breasts, cut into strips)

Preheat the oven to 400 degrees. Spray a large baking sheet with nonstick cooking spray.

Put the sour cream in a shallow bowl and stir in the mustard (optional), salt, and pepper. Put the dry stuffing in another large shallow bowl or on a plate and crush it into smaller pieces, without completely pulverizing it.

Dip each piece of chicken in the sour cream mixture, shake off the excess, then roll and press the chicken in the stuffing, coating each piece as well as possible. Put the coated chicken strips on the baking sheet and spray the tops of the chicken strips with cooking spray.

Bake the chicken strips for 20 minutes until they are cooked through and lightly golden.

{ **my favorite baby food trick** Set aside a little of whatever cooked fruit or vegtable you are making for dinner (before seasoning) and puree it in the blender for the baby. Fill clean ice cube trays with the pureed food, cover them with foil, and place them in the freezer. Once they are frozen solid, empty the cubes of food into a resealable plastic bag and mark the bag with the name of the food and the date. Remove a cube, microwave it, and voilà, you have a meal for the baby. Eventually you will have a virtual store shelf full of varieties to choose from.

This light pasta salad is great for an autumn picnic or potluck, as it tastes great served at room temperature or cold. You can also experiment by adding your favorite ingredients, like diced pea pods, slivered almonds, or water chestnuts. I made this with whole wheat pasta for extra nutrition, and the family didn't mind a bit. Serve it with lightly steamed snap peas or green beans tossed with 1 tablespoon melted butter.

asian pasta salad with ginger-soy dressing

Prep + Cook = 20 minutes

8 servings

Nutritional Information per serving:

Calories 280, Total Fat 4g, 6%, Saturated Fat 0.5g, 3%, Cholesterol 0mg, 0%, Sodium 670mg, 28%, Total Carbohydrate 50g, 17%, Fiber 3g, 12% Protein 11g, Sugar 5g

1 package (16 ounces) pasta spirals (whole wheat or regular)

2 tablespoons fresh lime juice (about ½ lime)

5 tablespoons soy sauce

1 tablespoon + 2 teaspoons sugar (use superfine if you have it)

1 tablespoon sesame oil

1 teaspoon fresh ginger, minced, or ⅓ teaspoon ground ginger

2 cups shredded carrots (also called matchstick cut)

¼ cup chopped scallions (about 4 scallions)

½ cake (8 ounces) extra-firm tofu, drained and diced or 1½ cups cooked chicken, diced (optional)

1 teaspoon black or white sesame seeds

Cook the noodles according to the package directions.

In a medium bowl, whisk together the lime juice, soy sauce, all the sugar, oil, and ginger.

In a large serving bowl, combine the carrots, scallions, and tofu.

Briefly toast the sesame seeds on the lightest setting in the toaster oven for about 2 minutes, or toast them in the oven for about 3 to 5 minutes at 350 degrees, until they are lightly browned.

Rinse the cooked pasta with cold water until it cools, drain it thoroughly, and add the noodles to the bowl with the carrots. Toss everything with the ginger-soy sauce. Sprinkle it with the sesame seeds. Refrigerate it until you are ready to serve it.

This is a tantalizing twist on traditional burritos. It may sound odd, but it's not overly sweet and is quite delicious. Serve the burritos with sour cream, salsa, chips and guacamole, or whatever Mexican condiments your family enjoys.

sweet potato burritos

Prep (15 minutes) +
Cook (25 minutes)

10 servings

Nutritional
Information per
serving:

Calories 270, Total
Fat 3.5g, 6%, Satu-
rated Fat 0g, 0%,
Cholesterol 5 mg,
1%, Sodium 730mg,
31%, Total Carbohy-
drate 44g, 15%, Di-
etary Fiber 3g, 14%,
Protein 14g, Sugar 5g

3 medium sweet potatoes, peeled and cut into ½-inch chunks

1 can (15 ounces) kidney beans (preferably unsweetened) with their liquid

2 tablespoons chili powder

1 teaspoon cumin

1 tablespoon Dijon mustard

2 tablespoons soy sauce

10 soft-taco-sized (8-inch) flour or whole wheat tortillas

2 cups shredded Cheddar cheese

Place the chopped sweet potatoes in a microwave-safe dish with about 2 table-spoons of water. Microwave them on high until they are soft, about 10 minutes. (Or immerse the sweet potatoes in just enough water to cover them completely and bring it to a boil. Simmer the potatoes until they are soft when pierced with a fork, about 30 minutes.)

Preheat the oven to 350 degrees.

Mash the sweet potatoes, beans with their liquid, chili powder, cumin, mustard, and soy sauce until the mixture is soft and well blended.

If the tortillas are stiff, warm them briefly in the microwave to soften them. Divide the mixture evenly among the tortillas. Top each with a generous handful of cheese. Fold the tortillas up burrito style and place them in a 9 × 13-baking dish. Bake them for 12 minutes, or longer if you want them a little crispy. Serve them hot.

After trying several versions, I finally concocted a butternut squash soup I love. The soup is easy to make, but it takes a little while for the squash to bake. (I don't think the squash is quite as good if cooked in the microwave—it gets slightly caramelized in the oven.) This would be a delicious Thanksgiving soup to enjoy while the turkey is cooling, and it can be made a day or two in advance. Serve it with bread and a salad topped with diced apples and Gorgonzola cheese.

butternut squash soup

Prep (20 minutes) +
Cook (1 hour +)

6 servings

Nutritional
Information per
serving:

Calories 160, Total
Fat 4g, 7%, Saturated
Fat 2.5g, 12%, Choles-
terol 10 mg, 3%,
Sodium 240mg, 10%,
Total Carbohydrate
30g, 10%, Dietary
Fiber 7g, 27%, Pro-
tein 3g, Sugar 11g

1 medium-large butternut squash
2 tablespoons butter
1 teaspoon chopped garlic (about 2 cloves)
1 large onion, chopped
2 celery stalks, chopped
¼ teaspoon cinnamon
¼ teaspoon ground ginger
2 cups chicken or vegetable broth
½ teaspoon salt
1 tablespoon honey

Preheat the oven to 400 degrees. Line a rimmed cookie sheet with aluminum foil and spray the foil with nonstick cooking spray.

Slice the ends off the squash, stand it on one end, and slice the squash in half lengthwise. Scrape out the seeds and place the two halves, cut side down, on the baking sheet. Bake the squash until it is very tender when pierced with a fork, 50 to 60 minutes.

After the squash has baked for 50 minutes, melt the butter over medium heat in a heavy saucepan. Add the garlic and cook it for about 1 minute. Add the onions, celery, cinnamon, and ginger and continue cooking, stirring occasionally, until the onions and celery are softened, 5 to 8 minutes.

When the squash is tender, remove it from the oven and let it cool for a few minutes. Peel off the skin or scrape out the flesh (whichever is easier) and add the flesh to the pot with the onions. Add the broth and bring it to a boil. Stir it thoroughly and simmer it gently for about 10 minutes.

Puree the soup in a blender and return it to the pot. Stir in the salt and honey. Serve the soup hot.

This recipe from my mom looks elegant yet is very easy to make. Serve it with wild rice and steamed broccoli spears.

baked stuffed rainbow trout or salmon

Prep (15 minutes) +
Cook (25 minutes)

4 servings

Nutritional
Information per
serving:

Calories 360, Total
Fat 17g, 26%, Satu-
rated Fat 4.5g, 23%,
Cholesterol 110mg,
37%, Sodium 170mg,
7%, Total Carbohy-
drate 6g, 2%, Dietary
Fiber <1g, 4%, Pro-
tein 41g, Sugar 1g

- 2 tablespoons butter or olive oil
- ½ teaspoon minced garlic (about 1 clove)
- 4 ounces sliced mushrooms
- ¼ cup white wine
- ½ cup bread crumbs
- ¼ cup grated Parmesan cheese
- ¼ cup fresh chopped parsley or cilantro
- ¼ cup fresh lemon or lime juice (about 1 lemon or lime)
- 4 (½ pound each) whole boned trout or whole small salmon, cleaned and heads removed or intact (1 fish per person)

Preheat the oven to 400 degrees. Coat a 9 × 13-inch baking dish with nonstick cooking spray.

In a medium skillet, heat 1 tablespoon of the butter or oil over medium heat. Add the garlic and mushrooms and sauté them until the mushrooms shrink and become tender, 5 to 8 minutes. Add half of the wine and let it cook down for about 5 minutes. Add the remaining butter or oil, the bread crumbs, the Parmesan cheese, the parsley or cilantro, and half of the lemon or lime juice. Mix it well.

Distribute the mixture evenly inside the 4 fish, putting it on top of the flesh inside and gently pressing the fish closed around the stuffing. Place the fish in the baking dish and pour the remaining wine and lemon or lime juice over them. Bake the fish, uncovered, for 25 minutes. Do not flip the fish while they are cooking.

Serve the fish whole.

unpacking groceries: start at the store

Whenever I can, I try to pack frozen and refrigerator items in separate bags so that when I arrive home, if chaos meets me at the door, I need only unpack my "priority" bags and the rest can be left for a calmer moment. It's simple: As you unload your grocery cart, take out the cold items first and ask that they be packed separately.

Our friend Linda Singer suggested this healthy and delicious recipe. We cook the chimichangas until they are crispy and top them with sour cream, salsa, and guacamole—yum! Serve them with chips and salsa and the extra half can of corn.

baked turkey chimichangas

Prep (20 minutes) +
Cook (20 minutes)

10–12 servings

Nutritional
Information per
serving:

Calories 300, Total
Fat 9g, 14%, Saturated Fat 3g, 15%,
Cholesterol 45mg,
15%, Sodium 820mg,
34%, Total Carbohydrate 49g, 16%, Dietary Fiber 13g, 52%,
Protein 19g, Sugar 4g

1 pound ground turkey

1 can (15 ounces) vegetarian refried beans

1 cup mild salsa, plus additional for serving

1 cup unsweetened corn kernels

1 cup shredded Monterey Jack cheese

10–12 large flour or whole wheat tortillas

fat-free sour cream for serving

guacamole for serving (optional)

Preheat the oven to 375 degrees. Coat a 9 × 13-inch baking dish with nonstick cooking spray.

In a large nonstick skillet, brown the turkey over medium-high heat until it is cooked through, about 5 minutes. Add the beans, salsa, and corn. Cook the mixture until it is heated through. Remove it from the heat and stir in the cheese.

Warm the tortillas in the microwave for approximately 1 minute on high to soften them.

To assemble the chimichangas, put a large spoonful of the turkey-bean mixture into each tortilla, fold in the sides, and roll it up. Place the rolled chimichangas into the baking dish.

Bake the chimichangas, uncovered, until they are crisp and lightly browned, about 20 minutes. Serve them topped with salsa, sour cream, and guacamole (optional).

cooking with wine Do you worry that cooking with wine will make your kids tipsy? Don't worry; when you cook with wine, nearly all the alcohol evaporates, while the wine's flavors get more concentrated. For the best flavor, use drinking, rather than cooking, wine.

My neighbor Deb Ford often serves this creamy and delectable pasta when she has company over. When I brought it to a potluck, it disappeared in a flash. Serve it with warm bread sticks and sautéed onions and zucchini.

fettuccine with melted brie and tomatoes

Prep + Cook =
20 minutes

8 servings

Nutritional
Information per
serving:

Calories 380, Total
Fat 16g, 25%, Saturated Fat 6g, 30%,
Cholesterol 30mg,
10%, Sodium 180mg,
8%, Total Carbohydrate 45g, 15%, Dietary Fiber 2g, 8%,
Protein 14g, Sugar 4g

½ pound Brie cheese

4 large ripe tomatoes, diced (about 4 cups), or 2 cans (15 ounces each) diced tomatoes, mostly drained

1 cup fresh basil leaves, cut into strips

1½ teaspoons minced garlic (about 3 cloves)

¼ cup olive oil

1 package (16 ounces) fettuccine

Take the Brie out of the refrigerator at least 2 hours before cooking, if possible—otherwise, warm it in the microwave on high heat for 30 seconds to 1 minute until it is softened. Remove the rind and tear the cheese into irregular pieces into a large serving bowl. Add the tomatoes, basil, garlic, and oil to the bowl.

Cook the pasta according to the package directions until it is al dente. Drain it and immediately toss the pasta with the sauce in the bowl until the Brie has melted. Serve it immediately.

TIP: If you can't find perfectly ripe tomatoes for this recipe, the diced canned tomatoes reduce chopping time and have a fresh flavor.

This one-pan salmon cooks quickly and is simply delicious for the whole family. If possible, use wild Alaskan salmon (sometimes called coho or sockeye), which is better for people and the earth. Serve it with couscous or quinoa (a quick-cooking, healthy whole grain) and roasted asparagus (see p. 299).

seared salmon with lime butter

Prep + Cook =
10 minutes

4 servings

Nutritional
Information per
serving:

Calories 340, Total
Fat 18g, 28%, Satu-
rated Fat 4.5g, 22%,
Cholesterol 130mg,
44%, Sodium 500mg,
21%, Total Carbohy-
drate 1g, 0%, Dietary
Fiber 0g, 0%, Protein
39g, Sugar 1g

1 tablespoon butter

1½ pounds salmon fillet

2–4 teaspoons lime juice (about ½ lime)

½ teaspoon kosher salt

Spray a large cast-iron or stainless-steel skillet with nonstick cooking spray and heat it over medium-high heat. When the pan is hot, add half of the butter and let it melt. The pan should be hot enough that the butter bubbles but doesn't brown. Add the salmon, skin side down, and top it with half of the lime juice and half of the salt.

Sear the salmon (cook it without moving it) for about 5 minutes until it starts to cook through. Add the remaining half of the butter to the pan and flip the salmon. Reduce the heat slightly. Top the salmon with the rest of the lime juice and a little more salt. Cook it for 3 to 5 more minutes until the salmon flakes easily and is cooked through. Remove the salmon to a plate and top it with any pan drippings.

freshest fish For the freshest taste, try to buy fish within 24 hours of using it.

I was inspired to make black bean soup after enjoying some at a friend's house. We topped it at the table with sour cream, crushed tortilla chips, Monterey Jack cheese, and Tabasco sauce. Serve it with baked sweet potatoes (see p. 300) and cornbread.

black bean soup

Prep + Cook =
25 minutes

8 servings

Nutritional
Information per
serving:

Calories 210, Total
Fat 2.5g, 4%, Saturated Fat 0g, 0%,
Cholesterol 0mg, 0%,
Sodium 1070mg, 45%,
Total Carbohydrate
36g, 12%, Dietary
Fiber 13g, 52%, Protein 12g, Sugar 5g

1 tablespoon olive oil

1½ cups chopped onion (about ½ large onion)

1 teaspoon minced garlic (about 2 cloves)

3 cans (15 ounces each) black beans with their liquid

1 can (14½ ounces) chicken broth

1 can (15 ounces) diced tomatoes with juice

1 can (15 ounces) tomato sauce

1 tablespoon chili powder

½ cup red wine (optional)

Stir-ins: low-fat sour cream, crushed tortilla chips, shredded part-skim mozzarella cheese, Tabasco sauce

In a large stockpot, heat the oil over medium heat. Add the onions and garlic and sauté them until the onions start to brown, about 5 minutes. Add the beans, chicken broth, tomatoes, tomato sauce, and chili powder. Bring the soup to a boil. Reduce the heat and simmer the soup until the flavors blend and it thickens slightly, about 15 to 20 minutes. After about 10 minutes of simmering, add the red wine (optional) and stir it into the soup.

Puree some (at least 2 cups) or all of the soup in a blender to the desired consistency and stir the pureed soup back in with the rest of the soup in the pot.

soup's on: If you make lots of soups, a hand (immersion) blender is a great investment, so you don't have to transfer hot soup to the blender to puree it. The prices vary widely, but my $20 version works just fine.

This versatile recipe can be served as a frittata, or with tomato sauce and toppings as a zucchini-crusted pizza, or even as a filling for a sandwich. However you choose to serve it, this dish is light, healthy, and delicious. Serve it with whole grain bread and a salad of mixed greens, mandarin oranges, and sliced almonds. For a heartier meal, serve it with a roast chicken from the supermarket.

zucchini frittata with red peppers and basil

Prep (15 minutes) +
Cook (30 minutes)

6 servings

Nutritional
Information per
serving:

Calories 120, Total
Fat 5g, 8%, Saturated
Fat 2.5g, 13%, Choles-
terol 115mg, 38%,
Sodium 330mg, 14%,
Total Carbohydrate
9g, 3%, Dietary Fiber
1g, 4%, Protein 9g,
Sugar 2g

3 cups grated zucchini (about 2 medium zucchini)

3 eggs, lightly beaten

$\frac{1}{3}$ cup flour

$\frac{2}{3}$ cup shredded mozzarella cheese

$\frac{1}{3}$ cup shredded Swiss cheese

$\frac{1}{4}$ teaspoon garlic powder

$\frac{1}{2}$ teaspoon salt

$\frac{1}{2}$ red bell pepper, cut into 1-inch strips

15 fresh basil leaves, chopped

Preheat the oven to 400 degrees. Spray a 9 × 13-inch pan with nonstick cooking spray.

Wrap the grated zucchini in a clean dishcloth and let it sit for a few minutes to draw the moisture out.

In a large bowl, combine the eggs, the flour, $\frac{1}{3}$ cup of the mozzarella cheese, the Swiss cheese, the garlic powder, and the salt. Add the zucchini. Spread the mixture in the pan. Bake it for 20 minutes.

Remove the frittata from the oven and top it with the red pepper, the basil, and the remaining $\frac{1}{3}$ cup of the cheese. Return the frittata to the oven for 10 to 15 minutes until it is firm and lightly browned at the edges. Serve it hot or cold.

This is a very satisfying and nutritionally complete dinner. I love the combination of spinach and feta cheese, but if feta is not one of your favorite cheeses or it's too strong for your kids, substitute shredded or fresh chopped mozzarella cheese. Serve the ravioli with whole-grain bread sticks and baby carrots.

creamy ravioli and spinach bake

Prep + Cook =
30 minutes

8 servings

Nutritional
Information per
serving:

Calories 330, Total
Fat 12g, 18%, Saturated Fat 7g, 35%,
Cholesterol 75mg,
25%, Sodium 730mg,
30%, Total Carbohydrate 37g, 12%, Dietary Fiber 4g, 16%,
Protein 17g, Sugar 6g

1 family-sized package (20 ounces) cheese ravioli

1 package (10 ounces) frozen chopped spinach

1 can (15 ounces) diced tomatoes with their liquid

½ teaspoon garlic powder

1 cup light sour cream

½ teaspoon salt

1 teaspoon dried basil

4 ounces feta cheese, crumbled

In a large pot of boiling water, cook the ravioli for about 3 minutes and drain it. Defrost the spinach and drain it. Preheat the oven to 375 degrees.

In a large bowl, combine all the remaining ingredients. Gently but thoroughly stir in the ravioli.

Smooth the mixture into an 8 × 8-inch flat baking dish and cover it with aluminum foil. Bake the ravioli for 15 to 20 minutes until it is heated through.

do it yourself It is much cheaper to buy feta cheese that is not crumbled, rather than the precrumbled variety, and takes only seconds to crumble it yourself.

If your family doesn't like spicy food, be sure to use mild salsa when making this delicious Mexican casserole, which is a bit like heartier nachos. Serve it with chopped cantaloupe and additional chips (or warm tortillas) and salsa.

texas black bean casserole

Prep (20 minutes) +
Cook (40 minutes)

8 servings

Nutritional
Information per
serving:

Calories 320, Total
Fat 12g, 19%, Saturated Fat 3g, 16%,
Cholesterol 15 mg,
5%, Sodium 1030 mg,
43%, Total Carbohydrate 43g, 14%, Dietary Fiber 9g, 37%,
Protein 12g, Sugar 8g

2 tablespoons vegetable oil

1 large onion, chopped

1 red or green bell pepper, chopped

1 can (14 ounces) unsweetened corn kernels, drained

⅓ cup chopped pitted Spanish (green) olives (about 6 large olives)

1 can (15 ounces) vegetarian refried beans

1 can (15 ounces) black beans

Several large handfuls tortilla chips (about 3 cups total)

1 jar (15 ounces) mild salsa

1 cup shredded Cheddar cheese

Preheat the oven to 375 degrees.

In a frying pan, heat the oil over medium-high heat. Add the onions and peppers and sauté them until the onions are translucent, about 5 minutes, stirring them occasionally. Add the drained corn kernels to the pan. Remove the pan from the heat and stir in the olives.

In a medium bowl, mix together the refried beans and black beans.

To assemble the casserole, spray a 9 × 13-inch casserole dish with nonstick cooking spray and line the bottom of the dish with the tortilla chips, breaking them up a little with your hands.

Spread the beans over the chips and top the beans with the onion mixture. Pour the salsa over everything and top it with the Cheddar cheese.

Cover the casserole with foil and bake it for 30 to 35 minutes until the cheese is bubbly. Uncover the casserole and bake it for 5 to 10 minutes more until the edges begin to brown. Cut it into squares to serve it.

This is a fun recipe for the kids to help you make. You can use different fillings in place of mushrooms and onions. Try spinach, sausage, or chopped tomato. Serve the calzones with a salad and sliced fresh or canned pineapple.

mushroom and onion calzones

Prep (15 minutes) +
Cook (12 minutes)

4 servings

Nutritional
Information per
serving:

Calories 320, Total
Fat 9g, 14%, Satu-
rated Fat 4g, 20%,
Cholesterol 20mg,
7%, Sodium 840mg,
35%, Total Carbohy-
drate 44g, 15%, Di-
etary Fiber 3g, 12%,
Protein 15g, Sugar 8g

1 can (10 ounces) refrigerated pizza crust dough

2 teaspoons minced garlic (about 4 cloves)

1 cup (or less) red pasta sauce

1 cup diced onion (about ½ medium onion)

1 cup sliced mushrooms (about 4 ounces)

1 cup shredded mozzarella or crumbled feta cheese (about 4 ounces)

Preheat the oven to 425 degrees. Coat a baking sheet with nonstick cooking spray.

Unroll the pizza crust dough onto the baking sheet. Using a pizza cutter or sharp knife, cut it into 4 squares. Pat each square into a 6 × 5-inch rectangle.

Sprinkle the garlic evenly over the rectangles (or leave the kids' portions plain). Top each rectangle with a spoonful of the sauce and a handful of mushrooms, onion, and cheese.

For each rectangle, bring 2 opposite corners to the center and pinch them to seal them shut. Repeat with the other 2 corners.

Bake the calzones for 12 minutes or until they are golden.

My neighbor Annie Canby suggested this simple preparation for shrimp. It's delicious (our eight-year-old son, Solomon, loved it) and couldn't be easier. If you prefer, grill the shrimp on skewers or a grilling tray. If you don't eat shrimp, you can use a pound of boneless, skinless chicken breasts or Halibut instead. Serve it with rice and steamed edamame (Japanese soybeans).

honey-dijon shrimp

Prep + Cook = 15 minutes + Marinate

4 servings

Nutritional Information per serving:

Calories 200, Total Fat 6g, 9%, Saturated Fat 1g, 4%, Cholesterol 170 mg, 57%, Sodium 860 mg, 36%, Total Carbohydrate 11g, 4%, Dietary Fiber 0g, 0%, Protein 25g, Sugar 8g

¼ cup Dijon mustard

2 tablespoons honey

2 tablespoons soy sauce

1 tablespoon olive oil

¼ teaspoon pepper

1 pound large shrimp, peeled and deveined

In a measuring cup, mix together the mustard, honey, soy sauce, oil, and pepper. In a medium bowl, mix the shrimp and marinade together. If time allows, refrigerate the shrimp for 1 to 2 hours. If not, proceed to the next step.

In a medium nonstick skillet, cook the shrimp and sauce for 3 to 5 minutes over medium heat until the shrimp become opaque. Serve the shrimp and sauce over rice.

This tangy, aromatic soup re-creates a delicious Thai flavor with ingredients available in most supermarkets. Look for light coconut milk, which is much lower in fat than the traditional version. Serve the soup with steamed dumplings and steamed broccoli with sesame-soy-ginger sauce (see p. 298).

thai chicken noodle soup

Prep (25 minutes) +
Cook (15 minutes)

6 servings

Nutritional
Information per
serving:

Calories 300, Total
Fat 15g, 23%, Saturated Fat 8g, 40%,
Cholesterol 55mg,
18%, Sodium 470mg,
20%, Total Carbohydrate 16g, 5%, Dietary Fiber 3g, 12%,
Protein 24g, Sugar 4g

1 tablespoon vegetable oil

1 teaspoon minced garlic (about 2 cloves)

1 pound boneless, skinless chicken breasts, cut into ½-inch pieces

¾ teaspoon turmeric

¼ teaspoon cayenne pepper (optional)

6 cups chicken broth

¾ cup light unsweetened coconut milk

3 tablespoons fresh lime juice (about 1 lime)

3 tablespoons smooth peanut butter

2 cups thin (or thread) egg noodles

1 tablespoon sugar

2 tablespoons chopped fresh cilantro

salt and pepper to taste

In a medium stockpot, heat the oil over medium heat. Add the garlic and stir-fry it for 1 minute until it is a light golden color. Add the chicken, turmeric, and cayenne (optional) and stir-fry it for 3 to 4 more minutes.

Add the chicken broth, coconut milk, lime juice, peanut butter, and noodles. Bring the soup to a low boil, cover the pot, and simmer the soup for 15 minutes.

Add the sugar and cilantro. Season the soup with salt and pepper.

winter

week 1

Easy Chicken and Vegetable Pot Pie

Spaghetti and Meatballs

Black-Eyed Pea Tacos

Spinach, Feta, and Pine Nuts over Rice

Deli Dinner

week 2

Chicken Diablo

Flounder with Lemony Bread Crumb Topping

Greek Penne Pasta

Quesadillas with Spinach and Onions

Split Pea Soup with a Touch of Curry

week 3

Hot Dog Creole

Bowties Alfredo with Broccoli

Lentil and Cheese Casserole (Vegetarian Meatloaf)

Tomato and Wild Rice Soup

Wild Salmon or Artic Char with Chili-Lime Spice Rub

week 4

Easy Baked Ziti

Pumpkin Black Bean Soup

Mediterranean Chicken with Tomatoes and Olives

Baked Sausage and Egg Casserole

Southwestern Bulgur Pilaf

week 5

Fried Rice with Shrimp (or Tofu or Chicken)

Molly's Spiced Chicken Quesadillas

Baked Macaroni and Cheese with Tomatoes

Potato and Goat Cheese Spanish "Tortilla"

Soba Noodle Soup with Shiitake Mushrooms

week 6

Chicken Tarragon in a Pastry Packet

Broiled Salmon with Mustard-Soy Crust

Mushroom Tortellini with Roasted Vegetables

Easy-Cheesy Tortilla Skillet

Mushroom Barley Soup

week 7

Baked Spaghetti

California Rollos

Tuscan White Bean Soup with Sourdough Croutons

Ma Po Tofu (Chinese Tofu and Ground Pork)

Polenta Casserole with Roasted Red Peppers and Chopped Olives

week 8

Beef and Mushrooms in a
Light Cream Sauce

Savory Shrimp and
Mozzarella Melt

Light Cheese Tortellini with
Broccoli

Winter Vegetable Curry
with Lentils

Savory Udon Noodle Soup

week 9

Coconut Chicken with Mango

Black Bean Burgers

Creamy Broccoli Noodle
Casserole

Sautéed Tilapia with
Baby Spinach

Andrew's Amazing Pizza

week 10

Spiced Chicken with Maple
Butter Glaze

Manhattan Clam (or
Clam-less) Chowder

Warm Eggplant
Pita Sandwiches

Broccoli and Cheddar
Stuffed Potatoes

Rotini with Goat Cheese
and Bacon

week 11

Chicken (Nuggets!) with
Caramelized Onions

Quinoa and Black Bean
Burritos

Maryland Crab Cakes

Baked Artichoke Pasta

Cobb Salad

week 12

Taco Chili with Cilantro Sour
Cream

Ravioli Lasagna

Tangy Flank Steak

Zesty Baked Salmon

Spinach and Mushroom
Omelets

week 13

Moroccan Chicken

Fettuccine with Chickpea
Sauce

Breaded Tilapia with
Garlic-Lime Sauce

Baked Eggplant Parmesan

Wild Rice and Corn Casserole

This recipe is easier and more vegetable-laden than a traditional pot pie, but it retains that nostalgic flavor. For a meatless version, substitute cream of mushroom soup and add 8 ounces of diced tofu, if desired. Cut the vegetables in small cubes so they cook quickly, and serve the pot pie with additional peas on the side.

easy chicken and vegetable pot pie

Prep (30 minutes) +
Cook (20 minutes)

8 servings

Nutritional
Information per
serving:

Calories 200, Total
Fat 10g, 15%, Satu-
rated Fat 3.5g, 17%,
Cholesterol 35mg,
12%, Sodium 380 mg,
16%, Total Carbohy-
drate 17g, 6%, Di-
etary Fiber 2g, 9%,
Protein 11g, Sugar 4g

1 package (2 crusts) refrigerated 9-inch pie crusts

2 tablespoons butter

½ large onion, diced

2 large carrots, peeled and cut into ¼-inch cubes

2 large potatoes, peeled and cut into ¼-inch cubes

2 stalks celery, diced

½ cup frozen peas

1 can (10¾ ounces) condensed reduced-fat cream of chicken soup (or use cream of mushroom soup)

1 cup cooked and diced chicken (optional)

¼ cup water

Preheat the oven to 375 degrees. If the pie crusts are frozen, set them out to soften (if they don't soften in time, warm them in the microwave for about 15 seconds).

In a stockpot, melt the butter over medium-high heat. Add the onions, carrots, potatoes, and celery. Cook, partially covered, until softened, about 5 to 8 minutes. (The vegetables in this recipe retain some crunch after the pie is cooked. If you like your veggies softer, cook them for a few extra minutes.)

Add the peas, cream of chicken soup, chicken (optional), and water to the pot. Simmer it gently for a few minutes while you prepare the crust.

Line a pie plate with 1 pie crust. Add the filling mixture and top it with the remaining pie crust. Cut slits in the top, pinch the sides of the crusts together, and trim the excess crust with a paring knife or scissors.

Place the pie on a cookie sheet (to help catch spills) and bake it for 20 minutes. Remove it from the oven and allow it to cool for a few minutes before serving.

This family-friendly dinner goes well with sourdough bread and a green salad with Gorgonzola cheese and dried cranberries.

spaghetti and meatballs

Prep + Cook = 25 minutes

8 servings

Nutritional Information per serving:

Calories 460; Total Fat 17g, 26%, Saturated Fat 5g, 25%, Cholesterol 65mg, 22%, Sodium 550mg, 23%, Total Carbohydrate 55g, 18%, Dietary Fiber 3g, 12%, Protein 21g, Sugar 8g

1 package (16 ounces) spaghetti

1 pound lean ground beef (or use ground chicken or turkey)

1 egg

½ cup bread crumbs

2 tablespoons ketchup

¼ teaspoon garlic powder

1 tablespoon olive oil

1 jar (26 ounces) red pasta sauce

grated Parmesan cheese for serving

Cook the spaghetti according to the package directions.

Meanwhile, in a medium bowl, mix together the meat, egg, bread crumbs, ketchup, and garlic powder. Form the mixture into meatballs 1 inch across.

In a large skillet, heat the oil over medium-high heat. Add the meatballs and cook them, turning them frequently, until they are browned on all sides, 5 to 8 minutes. Add the sauce and cook it until it is warmed through. Simmer it gently, partially covered, until the spaghetti is ready.

Serve the meatballs and sauce over the spaghetti and sprinkle it with Parmesan cheese.

TIP: To make homemade tomato sauce instead of using a jar: Sauté 1 teaspoon minced garlic (about 2 cloves) in 2 tablespoons olive oil over medium heat for about 30 seconds. Add 1 medium-sized chopped onion and cook it until the onion is soft and translucent, about 5 minutes. Add 5 fresh tomatoes or 1 can (15 ounces) diced tomatoes and 1 can (15 ounces) tomato sauce. Add 2 teaspoons dried or 2 tablespoons fresh chopped basil, ½ teaspoon salt and ¼ teaspoon pepper. Simmer it until the sauce thickens, about 10-15 minutes. Add the meatballs to the sauce and proceed with the recipe.

These meatless tacos are a delicious way to get healthy legumes into your family's diet. We easily went through twelve of those crisp little taco shells in one sitting. Our daughter, Celia, actually prefers eating the fillings and shells separately, while our son, Solomon, has a great time creating the taco and then trying to stuff the whole thing in his mouth before it falls apart. Heating the taco shells makes a world of difference, giving them a good crunch. Serve the tacos with yellow rice.

black-eyed pea tacos

Prep + Cook =
20 minutes

12 small tacos

Nutritional
Information for 1
taco:

Calories 210, Total Fat 6g, 10%, Saturated Fat 2g, 11%, Cholesterol 5mg, 2%, Sodium 210mg, 9%, Total Carbohydrate 30g, 10%, Dietary Fiber 6g, 26%, Protein 9g, Sugar 5g

1 tablespoon olive oil

½ medium onion, diced

1 tomato, diced

2 cans (15 ounces each) black-eyed peas (or use pinto beans)

1 can (15 ounces) unsweetened corn kernels

¼ cup mild salsa, plus additional for serving

¼ cup chopped fresh cilantro (optional)

12 taco shells (or use warmed corn or flour tortillas)

1 cup shredded Cheddar cheese

2 cups chopped iceberg lettuce

Preheat the oven to 350 degrees.

In a large skillet, heat the oil over medium-high heat. Add the onion and cook it, stirring it occasionally, until it starts to brown, about 5 minutes. Meanwhile, dice the tomato, and drain and rinse the beans and corn in a colander. (At this point, you may want to remove some of the beans and corn to leave them plain for picky eaters.)

When the onion begins to brown, add the tomato and sauté it for about 2 more minutes. Add the beans, corn, salsa, and cilantro and stir the mixture until it is heated through.

Heat the taco shells on a baking sheet in the oven for about 5 minutes. (Set the timer to be sure they don't burn.)

Assemble the tacos at the table, with the bean mixture, Cheddar cheese, lettuce, and extra salsa as desired.

Invented by our friend Mark Spindel, this light and healthy dinner fuses Asian and Greek cuisines. Serve it with peeled and sliced cucumbers drizzled with balsamic vinaigrette.

spinach, feta, and pine nuts over rice

Prep + Cook =
30 minutes

4 servings

Nutritional
Information per
serving:

Calories 440, Total
Fat 16g, 25%, Satu-
rated Fat 5g, 25%,
Cholesterol 25mg,
8%, Sodium 700mg,
29%, Total Carbohy-
drate 61g, 20%, Di-
etary Fiber 3g, 12%,
Protein 13g, Sugar 2g

1½ cups dry white rice

¼ cup pine nuts

1 tablespoon olive oil

½ teaspoon minced garlic (about 1 clove)

pinch of salt

12–16 ounces baby spinach

1 tablespoon lemon juice (about ¼ lemon)

¼ cup golden raisins or currants (optional)

4 ounces feta cheese, crumbled

pepper for serving

Cook the rice according to the package directions. Meanwhile, toast the pine nuts lightly in a toaster oven and set them aside.

Meanwhile, in a large skillet, heat the oil over medium heat. Add the garlic and sauté it for about 30 seconds (but don't let it brown). Add a pinch of salt and the spinach, stir it, and cover the skillet. Steam the spinach until it is just wilted, about 3 minutes. Reduce the heat to low.

To the spinach, add the lemon juice, pine nuts, and raisins or currants and stir it gently until it is warmed through.

Serve the spinach in bowls over the rice, topped with the cheese. Season it with pepper at the table, in case the kids aren't fond of its flavor.

a note on nuts Those delicious, good-for-you nuts will taste fresh longer if you keep them tightly sealed in your freezer. Because of their high oil content, they will not freeze and will stay fresh for many months.

This "deli" dinner was one of my favorites when I was a kid, and now our kids love it, too. It's a great alternative to takeout on those nights when you're extra tired, and the kids get a kick out of having "breakfast" for dinner. If you have an authentic deli nearby, try to get nova rather than lox, as it is usually less salty. Serve this dinner with sliced red onions and tomatoes.

deli dinner

Prep Time =
10 minutes

4 servings

Nutritional
Information per
serving:

Calories 400, Total
Fat 14g, 22%, Saturated Fat 3.5g, 18%,
Cholesterol 330mg,
110%, Sodium
1680mg, 70%, Total
Carbohydrate 39g,
13%, Dietary Fiber
2g, 8%, Protein 28g,
Sugar 2g

1 tablespoon butter or margarine

6 eggs

1 heaping tablespoon plain yogurt

1 heaping tablespoon cottage cheese

salt to taste

4 bagels, sliced

cream cheese to taste (about 4 ounces)

8 ounces sliced smoked salmon (nova or lox)

In a medium nonstick skillet, melt the butter over medium-low heat.

In a medium bowl, beat together the eggs, yogurt, and cottage cheese. Add the eggs to the skillet and cook them over medium-low heat, stirring them occasionally, until they are light and fluffy. Remove the skillet from the heat and season the eggs with salt. Cover the skillet to keep the eggs warm while you toast the bagels.

Serve the eggs with the toasted bagels topped with cream cheese, smoked salmon, tomatoes, and onion.

kids and table manners, or the virtues of a fork

If your children are in preschool or older, you might wonder what kind of behavior to expect from them at the dinner table. My husband and I also struggle with the line between enforcing good manners and enjoying a family meal. For example, at what age is it no longer appropriate for children to use their hands to pick up spaghetti? Can they really be expected to stay seated until everyone is done? Is it okay for our first grader to tell a story with an entire piece of bread in his mouth?

There are no right answers, of course. As with other parenting decisions, we make up the rules as we go. Around the time our kids turned four we started insisting they use silverware at the dinner table. We also expect them to wait until everyone is seated to start eating, wait their turn in a conversation, ask to be excused before leaving the table, and clear their plates when they're done. I'm not sure if these standards are tough or lax, but they feel right for our family. Table manners can certainly be phased in, so kids don't become disheartened by constant nagging.

When I asked our kids to suggest some rules for the table, they had several good ideas. Solomon said that you shouldn't use your spoon as a cannon (he got this idea from the school lunchroom!), and Celia said it's not nice to say "Ewww, yuck" about the food, especially before you taste it.

One thing I've realized is that Andrew and I need to set good examples. If I find myself slouching at the table or talking with my mouth full, I feel hypocritical expecting better from them. We've tried to improve our own manners, too.

We hope that Solomon and Celia's associations with family dinners are positive and that they don't feel constantly criticized about manners. But we also want to feel reasonably comfortable that if our children eat at a restaurant or a friend's house, they won't stick the asparagus in their ears.

P.S. Don't forget to give the kids lots of great feedback when they show off their good manners at dinner!

This great family-friendly chicken dish comes from our friend Monica Medina. Monica prepares the chicken in the morning before work, so it's ready to pop in the oven when she gets home. Serve it with couscous and lemon-pepper asparagus (see p. 299).

chicken diablo

Prep (15 minutes) +
Cook (50 minutes)

6 servings

Nutritional
Information per
serving:

Calories 250, Total
Fat 10g, 15%, Satu-
rated Fat 6g, 30%,
Cholesterol 85mg,
28%, Sodium 200mg,
8%, Total Carbohy-
drate 13g, 4%, Dietary
Fiber 0g, 0%, Protein
27g, Sugar 12g

4 tablespoons butter

¼ cup Dijon mustard

½ cup honey

1 teaspoon curry powder

1 whole chicken, cut up (or 8–12 chicken pieces of your choice)

Preheat the oven to 350 degrees.

In a small saucepan, melt the butter over medium-low heat. Add the mustard, honey, and curry powder and continue cooking and stirring until the sauce is well mixed, about 2 minutes.

Arrange the chicken pieces in a large baking pan. Pour the sauce over the chicken. (At this point you can refrigerate the chicken and sauce for up to 24 hours or bake it right away.)

Bake the chicken for 50 minutes. Halfway through, turn the chicken over and baste it with the sauce. For browner tops, put the chicken under the broiler for the final 5 minutes of cooking.

When I first made this fish, all three kids at the table (ours plus guest Sophie Martel) surprised us by finishing their entire servings, including the Asian Rice Pilaf (see p. 300) on the side. Solomon even licked his plate clean. What better testament can there be for this dish than three members of the clean plate club?

flounder with lemony bread crumb topping

Prep + Cook =
30 minutes

4 servings

Nutritional
Information per
serving:

Calories 430, Total
Fat 23g, 35%, Saturated Fat 4g, 20%,
Cholesterol 65mg,
22%, Sodium 690mg,
29%, Total Carbohydrate 31g, 10%, Dietary Fiber <1g, 4%,
Protein 25g, Sugar 5g

2 flounder fillets (about 1–1½ lbs. total)

⅓ cup bread crumbs

1 tablespoon olive oil

¼ cup chopped fresh parsley

2 tablespoons fresh lemon juice (about ½ lemon), plus additional for serving

½ teaspoon minced garlic (about 1 clove)

¼ teaspoon kosher salt

1 teaspoon Dijon mustard

Preheat the oven to 425 degrees. Coat a baking sheet with aluminum foil and spray the top of the foil with nonstick cooking spray. Lay the fish fillets on the baking sheet.

In a medium bowl, combine the bread crumbs, oil, parsley, lemon juice, garlic, salt, and mustard and mix them together well with a fork.

Press an equal amount of the bread crumb mixture onto the top of each fillet.

Bake the fish until it is white and flakes easily in the center, about 10 minutes. For a browner topping, broil it for the final 2 minutes of cooking. Sprinkle the fish with additional lemon juice before serving, if desired.

This is a fresh-tasting dish for weeknight dinner, and it's good hot or cold. Arugula has a mild taste that adventurous children may like, but leave some noodles plain just in case. Serve with a loaf of bread with olive oil for dipping.

greek penne pasta

Prep + Cook =
25 minutes

8 servings

Nutritional
Information per
serving:

Calories 300, Total
Fat 9g, 14%, Satu-
rated Fat 3g, 5%,
Cholesterol 10mg,
3%, Sodium 370mg,
15%, Total Carbohy-
drate 45g, 15%, Di-
etary Fiber 2g, 8%,
Protein 10g, Sugar 3g

1 package (16 ounces) penne or other similarly shaped pasta

1 bunch arugula (¼ pound), stemmed and roughly chopped

4 plum tomatoes, chopped

4 ounces feta cheese, crumbled

½ cup pitted kalamata olives, chopped

10 fresh basil or mint leaves

1 teaspoon balsamic vinegar

2 tablespoons olive oil

salt and pepper to taste

Cook the pasta according to the package directions.

Meanwhile, soak the arugula in a bowl of cold water for a few minutes to clean it thoroughly, then drain it. In a large serving bowl, combine the arugula, tomatoes, feta cheese, olives, basil or mint leaves, vinegar, and oil.

When the pasta is done, drain it and toss it with the ingredients in the large bowl. Season it with salt and pepper and serve it warm.

These quesadillas are a staple on busy nights in our house. Sometimes we add cooked chicken or steak, or make a quick version in the microwave for lunch. Some kids prefer them without the veggies, so you may want to leave one or two plain. Serve with corn on the cob or corn kernels.

quesadillas with spinach and onions

Prep Time = 20 minutes

8 servings

Nutritional Information per serving:

Calories 240, Total Fat 13g, 20%, Saturated Fat 7g, 35%, Cholesterol 30mg, 10%, Sodium 370mg, 15%, Total Carbohydrate 20g, 7%, Dietary Fiber 4g, 16%, Protein 11g, Sugar <1g

- 1 tablespoon olive oil
- 1 onion, halved and sliced into thin half rings
- 1 bag (6–9 ounces) baby spinach
- 8 soft-taco-sized flour or whole wheat tortillas
- 2 cups shredded Cheddar cheese (or a mixture of Cheddar and Monterey Jack cheeses)
- salsa for serving

Preheat the oven to 300 degrees.

In a medium skillet, heat the oil over medium-high heat. Add the onions and sauté them until they are browned, about 5 minutes. Add the spinach and cook it until it is wilted.

Meanwhile, heat a large frying pan over medium-high heat. Place 2 tortillas at a time in the frying pan (they will overlap). Put a handful of cheese and a spoonful of the onions and spinach in each (staying away from the edges of the tortilla) and fold the tortillas in half, so 2 tortillas fit in a round pan. Flip when the bottoms of the tortillas are golden brown, about 4 minutes. Cook them on the second side until they are golden brown.

Carefully transfer the cooked quesadillas to a baking sheet and put them in the oven so they stay warm until all are cooked. Serve them hot, sliced in wedges, with salsa.

shredding your own cheese vs. preshredded

If you are more concerned about saving money than time, buy cheese by the block and grate it yourself. If saving time is a bigger concern, purchase bags of shredded cheese.

My parents' hometown of Santa Barbara is right near Buellton, California, home of Andersen's Pea Soup. Andersen's Pea Soup is a tourist mecca for devotees of this humble stew—I was shocked that split peas have such a following! This concoction may not be Andersen's secret recipe, but it's darn good. Serve it with whole wheat bread and a spinach salad with chopped oranges, avocados, and Gorgonzola cheese.

split pea soup with a touch of curry

Prep (30 minutes) +
Cook (45 minutes)

8 servings

Nutritional
Information per
serving:

Calories 180, Total
Fat 4.5g, 7%, Saturated Fat 1g, 5%,
Cholesterol 0mg, 0%,
Sodium 210mg, 9%,
Total Carbohydrate
27g, 9%, Dietary
Fiber 7g, 29%, Protein 8g, Sugar 9g

2 tablespoons olive oil

1 large yellow onion, chopped

2 teaspoons minced garlic (about 4 cloves)

4 large carrots, diced

4 stalks celery, chopped

3 new potatoes, chopped into ½-inch pieces

2 cans or 1 box (29–32 ounces) chicken or vegetable broth

2½ soup cans (about 36 ounces) water

¾ teaspoon salt

½ teaspoon pepper

2 teaspoons curry powder

1 pound dried split green peas, thoroughly rinsed

low-fat sour cream or plain yogurt for serving (optional)

In a large stockpot, heat the oil over medium heat. Add the onions and garlic and sauté them for several minutes while you chop the carrots and celery. Add the carrots and celery and sauté the mixture for several more minutes while you chop and add the potatoes.

Add the chicken broth, water, salt, pepper, curry powder, and split peas and bring the soup to a boil. Simmer it, uncovered, for 45 minutes until the peas are very soft. Serve it hot, stirring in a spoonful of sour cream or yogurt, if desired.

It might not sound tantalizing to many adults, but this dish, invented by our friend Sara Emley, tastes great and is a perfect solution for that opened package of hot dogs you need to use up. Serve it with steamed rice and Sweet Potato Fries (see p. 300)

hot dog creole

Prep + Cook =
20 minutes

6 servings

Nutritional
Information per
serving:

Calories 330, Total
Fat 21g, 33%, Satu-
rated Fat 7g, 36%,
Cholesterol 30mg,
10%, Sodium 1520
mg, 63%, Total Car-
bohydrate 29g, 10%,
Dietary Fiber 4g,
17%, Protein 10g,
Sugar 11g

- 1 tablespoon olive oil
- 4–5 hot dogs, sliced in semicircles (beef, chicken, turkey, or meatless)
- ½ onion, diced
- ½ green, red, or yellow bell pepper, diced
- 1 can (10 ounces) unsweetened corn kernels, drained
- 1 can (15 ounces) tomato sauce
- 1 teaspoon chili powder
- a few shakes hot pepper sauce (such as Tabasco), to taste

In a large skillet, heat the olive oil over medium heat. Add the hot dogs, onions, and peppers and sauté them until the onions and peppers are softened, about 8 minutes.

Add the corn, tomato sauce, chili powder, and hot pepper sauce to taste. Cook it until it is heated through. Serve it over rice.

I was in high school when I first tasted fettuccine Alfredo. I couldn't believe how creamy and delicious it was—but I also remember the disappointment of learning it was very high in fat so could only be an occasional indulgence. At last, here's a recipe, from Scramble contributor Sherry Ettleson, for a low-fat Alfredo sauce that is also high in protein and calcium. The sauce can also double as a delicious dip for crackers or baby carrots. Serve the pasta with additional steamed broccoli tossed with Parmesan cheese.

bowties alfredo with broccoli

Prep + Cook =
25 minutes

8 servings

Nutritional
Information per
serving:

Calories 350, Total
Fat 12g, 18%, Saturated Fat 2.5g, 12%,
Cholesterol 10mg,
3%, Sodium 130mg,
5%, Total Carbohydrate 47g, 16%, Dietary Fiber 3g, 14%,
Protein 15g, Sugar 4g

- 1 pkg. (16 ounces) bowtie pasta
- ½ pound (about 1 head) broccoli florets
- ½ cup reduced-fat ricotta or cottage cheese
- ½ cup plain nonfat or low-fat yogurt
- 1 tablespoon butter
- 1 teaspoon chopped garlic (about 2 cloves)
- ½ cup chopped walnuts
- ¼ cup grated Parmesan cheese
- 1 teaspoon dried basil
- ¼ teaspoon pepper
- ½ teaspoon salt

Bring a large pot of water to a boil. Add the pasta and cook it until it is 2 minutes short of being done, then add the broccoli for the final 2 minutes of cooking.

While the pasta cooks, use a blender or food processor to combine the ricotta or cottage cheese, yogurt, butter, garlic, walnuts, Parmesan cheese, basil, pepper, and salt. Blend it until it is smooth.

When the pasta and broccoli are cooked, drain them and toss them with the sauce. (Make sure to scrape all the sauce out of the blender or food processor.) Serve the pasta warm.

TIP: While dinner is cooking tonight, soak the lentils to save time on tomorrow night's dinner.

Believe it or not, many kids and adults who have tried it love this twist on the traditional meat dish. It's definitely not a looker, but it tastes great. The only challenge is finding time during the day (or the day before) to cook the lentils, which is easy but requires a little planning. My husband likes his vegetarian meatloaf on a toasted English muffin topped with the tomato sauce, while some people prefer to eat it over rice. Serve it with Lemony-Garlic Spinach (see p. 298).

lentil and cheese casserole (vegetarian meatloaf)

Prep (20 minutes) + Cook (45 minutes)

8 servings

Nutritional Information per serving:

Calories 230, Total Fat 9g, 14%, Saturated Fat 5g, 25%, Cholesterol 50mg, 17%, Sodium 620mg, 26%, Total Carbohydrate 25g, 8%, Dietary Fiber 5g, 20%, Protein 14g, Sugar 4g

2 cups shredded regular or reduced-fat Cheddar cheese

2 cups cooked lentils (see directions below)

½ small onion, finely chopped

¼ teaspoon pepper

¼ teaspoon dried thyme

1 cup bread crumbs

1 egg, slightly beaten

1 tablespoon butter, softened

1 can (15 ounces) tomato sauce

Preheat the oven to 350 degrees. In a large bowl, mix together all the ingredients except the tomato sauce.

Spread the mixture evenly in a loaf pan coated with nonstick cooking spray. Cover it with aluminum foil and bake it for 45 minutes.

Serve sliced with warm tomato sauce, or make sandwiches on English muffins.

TIP: To cook the lentils, in a medium saucepan with a lid, bring 3 cups of water to a boil. Rinse 1½ cups of lentils in a colander or bowl. Add the lentils to the boiling water, reduce the heat, cover the pan, and simmer the lentils for 25 to 30 minutes until they are tender to the bite. Drain any remaining liquid. This may produce more than 2 cups of lentils, so measure them before mixing them into the loaf. Soaking the lentils overnight cuts the cooking time by about half, so if you have soaked them, check for doneness after 10 or 15 minutes.

My brother, Lincoln, introduced me to this simply delicious one-pot soup. It is so simple to make, and elegant enough to serve to your book club or other casual gathering. Serve it with steamed artichokes and a loaf of fresh bread.

tomato and wild rice soup

Prep (20 minutes) + Cook (30–40 minutes)

8 servings

Nutritional Information per serving:

Calories 150, Total Fat 4.5g, 7%, Saturated Fat 0.5g, 3%, Cholesterol 0mg, 0%, Sodium 420mg, 18%, Total Carbohydrate 26g, 9%, Dietary Fiber 5g, 20%, Protein 5g, Sugar 9g

- 2 tablespoons olive oil
- 1 large onion, chopped
- 3 large carrots, chopped
- 2 stalks celery, chopped
- ¾ cup wild rice
- 1½ cups water
- 3 pounds fresh tomatoes (6–8 tomatoes), chopped, or 1 can (28 ounces) crushed tomatoes
- 1 teaspoon sugar
- ½ teaspoon salt
- ¼ teaspoon pepper
- 2 bay leaves
- 1 box (32 ounces) chicken or vegetable broth

In a large stockpot, heat the oil over medium-high heat. Add the onion, carrots, and celery. Cook them until they are softened, 6 to 8 minutes.

Add the remaining ingredients. Bring it to a boil, lower the heat, cover the pot, and simmer the soup for 30 to 40 minutes, until the rice and vegetables are tender. Remove the bay leaves before serving. If the soup is too thick, add more broth or water to thin it.

chop your chopping time To chop long, thin vegetables like celery and carrots, lay them side by side (flat side down for celery) and cut 2 or 3 at a time with a large chef's knife. With round vegetables such as zucchini, onions, and mushrooms, cut them in half lengthwise first and put the flat side down on the cutting board so they don't roll around while you try to slice them.

A simple spice rub really livens up mild fish. This spice combination would also be great on chicken, and it works really well with the delicate flavor of Artic Char (a close relative of salmon that comes mostly from Iceland) or trout. Serve it with rice pilaf with lentils (made by Near East) and a Tropical Fruit Salad (see p. 297).

wild salmon or arctic char with chili-lime spice rub

Prep + Cook = 20 minutes

4 servings

Nutritional Information per serving:
Calories 250, Total Fat 11g, 17%, Saturated Fat 1.5g, 8%, Cholesterol 95mg, 32%, Sodium 220mg, 9%, Total Carbohydrate 1g, 0%, Fiber 0g, 0%, Protein 34g, Sugar <1g

- **1–1½ pounds Arctic Char or Wild Salmon fillet**
- **1 teaspoon brown sugar**
- **½ teaspoon chili powder**
- **¼ teaspoon cinnamon**
- **¼ teaspoon salt**
- **2 teaspoons fresh lime juice (about ¼ lime)**

Preheat the broiler and set the oven rack about 6 inches from the heating element.

Line a baking sheet with foil and lay the fish flat on top of the foil, skin side down.

In a small bowl combine the brown sugar, chili powder, cinnamon, and salt.

Sprinkle the fillet with the lime juice and then sprinkle and press the spice mixture evenly over the flesh of the fish (for picky eaters, leave some fish plain or very lightly coated).

Broil the fish for 10 to 12 minutes until the spice rub is browned but not blackened and the fish is cooked through in the thickest part of the fillet. (Alternatively, bake the fish for 10 to 15 minutes at 450 degrees.) Remove it from the oven, cut it into 4 pieces, and serve.

do you or don't you dessert?

"Did I eat enough broccoli to get dessert?" This used to be a typical dinnertime query at our house. Andrew and I got tired of using vegetables as pawns in the game of control over our kids' diets, so we've made desserts the exception, rather than the rule. Our kids still get plenty of treats at parties and special occasions, but they no longer expect after-dinner sweets most nights. I was curious about how other parents navigated the dessert maze, so I convened an informal focus group of parents we know. Like us, nearly every parent I spoke to has set some dessert boundaries, but each family had a slightly different approach.

Some families find that nightly dessert helps encourage their kids to eat decent dinners, and some even found that the kids stopped negotiating so much once they got used to the rules. Some of these families offer only healthy desserts, such as diced melon, strawberries and whipped cream, smoothies, or applesauce.

The parents in one family we know let their child pick a small (such as a lollipop) and a big (such as a cupcake) sweet each day, so if they haven't already consumed their allotment, they can have dessert after dinner. Another family in our neighborhood rarely has dessert during the week. The kids are used to holding out for "treat day" every Sunday, when the family makes an outing to a convenience store where each kid gets to select something sweet. Other parents reserve dessert for babysitter nights to help smooth the transition. I even learned of a mom who gives her kids dessert before dinner and swears the kids go on to eat healthy dinners after their sweet tooth is sated.

For many of us, dessert carries a certain nostalgia (or sense of deprivation) associated with our own childhoods. My dad was one of the original "health nuts," so at our house dessert was rarely an option. My brother and sister and I eagerly anticipated Friday night dinners at our grandparents' house, where we got to pick two pieces of candy from a jar normally kept out of reach.

Sometimes I'm overwhelmed by the abundance of sweets that surrounds our kids, from piñatas at parties, birthday celebrations at schools, even lollipops at the grocery store and bank. I know several parents who are already concerned about their kids' weight. Yet it's so hard to carefully manage what they are exposed to and how much of it they eat, or to deny your children something that brings them—and probably you—great pleasure. The dinner table is an opportunity for parents to exert some manner of control over our kids' diets, whether or not we seize it. And, like everything else, the example we set in our own eating habits surely influences how our kids view food, including dessert.

P.S. We keep a kitchen drawer stocked with sugarless gum. A piece in the afternoon often hits the after-school sweet spot for Solomon and Celia.

My friend and first cookbook coauthor, Lisa Flaxman, introduced me to her simple baked ziti years ago. Depending on what's in the fridge or freezer, we make it more interesting by adding vegetables or cooked meat. Serve it with Italian-style Cauliflower (see p. 298).

easy baked ziti

Prep (20 minutes) +
Cook (20 minutes)

8 servings

Nutritional
Information per
serving:

Calories 330, Total
Fat 7g, 11%, Saturated Fat 2.5g, 13%,
Cholesterol 10mg,
3%, Sodium 630mg,
26%, Total Carbohydrate 50g, 17%, Dietary Fiber 3g, 12%,
Protein 16g, Sugar 7g

1 package (16 ounces) ziti pasta

1 jar (26 ounces) red pasta sauce

1 cup low-fat cottage cheese

1 cup chopped or shredded mozzarella cheese

1–2 cups chopped raw vegetables (such as peas, bell pepper, mushrooms, or zucchini) or cooked meat (such as sausage or chicken) (optional)

2 tablespoons grated Parmesan cheese

Preheat the oven to 350 degrees. Spray a large, deep casserole dish with nonstick cooking spray.

Cook the pasta according to the package directions and drain it. Return it to the pot and toss it with the pasta sauce, cottage cheese, mozzarella cheese, and any vegetables or cooked meat (optional).

Spread the mixture evenly in the casserole dish and top it with the Parmesan cheese. Bake it, uncovered, for 20 minutes, or longer for a firmer top.

healthier pasta Whole wheat pasta has much more fiber than refined pasta plus extra vitamins and minerals. If you use it in recipes with lots of sauce and flavor, your family will probably not notice the difference in taste.

My friend Jackie Cohen put this soup in decorative jars and gave it to our daughters' teachers as holiday gifts (she reminded them to refrigerate it right away). It's unusual, very healthy, and good enough to share. Serve it with corn muffins and a green salad with diced (canned) beets, glazed walnuts, and crumbled goat cheese.

pumpkin black bean soup

Prep + Cook =
30 minutes

6 servings

Nutritional
Information per
serving:

Calories 140, Total
Fat 3.5g, 5%, Saturated Fat 0g, 0%,
Cholesterol 0mg, 0%,
Sodium 580mg, 24%,
Total Carbohydrate
23g, 8%, Dietary
Fiber 6g, 24%, Protein 5g, Sugar 7g

1 tablespoon vegetable oil

1½ cups chopped onion (about 1 small onion)

3 garlic cloves, chopped

1 can (15 ounces) black beans, drained

1 can (15 ounces) whole tomatoes, drained

½ teaspoon salt

pepper to taste

1 can (15 ounces) pumpkin

3½ cups vegetable or chicken broth

1 teaspoon cumin

2 tablespoons dry sherry

sour cream for serving

In a stockpot, heat the oil over medium-high heat. Add the onions and garlic and sauté them until they are softened, about 5 minutes.

Chop the beans and tomatoes in a food processor or blender until they are pureed with some chunks remaining. Add them to the onions and garlic. Add the remaining ingredients, except the sour cream.

Mix the soup well, bring it to a gentle boil, and simmer it for 20 minutes. Serve it with a dollop of sour cream.

This chicken dish, from Ruth Marcus, is impressive for casual entertaining but easy enough for a weeknight meal. For a more elegant presentation, leave the chicken breasts whole and spoon the sauce over the chicken. Serve it with couscous.

mediterranean chicken with tomatoes and olives

Prep + Cook = 20 minutes

6 servings

Nutritional Information per serving:

Calories 220, Total Fat 5g, 8%, Saturated Fat 1g, 5%, Cholesterol 90 mg, 30%, Sodium 250 mg, 10%, Total Carbohydrate 5g, 2%, Dietary Fiber <1g, 5%, Protein 37g, Sugar 3g

3 teaspoons olive oil

4 boneless, skinless chicken breast halves, cut into 1-inch pieces

1 medium onion, chopped

1 teaspoon minced garlic (about 2 cloves)

1 can (15 ounces) diced tomatoes with their liquid

½ cup pitted green olives, coarsely chopped

1 teaspoon dried oregano or 1 tablespoon fresh

1 teaspoon dried basil or 1 tablespoon fresh

In a large nonstick skillet, heat 2 teaspoons of the oil over medium-high heat. Add the chicken and sauté it until it is browned on all sides and just cooked through, about 5 to 7 minutes. Remove the chicken from the pan and set it aside. (If you have picky eaters, you may want to keep some of the chicken plain at this point.)

Add the remaining 1 teaspoon of the oil and the onions to the skillet. Cook the onions until they are slightly tender, about 3 minutes. Add the garlic and cook it for 1 more minute. Add the tomatoes, olives, oregano, and basil and cook the sauce for 5 to 8 more minutes. Add the chicken and stir it until it is heated through.

This easy casserole recipe comes from my friend and neighbor Christina McHenry. She serves it for brunch, assembling the casserole the night before and baking it in the morning. It also makes a hearty dinner. For a vegetarian alternative, make it using vegetarian sausage patties. Serve it with biscuits and strawberries or with salsa and tortillas for a Southwestern flare.

baked sausage and egg casserole

Prep (10 minutes) +
Cook (35–40 minutes)

8 servings

Nutritional Information per serving:

Calories 320, Total Fat 21g, 32%, Saturated Fat 9g, 45%, Cholesterol 305 mg, 102%, Sodium 750mg, 31%, Total Carbohydrate 5g, 2%, Dietary Fiber 0g, 0%, Protein 29g, Sugar 4g

1 pound sausage (turkey, pork, or vegetarian)

2 cups shredded Cheddar cheese

1 can (4 ounces) chopped green chilies, drained (optional)

9 eggs

2 cups skim milk

¾ teaspoon dry mustard

½ teaspoon salt

Preheat the oven to 350 degrees. Spray a 9 × 13-inch baking dish with nonstick cooking spray.

Brown the sausage in a nonstick skillet (or in the oven, if you're using vegetarian sausage) and drain the excess liquid.

Crumble the sausage in the bottom of the baking dish and sprinkle it with the cheese and chilies (optional).

In a medium bowl, whisk together the eggs, milk, mustard, and salt. Pour the mixture over the sausage and cheese.

Bake the casserole for 35 to 40 minutes until the eggs set. Serve it hot.

Bulgur wheat is one of my recent favorite foods. This ancient Mediterranean grain cooks quickly and has a mild, nutty flavor that works well for casseroles, stews, and pilafs. In this flavorful version, the Middle East finally meets the Southwest! Serve it with Carrot and Apple Salad (see p. 298). The pilaf is also great wrapped in a tortilla or inside a pita pocket.

southwestern bulgur pilaf

Prep + Cook =
20 minutes

8 servings

Nutritional
Information per
serving:

Calories 240, Total
Fat 6g, 9%, Saturated
Fat 3g, 15%, Cholesterol 15mg, 5%,
Sodium 510mg, 21%,
Total Carbohydrate
37g, 12%, Dietary
Fiber 10g, 39%, Protein 11g, Sugar 6g

1½ cups bulgur wheat

2 cans (15 ounces each) chicken or vegetable broth

¼ teaspoon cinnamon

1 small green or red bell pepper, finely diced

1 can (15 ounces) black beans, drained and rinsed

1 can (15 ounces) unsweetened corn kernels, drained

1 tablespoon fresh lemon juice (about ¼ lemon)

1 cup (more or less to taste) shredded Cheddar cheese for serving

salsa for serving

In a medium pot with a tight-fitting lid, bring the bulgur wheat and broth to a boil. Add the cinnamon and diced peppers. Cover the pot, reduce the heat, and simmer it for 15 minutes. When the bulgur is cooked, stir in the beans, corn, and lemon juice and stir the mixture over low heat for 1 minute to warm it through.

Serve this dish topped with Cheddar cheese and salsa.

juicy fruit You will get more juice from a lemon, lime, or orange if you roll it, pressing it firmly, on the counter before juicing it.

This recipe, popular with Scramble newsletter subscribers, can be a side dish or a main course, depending on what you choose to mix in. Serve it with prepared Asian dumplings or egg rolls.

fried rice with shrimp (or tofu or chicken)

Prep + Cook =
30 minutes

6 servings

Nutritional
Information per
servings:

Calories 300, Total
Fat 7g, 11%, Satu-
rated Fat 1.5g, 8%,
Cholesterol 130mg,
43%, Sodium 600mg,
25%, Total Carbohy-
drate 43g, 14%, Di-
etary Fiber 2g, 8%,
Protein 16g, Sugar 2g

1½ **cups dry white rice**

2 **tablespoons peanut or vegetable oil**

½ **pound shrimp, peeled and deveined (or use extra-firm tofu or diced chicken breast)**

2 **eggs**

¼ **cup chopped scallions (about 4 scallions)**

1 **cup frozen peas, thawed slightly (or use water chestnuts, straw mushrooms, or diced and lightly steamed carrots)**

3 **tablespoons soy sauce, or more to taste**

¼–½ **teaspoon black pepper to taste**

Cook the rice according to the package directions.

Meanwhile, in a large nonstick skillet or wok, heat 1 tablespoon of oil over medium-high heat. Add the shrimp and sauté it for several minutes until it turns pink. (Cooked chicken will no longer be pink and tofu will be lightly browned and firm.) Remove the shrimp from the pan and set it aside.

When the rice is nearly done, heat the remaining 1 tablespoon of the oil in the pan over medium-high heat.

Crack the eggs into the heated oil and cut them into small pieces with a spatula. Add the scallions and stir-fry them for a moment. Add the rice, peas, soy sauce, and pepper, and toss thoroughly.

Add the cooked shrimp and stir the mixture together thoroughly.

perfect cooked tofu Use extra-firm tofu packed in water. Drain the tofu thoroughly and wrap it in a clean dish towel for a few minutes to absorb the extra water. Dice the tofu into ½-inch pieces. In a nonstick skillet, heat 1 tablespoon peanut or vegetable oil over medium-low heat. Add the diced tofu and sauté it for 10 minutes or more, tossing it occasionally, until it is lightly browned and firm.

Nine-year-old Molly Rubel makes these superb chicken quesadillas for her family. Your family will love them, too. For an extra healthy touch, add arugula or spinach to the quesadillas. Serve them with a Southwestern Bean Salad (see p. 298).

molly's spiced chicken quesadillas

**Prep + Cook =
30 minutes**

10 servings

**Nutritional
Information per
serving:**

Calories 370, Total
Fat 14g, 22%, Satu-
rated Fat 6g, 30%,
Cholesterol 80mg,
27%, Sodium 560mg,
23%, Total Carbohy-
drate 27g, 9%, Di-
etary Fiber 0g, 0%,
Protein 31g, Sugar 1g

1 tablespoon olive oil

1½ pounds boneless, skinless chicken breasts, cut into ½ -inch strips

1 small red onion, diced

½ teaspoon cumin

½ teaspoon salt

½ teaspoon cinnamon

½ teaspoon chili powder

2 cups shredded Monterey Jack or Cheddar cheese

10 soft-taco-sized flour or whole wheat tortillas

2 cups baby arugula or baby spinach leaves (optional)

Spray a large heavy skillet with nonstick cooking spray, add the oil, and heat it over medium heat. Add the chicken and onions and sauté them until the chicken is no longer pink, about 5 minutes. Add the cumin, salt, cinnamon, and chili powder and cook it for 1 to 2 more minutes. Remove the chicken mixture from the heat.

Heat a large nonstick skillet over medium heat. Spread a handful of cheese on half of each tortilla and top it with a layer of arugula or spinach (optional) and chicken. Fold the tortillas and cook them on each side until they are golden brown. You should be able to cook 2 or 3 quesadillas at a time, depending on the size of your skillet.

Slice each quesadilla in half and serve them.

TIP: An easy way to cut quesadillas is with clean kitchen shears or a pizza cutter.

cool! (yellow snow you *can* eat!) If snow has fallen recently, try making slushies with the kids. Scoop fresh snow into plastic cups, sprinkle it with lemonade powder and a few drops of food coloring, and let the kids mix them up and eat them for a frozen delight.

This super variation on mac 'n' cheese is fairly low in fat and quite delicious. The recipe only uses about half the box of macaroni, but you can make the whole box if someone in your family prefers plain pasta. Serve it with steamed broccoli spears.

baked macaroni and cheese with tomatoes

Prep (30 minutes) +
Cook (40–45
minutes)

8 servings

Nutritional
Information per
serving:

Calories 250, Total
Fat 10g, 16%, Saturated Fat 6g, 32%,
Cholesterol 30mg,
11%, Sodium 370 mg,
15%, Total Carbohydrate 27g, 9%, Dietary Fiber 2g, 7%,
Protein 13g, Sugar 5g

8 ounces (2 cups dry) macaroni

1 cup skim milk

½ teaspoon salt

1 teaspoon dry mustard

1 teaspoon butter

1 egg, beaten

2¼ cups shredded Cheddar cheese

3 tomatoes, diced, or 1 can (15 ounces) diced tomatoes, drained

2 tablespoons bread crumbs

Preheat the oven to 350 degrees. Spray a large casserole dish with nonstick cooking spray.

Cook the macaroni according to the package directions and drain it.

Meanwhile, in a medium bowl, mix together the milk, salt, and mustard. Set it aside.

In a large microwave-safe bowl, combine the macaroni with the butter, the beaten egg, and 2 cups of the cheese. Stir it thoroughly.

Place the macaroni mixture in the microwave on high for 2 minutes to melt the cheese more thoroughly. Mix it well.

Add the milk mixture and tomatoes to the macaroni and toss it. Place it in the casserole dish and smooth the top with a spatula. Sprinkle it with the remaining cheese and the bread crumbs and bake it, uncovered, for 40 to 45 minutes or until it is set.

These "oven omelets" make a delicious breakfast, brunch, or dinner. They can be served warm, cold or in between (think Spanish tapas). Though the recipe calls for goat or feta cheese, you can use any hard or soft cheese that you like. Serve them with chopped melon and bread or toast.

potato and goat cheese spanish "tortilla"

Prep + Cook =
20 minutes

6 servings

Nutritional
Information per
serving:

Calories 170, Total Fat 10g, 15%, Saturated Fat 2.5g, 13%, Cholesterol 180mg, 60%, Sodium 280 mg, 12%, Total Carbohydrate 12g, 4%, Dietary Fiber 1g, 4%, Protein 8g, Sugar 3g

2 medium Yukon Gold or russet potatoes (about ¾ pound), peeled and diced

2–3 tablespoons olive oil

1 medium onion, finely chopped

optional filings: ½ cup chopped ham or smoked turkey, sundried tomatoes, sliced mushrooms, or any combination

½ teaspoon dried rosemary

½ teaspoon salt

¼ teaspoon pepper

5 eggs

¼ cup skim milk

3 tablespoons crumbled goat cheese or feta cheese

In a medium bowl, sprinkle the diced potatoes with water. Lightly cover them and microwave them on high until they are fork-tender, about 3 to 5 minutes. Drain any excess liquid.

Preheat the broiler and set the rack 4 to 5 inches from the flame.

Spray a heavy-bottomed oven-proof 10-inch skillet with nonstick cooking spray. Add the oil and heat it over medium heat. Add the onions and sauté them until they are soft, 2 to 3 minutes. Add the softened potatoes (plus any optional ingredients), rosemary, salt, and pepper and sauté the mixture for a few more minutes.

In a bowl, mix the eggs, milk, and cheese and pour it over the potato mixture in the pan. Over medium-high heat, cook the egg mixture until the eggs just start to harden, about 2 minutes.

Place the skillet under the broiler and cook the tortilla until it is golden brown on top, about 3 to 5 minutes. Watch closely or the tortilla will burn. Remove it from the oven, let it cool, cut it, and serve it warm. In Spain, they eat these cold!

This soup is quick and satisfying for all ages. Soba noodles are healthy Japanese noodles made from buckwheat flour. If you can't find them in the Asian foods section of your supermarket, you can use whole wheat linguine or ramen noodles. You can also add diced tofu, chicken, or beef to the soup and let it cook for a few minutes in the boiling broth. Serve the soup with lightly salted edamame (Japanese soybeans).

soba noodle soup with shiitake mushrooms

Prep + Cook =
20 minutes

6 servings

Nutritional
Information per
serving:

Calories 210, Total
Fat 2g, 3%, Saturated
Fat 0.5g, 3%, Choles-
terol <5mg, 2%,
Sodium 1000mg, 42%,
Total Carbohydrate
43g, 14%, Dietary
Fiber 3g, 12%, Pro-
tein 10g, Sugar 2g

10 ounces soba noodles

8 dried shiitake mushrooms (about ¾ cup)

1 carton (32 ounces) chicken broth

2 individual packets miso soup mix or 2 tablespoons miso paste

4 scallions, sliced

a few dashes of five-spice powder (optional)

2 tablespoons soy sauce

In a large stockpot, cook the soba noodles for 4 minutes (or until al dente) and drain them.

In a medium bowl, soak the shiitake mushrooms in 2 cups of hot water (you can heat the water in the microwave).

When the noodles go into the boiling water, bring the chicken broth to a simmer in a separate pot. Add the miso soup mix or paste.

Reserving the water, remove the mushrooms to a cutting board. Add the mushrooms' water to the chicken broth. Chop the mushrooms into ½-inch pieces and add them to the broth, too. Add the cooked noodles, scallions, five-spice powder (optional), and soy sauce, return it to a simmer, and serve it hot.

meaty mushrooms Dried shiitake mushrooms are available in many supermarkets with Asian foods and are usually cheaper than fresh shiitakes. They soften up in the broth and have a meaty texture and nutty flavor that's great for enriching soups.

This chicken looks and sounds fancy but is actually simple to prepare. Your kids can help roll the dough and brush the egg on the packets. Serve it with corn on the cob.

chicken tarragon in a pastry packet

Prep (30 minutes) + Cook (15–20 minutes)

4 servings

Nutritional Information

Calories 470, Total Fat 17g, 26%, Saturated Fat 7g, 35%, Cholesterol 110mg, 37%, Sodium 310mg, 13%, Total Carbohydrate 35g, 12%, Dietary Fiber <1g, 4%, Protein 41g, Sugar 3g

2 tablespoons butter, softened

1 teaspoon lemon juice

½ teaspoon dried tarragon or 1 teaspoon minced fresh

⅛ teaspoon garlic powder

salt and pepper to taste

1 cup flour

1 can (8 ounces) refrigerated crescent roll dough

4 boneless, skinless chicken breast halves

1 egg, lightly beaten (optional)

Preheat the oven to 375 degrees. In a small bowl, using a fork, combine the butter, lemon juice, tarragon, garlic powder, salt, and pepper and set it aside. Put the flour in a shallow bowl or plate.

Combine the dough (which comes in 8 triangles) into 4 rectangles, by putting 2 triangles together for each. Using a rolling pin, roll each rectangle between 2 sheets of waxed paper to seal the divisions of the triangles and make the dough thinner, so it will be easier to wrap around the chicken breasts.

Coat the chicken breasts with flour. Place a chicken breast in the center of each rectangle. Spread the butter mixture evenly over the chicken breasts. Wrap the dough around each chicken breast and pinch the edges and ends of the dough to seal them. Place the packets seam side down on an ungreased baking sheet. Cut a small slit in the top of each packet to let the steam out. Bake them for 15 to 20 minutes or until the pastry is golden brown.

Optional step: For a shinier crust, remove the chicken from the oven after 15 minutes, brush the dough with beaten egg (kids can help), and bake it about 5 more minutes until the crust is a deep golden brown.

instant butter softening If you don't have time to soften butter on the counter for half an hour or so, you can soften it in the microwave for 10 to 15 seconds until it is just spreadable. Be careful not to melt it.

This dish, invented by my mother-in-law, Barbara Goldfarb, is delicious and quick to prepare. For a sweeter taste, use teriyaki sauce instead of the soy sauce. Serve it with Sesame Stir-fried broccoli (see p. 299).

broiled salmon with mustard-soy crust

Prep + Cook =
15 minutes

6 servings

Nutritional
Information per
serving:

Calories 260, Total
Fat 12g, 19%, Satu-
rated Fat 2g, 11%,
Cholesterol 100 mg,
33%, Sodium 370 mg,
15%, Total Carbohy-
drate 0g, 0%, Dietary
Fiber 0g, 0%, Protein
31g, Sugar 0g

1½–2 pounds salmon fillet

¼ cup grainy Dijon mustard

1 tablespoon soy sauce

Preheat the broiler and move the shelf so that the heat source is approximately 4 inches away.

Place the salmon skin side down in a shallow baking pan or on a cookie tray lined with foil. Brush the top of the fish with the mustard. Sprinkle soy sauce on top.

Broil the fish for 10 to 12 minutes, until the Dijon-soy crust is browned and the salmon flakes easily and is opaque throughout. Don't flip the fish during cooking.

fishy hands? Get the smell of fish (or garlic!) off your hands by washing them, then rubbing them with a slice of lemon.

Before I go to the grocery store each week, I try to create a new recipe using up what's left in the refrigerator. This dish, created from what I had on hand, was the fabulous result of a fridge clean out. Serve it with whole grain bread and sliced pears.

mushroom tortellini with roasted vegetables

Prep (10 minutes) + Cook (30 minutes)

6 servings

Nutritional Information per serving:

Calories 300, Total Fat 12g, 18%, Saturated Fat 4.5g, 23%, Cholesterol 25mg, 8%, Sodium 700mg, 29%, Total Carbohydrate 40g, 13%, Dietary Fiber 5g, 20%, Protein 10g, Sugar 4g

- ½ **pound fresh tomatoes (about 2 tomatoes), cut into 1-inch chunks**
- ½ **pound eggplant (use one small Asian eggplant if available), cut into 1-inch chunks**
- ½ **pound yellow squash (1–2 squash), cut into 1-inch pieces**
- 3 **tablespoons olive oil**
- 3 **tablespoons balsamic vinegar**
- ½ **teaspoon kosher salt**
- 1 **teaspoon (or more to taste) fresh chopped or ¼ teaspoon dried rosemary**
- 12 **ounces mushroom tortellini (use dried, rather than fresh tortellini, if possible)**
- ½ **cup dried mushrooms, such as porcinis or morels**
- ½ **cup warm water**
- 1 **tablespoon soy sauce**
- 1 **teaspoon fresh or ¼ teaspoon dried thyme**

Preheat the oven to 450 degrees. In a roasting pan, toss the tomatoes, eggplant, and squash with the oil, vinegar, salt, and rosemary. Roast the vegetables in the oven for 30 minutes, uncovered, tossing them after 15 minutes.

Meanwhile, cook the tortellini according to the package directions. Soak the mushrooms in a combination of the water and soy sauce. And 1 teaspoon fresh or ¼ teaspoon dried thyme to the broth. Set it aside.

When the vegetables come out of the oven, remove the mushrooms from the broth, reserving the liquid, and chop them coarsely.

In a large metal bowl, gently toss the tortellini with the roasted vegetables, mushrooms, and a couple of tablespoons of the mushroom broth. Serve it immediately.

TIP: Dried mushrooms can be kept in your pantry for years; then they can be added directly to soups or stews, or reconstituted with warm water or broth for a rich and delicious addition to meals.

This is a great meal for those nights when you don't really feel like cooking. It's warm, filling, and ready in a snap—and it tastes great, sort of like a Mexican omelet. (Beware: it doesn't get any extra points for looks.) If you are feeling ambitious, sauté some peppers and onions in the oil before you add the chips. Serve this dish with vanilla yogurt and clementines or tangerines.

easy-cheesy tortilla skillet

Prep + Cook =
10 minutes

4 servings

Nutritional
Information per
serving:

Calories 290, Total
Fat 15g, 23%, Saturated Fat 3g, 15%,
Cholesterol 215 mg,
71%, Sodium 840 mg,
35%, Total Carbohydrate 22g, 7%, Dietary Fiber 2g, 7%,
Protein 16g, Sugar 5g

1 tablespoon vegetable oil

2 cups broken tortilla chips

1 cup chunky salsa

4 eggs, beaten

⅔ cup shredded Cheddar cheese

In a 10- or 12-inch nonstick skillet, heat the oil over medium heat. Add the chips and sauté them in the oil for 1 minute. Add the salsa and stir it until the chips soak up some of the liquid.

Top this mixture with the beaten eggs. Cook it, stirring it gently, until the eggs are set and the mixture is somewhat dry, about 5 to 7 minutes. Top it with the cheese and serve it hot.

TIP: If you plan to make the Mushroom Barley Soup tomorrow night, soak the barley tonight.

silly game can get kids talking

Do you ever feel like getting your kids to talk about their day is harder than opening a new jar of pickles? We were eager to get our kids to join in the dinner-table conversation but wanted to get past the standard answers like "Nothing" and "I don't know." My husband, Andrew, developed a silly game that really gets them talking. Andrew asks them different questions each night that all begin "Tell me something that happened today that made you say…" The last word ranges from "Huh?" to "Cool!" to "I'm the Man" to "That's sad." It's amazing how this simple game has gotten them to share stories about their day and chime in on dinner-table talk. Now our kids often request the "Made You Say" game.

This meatless adaptation of the classic soup takes a while to cook, but my testers convinced me it is worth including in the Scramble because it is so healthy, delicious, and plentiful (we ate it for lunch all week). You can take half to a friend in need, or freeze some for a busy night. To halve the cooking time, use quick-cooking barley or soak regular barley in clean water overnight before cooking. Serve the soup with a loaf of bread and a Waldorf Salad (see p. 297).

mushroom barley soup

Prep + Cook =
30–60 minutes

10 servings

Nutritional
Information per
serving:

Calories 140, Total
Fat 4.5g, 7%, Satu-
rated Fat .5g, 3%,
Cholesterol 0mg, 0%,
Sodium 45mg, 2%,
Total Carbohydrate
22g, 7%, Dietary
Fiber 5g, 20%, Pro-
tein 5g, Sugar 4g

1 cup pearl barley (use quick-cooking if your market carries it)

3 boxes (32 ounces each) chicken or vegetable broth

2 tablespoons vegetable oil

1 large onion, chopped

1½ pounds (24 ounces) sliced fresh mushrooms

2 celery stalks, thinly sliced

½ teaspoon garlic powder

3 carrots, peeled and thinly sliced

3 tablespoons sherry

Rinse the barley in cold water (or drain the pre-soaked barley). Combine the broth and barley in a large pot and bring it to a boil. Reduce the heat and simmer it for 40 minutes, stirring it occasionally. (If you are using quick-cooking barley or you pre-soaked the barley, check if it's nearly tender after 10 to 20 minutes.)

Meanwhile, in a large heavy skillet, heat the oil over medium-high heat. Add the onions and sauté them until they are slightly browned, about 5 minutes. Add the mushrooms, celery, and garlic powder and sauté them until the mushrooms are softened, about 15 more minutes.

After the barley has simmered for 10 to 40 minutes (see note above), add the mushroom-onion mixture and carrots to the soup. Simmer it for 10 to 15 minutes (make sure the barley is tender to the bite). If the soup is too thick, add up to 1 cup of water. Stir in the sherry, warm the soup through, and serve it immediately.

This casserole is a great alternative to plain old spaghetti. Though this recipe only calls for half a package of spaghetti, you might want to make the whole package so you will have extra for picky eaters. Serve it with melon wedges.

baked spaghetti

Prep (25 minutes) +
Cook (40 minutes)

8 servings

Nutritional
Information per
serving:

Calories 230, Total Fat 7g, 11%, Saturated Fat 3g, 15%, Cholesterol 115mg, 38%, Sodium 420mg, 18%, Total Carbohydrate 29g, 10%, Dietary Fiber 3g, 12%, Protein 13g, Sugar 6g

½ pound spaghetti, broken into thirds

2 cups red pasta sauce

1 cup shredded part-skim mozzarella cheese

4 eggs, lightly beaten

½ red bell pepper, cut into ½-inch strips

2 cups frozen chopped broccoli, slightly thawed

¼ cup grated Parmesan cheese

Preheat the oven to 350 degrees. Spray a 9 × 13-inch baking dish with nonstick cooking spray.

Cook the spaghetti according to the package directions and drain it.

Meanwhile, in a large bowl, combine the pasta sauce, mozzarella cheese, eggs, red pepper strips, and broccoli.

When the spaghetti is cooked and drained, mix it well with the sauce mixture in the large bowl. Spread the mixture into the baking dish and top it with the Parmesan cheese. Bake it, uncovered, for 40 minutes until lightly browned.

knife news Use a serrated knife for cutting peppers and tomatoes to help ensure that the knife doesn't slip and cut your fingers. Their smooth skins can be hard to penetrate with a straight-edged chef's knife.

Japan meets Mexico with these sushi-taquitos! These rolls are reminiscent of real California rolls (one of Andrew's and my all-time favorite sushi rolls) without the hassle of trying to roll up seaweed and sticky rice. Imitation crab legs are made out of white fish and flavored and cut to resemble real crabmeat. Serve these with miso soup and cucumber slices dipped in ginger salad dressing. They also make a fun appetizer for a party.

california rollos

Prep + Cook = 20 minutes

8 servings

Nutritional Information per serving:

Calories 170, Total Fat 8g, 12%, Saturated Fat 1.5g, 8%, Cholesterol <5mg, 2%, Sodium 380mg, 16%, Total Carbohydrate 21g, 7%, Dietary Fiber 2g, 8%, Protein 5g, Sugar 0g

2 ripe avocados

½ cucumber, peeled

1 package (4 ounces) imitation crab legs (sometimes called surimi)

6 soft-taco-sized flour tortillas

1 package alfalfa or broccoli sprouts

soy sauce for serving

wasabi (Japanese horseradish) for serving (optional)

Cut the avocados in half and remove the pit, then scoop out the flesh with a large spoon. Thinly slice the avocados, cucumbers, and crab legs. Spread out some of each on half of each tortilla. Top it with sprouts and roll the tortilla up tightly. Slice the tortillas in half crosswise, or into 1-inch slices like sushi rolls.

Eat the rolls dipped in soy sauce. For a spicier dip, mix a little wasabi paste or powder into the soy sauce.

This is a lovely, mild, and healthy soup. It's great on its own but is even better topped with fresh sourdough croutons and a little Parmesan cheese. Serve it with the remaining sourdough bread and a spinach salad with Parmesan cheese, crumbled bacon, and sliced grapes.

tuscan white bean soup with sourdough croutons

Prep + Cook = 30 minutes

6 servings

Nutritional Information per serving:

Calories 270, Total Fat 7g, 11%, Saturated Fat 1.5g, 8%, Cholesterol <5mg, 2%, Sodium 670mg, 28%, Total Carbohydrate 38g, 13%, Dietary Fiber 7g, 28%, Protein 10g, Sugar 2g

- 2 tablespoons olive oil
- 1 large yellow onion (preferably a sweet Vidalia onion), chopped
- 2 teaspoons minced garlic (about 4 cloves)
- 2 cans (15 ounces each) cannellini beans
- 1 can (15 ounces) chicken or vegetable broth
- 2 tablespoons sherry (optional)
- 10 fresh basil leaves, finely chopped
- croutons for serving
- shredded Parmesan cheese for serving

croutons

- 2 large slices sourdough bread, cut into ½-inch cubes
- 1–2 tablespoons olive oil
- ¼ teaspoon kosher salt

Preheat the oven or toaster oven to 450 degrees for the croutons.

In a large stockpot, heat the oil over medium-high heat. Add the onion and garlic and cook them, stirring them occasionally, until the onion is tender, about 5 minutes. Add the cannellini beans and chicken broth and bring the soup to a boil.

While the soup is heating, puree it with a hand blender, if you have one. If not, remove it in batches and puree it in a standing blender, then return it to the pot. Simmer the soup for about 5 minutes.

Meanwhile, to make the croutons: in a medium bowl, toss the bread cubes with the oil and the salt. Place the croutons on a baking sheet in a single layer and bake them in the preheated oven for 3 to 5 minutes until they are slightly crisp and browned. Watch them carefully so they don't burn.

Add the sherry (optional) and basil to the soup and stir it until it is heated through. Ladle it into bowls and top it with the croutons and Parmesan cheese.

Yes, tofu—and the kids will like it. Scramble contributor Sherry Ettleson was surprised when everyone in her vegetarian family liked this dish (with veggie "meat" instead of pork, of course). It is a family-friendly way to get tofu into your diet. For extra spice, add ½ teaspoon of Chinese chili paste. If you prefer, you can use tortillas instead of lettuce leaves as wrappers. Serve this dish with steamed green beans.

ma po tofu (chinese tofu and ground pork)

Prep + Cook = 25 minutes

8 servings

Nutritional Information per serving:

Calories 210, Total Fat 9g, 14%, Saturated Fat 1.5g, 8%, Cholesterol 5 mg, 1%, Sodium 930 mg, 39%, Total Carbohydrate 11g, 4%, Dietary Fiber 3g, 12%, Protein 19g, Sugar 2g

1 tablespoon cornstarch

2 cups chicken or vegetable broth

1 teaspoon vegetable oil

1 teaspoon chopped garlic (about 2 cloves)

1½ tablespoons chopped ginger

6 scallions, green parts only, finely chopped

4 tablespoons hoisin sauce

1 pound ground pork (or use turkey or vegetarian ground "meat")

2 tablespoons soy sauce

1 pound extra-firm tofu, drained and cut into small cubes

8–10 large iceberg lettuce leaves

Stir the cornstarch into the vegetable broth and set it aside.

In a large skillet, heat the oil over high heat. Add the garlic, the ginger, and half of the scallions and stir-fry them for about 30 seconds, stirring them constantly to prevent burning. Add the hoisin sauce and ground meat. Stir-fry the mixture until the meat is almost cooked through, about 3 to 5 minutes.

Add the soy sauce, broth, and cornstarch mixture, and bring it to a low boil. Add the tofu and the remaining scallions. Simmer it for about 5 minutes. (Beware—it may look like slop, but it tastes really good.)

Wrap about ⅓ cup of the mixture inside each lettuce leaf and serve it like a burrito. It can be fun to do this at the table.

TIP: Wrap the tofu in a clean dishcloth after you drain it. Tofu is better able to absorb sauce if it is less "wet."

This delicious casserole was suggested by Scramble newsletter subscriber Leesa Hill. Our kids liked the soft texture of polenta, and I liked its easy preparation. You can make your own polenta from scratch, if you prefer, but I find the prepared variety quite acceptable in terms of nutrition and taste. Serve the casserole with peas and whole grain rolls.

polenta casserole with roasted red peppers and chopped olives

Prep (20 minutes) +
Cook (30 minutes)

8 servings

Nutritional
Information per
serving:

Calories 280, Total
Fat 9g, 14%, Saturated Fat 4g, 19%,
Cholesterol 20 mg,
6%, Sodium 640 mg,
27%, Total Carbohydrate 36g, 12%, Dietary Fiber 5g, 20%,
Protein 13g, Sugar
12g

2 cups red pasta sauce

2 tablespoons balsamic vinegar

1 can (7 ounces) chopped black olives, drained

1 jar (7½ ounces) roasted red peppers, drained and chopped

½ cup skim milk

1 tube (18–24 ounces) plain prepared polenta

2 cups shredded mozzarella cheese

Preheat the oven to 375 degrees. In a medium saucepan over medium heat, combine the pasta sauce, vinegar, olives, and red peppers. Simmer it for 10 minutes. Remove the pan from the heat and stir in the milk.

Cut the polenta into ½-inch cubes. Lay them in the bottom of a 9 × 13-inch casserole dish. Pour the sauce over the polenta, top it with the cheese, and bake it, uncovered, for 30 minutes.

This is a lighter and quicker version of beef Stroganoff that my family loves. It goes well with egg noodles and baked potatoes.

beef and mushrooms in a light cream sauce

Prep + Cook = 30 minutes

6 servings

Nutritional Information per serving:

Calories 330, Total Fat 20g, 31%, Saturated Fat 7g, 36%, Cholesterol 95 mg, 31%, Sodium 500 mg, 21%, Total Carbohydrate 9g, 3%, Dietary Fiber <1g, 3%, Protein 28g, Sugar 4g

- 1 cup reduced-fat sour cream
- 1 tablespoon Dijon mustard
- 2 tablespoons vegetable oil
- 1 pound cubed choice Angus stewing meat or beef tenderloin tips
- 2 tablespoons butter
- 8 ounces sliced mushrooms
- 3 large celery stalks, chopped
- 1 teaspoon minced fresh or dried dill
- ⅛ cup red wine
- ⅛ cup soy sauce

Remove the sour cream from the refrigerator so it warms slightly. Stir the mustard into the sour cream and set it aside.

In a large heavy skillet, heat the oil over medium-high heat. Sear the meat (cook without moving it) on all sides for about 1 minute until it is no longer pink on the outside. With a slotted spatula or spoon, transfer the meat to a plate.

Using the same skillet, reduce the heat to medium and add the butter. Add the mushrooms, celery, and dill and sauté them for about 5 minutes until they are softened. Add the wine and soy sauce and continue cooking the mixture for about 5 to 7 minutes until the vegetables are very tender and most of the liquid is absorbed. If the vegetables get too dry, add ¼ cup water to the skillet.

Return the meat to the skillet and cook it for 2 to 3 more minutes until it is cooked through. Reduce the heat to low, let the temperature lower for a minute, and stir in the sour cream mixture until it is warmed through (if the temperature remains too high, the sour cream may curdle). Remove it from the heat. Serve it over egg noodles.

This dreamy, creamy shrimp dish, from my friend Jessica Honigberg, is so delicious! If you chop the shrimp, it would also be a fabulous appetizer to spread on a warm baguette. Serve it with a green salad with Parmesan cheese and diced avocado and a loaf of crusty bread (such as a French boule).

savory shrimp and mozzarella melt

Prep (20 minutes) +
Cook (20 minutes)

5 servings

Nutritional
Information per
serving:

Calories 310, Total
Fat 15g, 24%, Saturated Fat 6g, 29%,
Cholesterol 165mg,
55%, Sodium 670mg,
28%, Total Carbohydrate 10g, 3%, Dietary Fiber 2g, 10%,
Protein 34g, Sugar 0g

2 teaspoons olive oil

1 teaspoon chopped garlic (about 2 cloves)

2 jars (6 ounces each) marinated artichoke hearts, drained and chopped into ½-inch pieces

pinch red pepper flakes (optional)

1 pound shrimp, peeled and deveined

8 ounces fresh mozzarella cheese, diced (or use 2 cups shredded)

2 tablespoons grated Parmesan cheese

Preheat the oven to 400 degrees.

In a large skillet, heat 1 teaspoon of the oil over medium heat. Add the garlic and sauté it for about 1 minute. Add the artichokes and red pepper flakes (optional) and cook them for about 3 minutes. Transfer the mixture to an 8 × 8-inch baking dish.

Heat the remaining 1 teaspoon of the oil in the skillet. Add the shrimp and sauté them for several minutes until they turn pink. Drain the excess liquid from the pan and put the shrimp on top of the artichokes in the baking dish. Top them with the mozzarella cheese and sprinkle the Parmesan cheese on top. Bake it for 20 minutes until the cheese is thoroughly melted and the dish is heated through.

This is a light and simple recipe to bring out the simply delicious flavors of broccoli and tortellini. It is popular with Scramble newsletter subscribers. Don't be concerned if the sauce is a little thin, as most of the liquid will be absorbed when you stir in the tortellini. Serve it with a loaf of whole-grain bread.

light cheese tortellini with broccoli

Prep + Cook = 20 minutes

8 servings

Nutritional Information per serving:

Calories 270, Total Fat 9g, 13%, Saturated Fat 3.5g, 18%, Cholesterol 30mg, 10%, Sodium 400mg, 17%, Total Carbohydrate 38g, 13%, Dietary Fiber 6g, 22%, Protein 14g, Sugar 6g

- **2 packages (9 ounces each) cheese tortellini**
- **1 tablespoon olive oil**
- **½ large red onion, thinly sliced, then cut into quarter circles**
- **1½ teaspoons chopped garlic (about 3 cloves)**
- **3 heads broccoli, cut into spears**
- **1½ cups vegetable or chicken broth**
- **⅛ teaspoon pepper (or more to taste)**
- **¼ cup shredded Parmesan cheese for serving**

Cook the tortellini according to the package directions.

Meanwhile, in a large heavy-duty skillet, heat the oil over medium heat and sauté the onion and garlic until the onion is softened, about 5 minutes.

Add the broccoli, broth, and pepper. Bring it to a boil, reduce the heat, cover the pan, and simmer it for about 10 minutes until the pasta is done.

Drain the tortellini, add it to the skillet, and toss it with the sauce. Serve the pasta topped with Parmesan cheese.

edgewise It's a really good idea to sharpen your straight-edged knives every week or two. You will be amazed by how much easier it is to chop with a sharp knife.

This is a mild, kid-friendly, and high fiber vegetable curry. We topped it at the table with a yogurt sauce (see the Tip below) and served it with steamed rice and warmed pita bread.

winter vegetable curry with lentils

Prep (30 minutes) +
Cook (30 minutes)

10 servings

Nutritional
Information per
serving:

Calories 160, Total
Fat 2g, 3%, Saturated
Fat 0g, 0%, Choles-
terol 0mg, 0%,
Sodium 260mg, 11%,
Total Carbohydrate
27g, 9%, Dietary
Fiber 10g, 40%, Pro-
tein 9g, Sugar 8g

- 1 tablespoon olive oil
- 1 large onion, diced
- 2 tablespoons curry powder
- ¼ teaspoon ground ginger
- 1½ pounds sweet potatoes (1 or 2 potatoes, depending on size), peeled and diced
- 1 head cauliflower, separated into florets
- 1 cup brown lentils, rinsed and drained
- 2 cans (15 ounce each) diced tomatoes with their juice
- 1½ cups water
- 1 teaspoon kosher salt

In a large nonstick pot, heat the oil over medium heat. Add the onion and cook it, stirring it frequently, until it is softened, about 5 minutes.

Add the curry powder and ginger and cook the mixture, stirring it constantly, for 1 minute. Add the sweet potatoes, cauliflower, lentils, tomatoes and their juice, water, and salt. Bring it to a boil, reduce the heat, cover the pot, and simmer it until the sweet potatoes are tender, about 30 minutes.

TIP: For a tasty sauce that goes well with this curry, mix 1½ cups low-fat plain yogurt with 1 teaspoon honey and ¼ teaspoon ground ginger.

This quick and light-tasting soup resembles a lemongrass soup, without the need for lemongrass, which is tough to find at many traditional supermarkets. Japanese udon noodles are made of wheat flour, which are healthier and have a great texture for kids. Serve the soup with asparagus with sesame soy ginger sauce (see p. 298).

savory udon noodle soup

Prep + Cook = 20 minutes

6 servings

Nutritional Information per serving:

Calories 210, Total Fat 3g, 5%, Saturated Fat 0g, 0%, Cholesterol 0mg, 0%, Sodium 590mg, 25%, Total Carbohydrate 37g, 12%, Dietary Fiber 3g, 12%, Protein 10g, Sugar <1g

- 1 package (10 ounces) udon noodles
- 4 cups chicken or vegetable broth
- 1 cup water
- ½ cake tofu or ½ pound shrimp, peeled and deveined
- 2 scallions, green parts only, sliced
- ¼–½ cup chopped fresh cilantro
- 1 tablespoon fish sauce (or use soy sauce)
- 2 tablespoons lime juice (about ½ lime)
- 1 package (8 ounces) sliced fresh mushrooms
- 1 cup baby spinach (optional)

In a large pot, boil the water to cook the noodles. When they go into the water, bring the chicken broth and water to a low boil in a separate saucepan, and add the rest of the ingredients except the spinach to the broth.

Cook the noodles for only 5 to 7 minutes or until they are al dente. Drain them and add them to the soup. Add the spinach (optional) to the soup, stir it, and serve it hot.

This dish is a staple in the home of my neighbor Annie Canby. The flavor is mild and slightly sweet, so her girls, Emma and Claire, ages 11 and 9, love it. The coconut milk and mango produce a sweet sauce, which is delicious scooped over rice. Serve the chicken with steamed peas and rice.

coconut chicken with mango

Prep + Cook = 30 minutes

6 servings

Nutritional Information per serving:

Calories 290, Total Fat 16g, 25%, Saturated Fat 11g, 55%, Cholesterol 65mg, 22%, Sodium 280mg, 12%, Total Carbohydrate 12g, 4%, Dietary Fiber 2g, 8%, Protein 28g, Sugar 7g

1 tablespoon olive oil

1–1½ pounds boneless, skinless chicken breasts, cut into 1-inch pieces

1¼ cups light coconut milk

3 tablespoons mango chutney (sold with Indian foods)

½ teaspoon salt

1 ripe mango, peeled and chopped, or 1 cup frozen mango, thawed and drained

In a large nonstick skillet, heat the oil over medium heat. Add the chicken and sauté it, tossing it occasionally, until it becomes slightly white on the outside, about 3 to 5 minutes. Add the coconut milk, chutney, and salt and simmer it for 15 to 20 minutes.

While the chicken is simmering, peel and chop the mango. Add it to the simmering chicken mixture for the final few minutes of cooking.

germ alert Be sure to wash your knife and cutting board thoroughly after cutting raw chicken, to avoid spreading dangerous bacteria.

These burgers, from Sherry Ettleson, are crispy on the outside and creamy on the inside, and full of wonderful fiber and protein for your family. Dress them up like any burgers, with lettuce, tomato, pickles, and your favorite toppings. They're also great topped with salsa. Serve them with Baked Potato Chips (see p. 300).

black bean burgers

Prep + Cook = 30 minutes

6 servings

Nutritional Information per serving:

Calories 300, Total Fat 6g, 9%, Saturated Fat 1g, 5%, Cholesterol 35mg, 12%, Sodium 690mg, 29%, Total Carbohydrate 50g, 17%, Dietary Fiber 7g, 28%, Protein 13g, Sugar 5g

1 can (15 ounces) black beans, drained
1 tablespoon tomato paste
½ cup minced red onion (about ¼ onion)
½ cup plain bread crumbs
¼ teaspoon dried oregano
1 tablespoon balsamic vinegar
1 egg, lightly beaten
salt and pepper to taste
¼ cup yellow cornmeal
3 tablespoons vegetable oil
6 whole grain hamburger buns

Coarsely chop the beans in a food processor or mash them slightly with a fork. Place the beans in a large mixing bowl and add all the ingredients except the cornmeal, oil, and buns. Mix them well and press the mixture into patties.

Place the cornmeal in a shallow bowl. Coat the patties on both sides in cornmeal. Set them on waxed paper. (You can store these in the refrigerator or freeze them until you want to use them.)

In a large nonstick skillet, heat the oil over medium heat. Fry the patties 2 to 3 minutes on each side, until they are lightly browned. Drain them on a paper towel. Serve them warm on buns with desired toppings.

"cubed" tomatoes Freeze 1-tablespoon dollops of tomato paste in an ice tray. Once they have frozen, you can transfer the cubes to a resealable plastic bag and keep them in the freezer for future recipes.

This big and satisfying casserole is a meal in itself, but it also goes well with a salad.

creamy broccoli noodle casserole

Prep (30 minutes) +
Cook (45 minutes)

10 servings

Nutritional
Information per
serving:

Calories 340, Total
Fat 20g, 30%, Saturated Fat 11g, 55%,
Cholesterol 150mg,
50%, Sodium 290mg,
12%, Total Carbohydrate 23g, 8%, Dietary Fiber 2g, 8%,
Protein 19g, Sugar 3g

- 1 bag (12 ounces) wide, flat egg noodles
- 3 tablespoons butter
- 2 stalks fresh broccoli (florets and stems), chopped
- 1 pound sliced mushrooms
- 1 large onion, chopped
- 3 eggs
- 3 cups low-fat ricotta or cottage cheese
- 1 cup reduced-fat sour cream
- ¼ cup white wine
- ½ cup bread crumbs
- 1 cup shredded Cheddar cheese

Preheat the oven to 350 degrees. Spray a 9 × 13-inch baking pan with nonstick cooking spray.

Cook the egg noodles in salted water until they are nearly done. Drain and toss them with 1 tablespoon butter.

While the noodles are cooking, melt 2 tablespoons of the butter in a large heavy duty skillet over medium-high heat. Add the broccoli, mushrooms, and onion and sauté them until they are tender, about 8 to 10 minutes.

While the vegetables are cooking, beat the eggs in a large bowl. Whisk in the ricotta or cottage cheese and sour cream.

Remove the vegetables from the heat and toss them with the white wine. Gently stir the vegetable mixture, the noodles, and ¼ cup of the bread crumbs into the egg mixture. Spread the mixture into the baking pan and top it with the Cheddar cheese and the remaining bread crumbs.

Cover the casserole with foil and bake it for 30 minutes, then remove the foil and bake it for 15 minutes more.

I love making tilapia because it cooks so quickly, is affordable, and is one of the safer fish for people and the planet. Also, my kids love its mild taste and chicken-like texture. I got the idea for this elegant recipe from Chris Hoge, owner of the gourmet food store Chris's Marketplace, in Bethesda, Maryland. Serve it with couscous.

sautéed tilapia with baby spinach

Prep + Cook =
10 minutes

4 servings

Nutritional
Information per
serving:

Calories 180, Total Fat 7g, 10%, Saturated Fat 1.5g, 7%, Cholesterol 70 mg, 23%, Sodium 85 mg, 4%, Total Carbohydrate 2g, 1%, Dietary Fiber <1g, 2%, Protein 26g, Sugar 0g

- 3 tablespoons olive oil
- ½ teaspoon minced garlic (about 1 clove)
- 9–12 ounces baby spinach
- 4 tilapia fillets (about 1½ pounds)
- 1 lemon, halved
- salt and pepper to taste
- lemon wedges for serving

In a large skillet, heat 1 tablespoon of the oil over medium heat. Add the garlic and sauté it until it is fragrant, about 30 seconds. Add the baby spinach, cover the pan, and cook the spinach, stirring it occasionally, until it is wilted, about 3 to 5 minutes. Uncover the pan and sprinkle the spinach with the juice of half the lemon and salt. Remove it from the heat, cover the pan, and set it aside.

In a large nonstick skillet, heat the remaining 2 tablespoons of the oil over medium-high heat. Place the fillets in the pan and press them down with a spatula to ensure each fillet is completely touching the pan. Cook the fillets on each side until they are lightly browned, 2 to 3 minutes. After flipping the fish, sprinkle the fillets with the juice of the other half of the lemon and season them with salt and pepper.

Put a scoop of spinach on each dinner plate and top it with the tilapia. Serve the dish with lemon wedges.

{ **healthy dessert** For a light and delicious dessert, try a fruit smoothie: Blend ripe bananas, fresh or frozen strawberries, blueberries, mangoes—or your favorite fruit—with nonfat vanilla yogurt and a splash of orange juice.

My husband is originally from New York, and our kids and I think that he makes the best New York pizza we've tasted. In this recipe, he shares his secrets. You can make your own dough if you have a bread machine, or purchase pizza dough from an Italian deli or supermarket. Serve it with a crisp salad topped with dried cranberries and Parmesan cheese.

andrew's amazing pizza

Prep + Cook =
30 minutes

2 (12-inch) thin-
crust pizzas

Nutritional
Information per
serving:

Calories 210, Total
Fat 9g, 14%, Satu-
rated Fat 3.5g, 18%,
Cholesterol 15mg,
5%, Sodium 560mg,
23%, Total Carbohy-
drate 21g, 7%, Di-
etary Fiber 1g, 4%,
Protein 12g, Sugar 2g

- 1 pizza dough
- 2–3 tablespoons olive oil
- 1 teaspoon cornmeal (if using pizza peel)
- flour (to keep dough from sticking)
- 1 cup tomato sauce or red pasta sauce
- 8 ounces diced fresh mozzarella or shredded mozzarella cheese

toppings (your choice) such as:
- 5–6 fresh mushrooms, sliced; ½ large onion, diced; ½ cup fresh basil leaves, washed (whole, torn, or cut to preference); fresh minced garlic or garlic powder to taste; pepperoni

Take the pizza dough out of the refrigerator *at least* ½ hour before beginning the preparation (for ease in rolling it out). Room temperature is best.

Preheat the oven to 500 degrees. If you're using a cookie sheet or pizza pan, brush it with a thin layer of olive oil. (If you're using a pizza stone and peel, preheat the stone on the bottom shelf of the oven and spread 1 teaspoon of cornmeal on the peel).

Sprinkle flour on a clean counter or pastry board. Put the pizza dough on it and cut it in half. Roll each half into approximately a 12-inch circle. Sprinkle flour as needed on the dough and/or rolling pin to prevent sticking.

Place the crust on the baking sheet or pizza peel and brush a thin layer of olive oil on top. Spread half of the tomato sauce on each pie, leaving a ½-inch rim around the edge. Spread half of the mozzarella cheese on each pie, followed by your chosen toppings. Bake the pies for 8 to 9 minutes, turning them around once, until the bottoms of the crusts are golden brown. Watch carefully so the bottoms don't burn. Remove them from the oven and let them cool for several minutes before you slice them.

TIP: Let your children make their own pizzas. Give them a piece of the dough on a cookie sheet sprinkled with flour to spread and play with, then supervise or help while they spread sauce and sprinkle cheese. Creative shapes encouraged!

This scrumptious chicken cooks so quickly because of the high heat and the chicken's proximity to the oven's heating element. Serve it with roasted asparagus (see p. 299).

spiced chicken with maple butter glaze

Prep + Cook =
  30 minutes

6 servings

Nutritional
Information per
serving:

Calories 310, Total
Fat 16g, 24%, Saturated Fat 5g, 26%, Cholesterol 105mg, 34%, Sodium 360mg, 15%, Total Carbohydrate 7g, 2%, Dietary Fiber 0g, 0%, Protein 33g, Sugar 6g

1½ teaspoons paprika

1 teaspoon salt

¾ teaspoon cinnamon

¾ teaspoon cumin

1 whole chicken, cut up (4–5 pounds)

3 tablespoons maple syrup (if possible, use pure maple syrup)

1½ tablespoons butter

1½ tablespoons Dijon mustard

Preheat the oven to 500 degrees. Line a baking sheet with aluminum foil and spray the foil with cooking spray. In a small bowl, combine the paprika, salt, cinnamon, and cumin.

Place the chicken pieces skin side up on the baking sheet. Sprinkle and rub the spice mixture evenly over the chicken (leave the drumsticks without spices for picky eaters). Position the sheet in the upper third of the oven, about 4 inches from the heating element, and bake the chicken, without turning it, for 15 minutes.

Meanwhile, in a small saucepan, combine the maple syrup, butter, and mustard. Stir it over low heat until the butter melts. Remove it from the heat.

After the chicken has baked for 15 minutes, brush it with the maple glaze and bake it for 5 minutes more. Brush the chicken with the glaze again and bake it for 5 minutes more.

This hearty soup, from my husband's grandmother Pearl Barnett (who lived in Manhattan until she was ninety-three), makes a great winter meal. If you don't eat clams, leave them out; the soup is still wonderful without them. This recipe makes enough soup to freeze half or share some with a friend. If you prefer to halve the recipe, go ahead and use the whole can of clams for a heartier soup. Serve it with soup crackers.

manhattan clam (or clam-less) chowder

Prep (30 minutes) +
Cook (30 minutes)

12 servings

Nutritional
Information per
serving:

Calories 190, Total
Fat 3.5g, 5%, Satu-
rated Fat 1.5g, 8%,
Cholesterol 20mg,
6%, Sodium 730mg,
30%, Total Carbohy-
drate 33g, 11%, Di-
etary Fiber 5g, 20%,
Protein 9g, Sugar 16g

- 2 tablespoons butter
- 4 large onions, chopped
- 2 celery stalks, chopped
- 6 carrots, chopped
- 2 cans (10¾ ounces each) condensed tomato soup
- 2 cans (15 ounces each) tomato sauce
- 4 tomato-sauce cans of water
- 2 large potatoes, peeled and diced
- ½ cup fresh parsley, chopped
- 2 tablespoons dried thyme
- 1 can (10 ounces) unsweetened corn kernels, drained
- 1 can (10 ounces) whole clams plus their juice (optional)
- salt and pepper to taste

In a large stockpot, melt the butter over medium heat. Add the onions and sauté them until they are slightly soft, about 5 to 8 minutes.

Add the celery, carrots, tomato soup, tomato sauce, and water. Raise the heat and bring the liquid to a boil.

Add the potatoes, parsley, and thyme. Reduce the heat and simmer the soup gently for 30 minutes. Add the corn and clams (optional) and warm it through. Season it with salt and pepper to taste. Serve the chowder hot.

The eggplant recipe comes from my husband's aunt, Annette Sherman. When I ran it in the newsletter, subscriber Mike Fisher raved that it tasted so good it was "like butter." This is a good dinner for the end of the week, because you can stuff the sandwiches with whatever's left over from the week's cooking. The sandwich resembles an Israeli falafel and tastes great with tahini sauce, yogurt, or red pasta sauce (which gives it more of an Italian flavor). Our kids enjoyed assembling their own sandwiches at the table. Serve them with a salad of chopped tomato, cucumber, and feta cheese—that can go inside the pita pockets, too!

warm eggplant pita sandwiches

Prep (15 minutes) +
Cook (30 minutes)

4 servings

Nutritional
Information per
serving:

Calories 290, Total
Fat 5g, 8%, Saturated
Fat 2g, 10%, Choles-
terol 10mg, 3%,
Sodium 600mg, 25%,
Total Carbohydrate
50g, 17%, Dietary
Fiber 4g, 15%, Pro-
tein 12g, Sugar 6g

2 eggs, beaten

1 cup bread crumbs (mix with ¼ cup grated Parmesan cheese,
   if desired)

1 large eggplant, peeled and cut into ½-inch round slices

4 ounces feta cheese, crumbled (or cheese of your choice)

1 tomato, chopped

tahini sauce (see the Tip below) red pasta sauce, or plain yogurt for serving
   (optional)

1 bag pita pockets

Preheat the oven to 375 degrees. Line a pan with foil and spray the foil with non-stick cooking spray.

In a shallow bowl, beat the eggs. In a separate shallow bowl, pour the bread crumbs and Parmesan cheese (optional). Using a fork, dip an eggplant slice in the egg, let the excess drip off, and dip both sides in the bread crumb mixture to coat it. Place the breaded eggplant slices on the pan and spray the tops with the cooking spray.

Bake the eggplant slices for 30 minutes, flipping them once, until they are soft and lightly browned. While the eggplant is cooking, put sandwich fixings, including sauce of your choice, in bowls on the table. Heat the pitas in the microwave oven before serving.

Transfer the eggplant slices to a plate and assemble the sandwiches at the table while the eggplant is still warm.

TIP: For tahini sauce, mix together ½ cup each of tahini (sesame paste) and plain yogurt. Add ½ teaspoon minced garlic and 1 tablespoon lemon juice. Season it with salt to taste.

Stuffed potatoes make an incredibly filling, healthy, and versatile dinner. I like the combination of broccoli and Cheddar cheese, but you can use spinach and feta cheese, mushrooms, or whatever you have in the vegetable drawer. This is a great one for kids to help make. They can mash the potatoes and broccoli and stuff the filling in the potato shells. For extra flavor, add a couple of tablespoons of salsa to the mashed potato. Serve the potatoes with a Waldorf Salad (see p. 297). For a heartier dinner, you can serve them with a prepared supermarket roast chicken.

broccoli and cheddar stuffed potatoes

Prep + Cook =
30 minutes

4 servings

Nutritional
Information per
serving:

Calories 430, Total
Fat 20g, 31%, Saturated Fat 10g, 51%,
Cholesterol 45, 15%,
Sodium 420 mg, 17%,
Total Carbohydrate
45g, 15%, Dietary
Fiber 7g, 29%, Protein 18g, Sugar 9g

4 large baking potatoes

1 head broccoli, cut into spears

2 tablespoons butter or margarine

⅓ cup low-fat milk

2 tablespoons salsa (optional)

1½ cups shredded Cheddar cheese

Prick the potatoes with a fork in several places and cook them in the microwave on high power until they are slightly softened, about 5 minutes per potato (but check every 5 minutes).

Preheat the oven to 400 degrees (use a toaster oven if you're making just one or two potatoes).

While the potatoes are cooking, steam the broccoli spears in a covered pot with about ½ inch of water for about 7 minutes until they are very tender. Drain and finely chop the broccoli.

When the potatoes are soft, carefully slice them in half lengthwise (use oven mitts—they're *hot*) and scoop out most of the flesh, leaving a layer of potato about ¼-inch thick inside the skin.

In a medium bowl, mash together the potato flesh, broccoli, butter or margarine, milk and salsa (optional) and 1 cup of the cheese. Mound the mixture back into the potato skins. Top them with the remaining cheese and bake them for about 6 to 8 minutes until the potatoes are heated through and the cheese is melted.

This is a creamy, flavorful pasta that's ideal for a chilly evening. For younger children, you may want to leave some pasta plain, as the goat cheese has a slightly strong taste. Herbes de Provence is a nice mix of dried French herbs, but you can substitute dried thyme if you don't have it. Serve the rotini with a spinach salad with diced oranges and walnuts.

rotini with goat cheese and bacon

Prep + Cook =
30 minutes

8 servings

Nutritional
Information per
serving:

Calories 330, Total
Fat 7g, 11%, Saturated Fat 2.5g, 13%,
Cholesterol 5mg, 2%,
Sodium 240mg, 10%,
Total Carbohydrate
50g, 17%, Dietary
Fiber 8g, 32%, Protein 15g, Sugar 4g

1 package (16 ounces) rotini or other spiral-shaped noodles

8 ounces bacon (turkey, pork, or vegetarian)

1 tablespoon olive oil

1 small red onion, slivered

1 teaspoon herbes de Provence (or use dried thyme)

½ cup chicken broth

4 ounces goat cheese

1 cup frozen peas (optional)

In a large stockpot, cook the pasta according to the package directions until it is al dente. Before you drain it, reserve ½ cup of the cooking water.

Meanwhile, in a nonstick skillet, cook the bacon over medium heat, turning it occasionally, until it is crisp. Remove it to a paper towel to drain. After it cools, cut the bacon into small pieces.

In a second skillet, heat the olive oil over medium heat. Add the slivered onion and Herbes de Provence and cook it until the onion is browned, stirring it occasionally, about 5 to 10 minutes.

Drain the pasta (don't forget to reserve some water). In a measuring cup, mix together the chicken broth and ½ cup of the pasta's cooking water, and heat it in the microwave until it is warm.

Return the pasta to the stockpot over low heat and crumble in the goat cheese. Add the chicken broth–water combination and stir. Add the bacon, cooked onion, and peas (optional) and stir until warmed through. If the pasta needs to be creamier add additional water or broth.

This dish, invented by Cindy Flaxman, is sweet and delicious. For the kids, it's essentially chicken nuggets, and for their parents, it's a gourmet meal! Serve it with couscous and grapes.

chicken (nuggets!)
with caramelized onions

Prep + Cook =
30 minutes

6 servings

Nutritional
Information per
serving:

Calories 360, Total
Fat 13g, 20%, Saturated Fat 4.5g, 22%,
Cholesterol 175mg,
59%, Sodium 590mg,
24%, Total Carbohydrate 20g, 7%, Dietary Fiber 2g, 8%,
Protein 40g, Sugar 6g

2 tablespoons butter

3 large sweet onions (preferably Vidalia), sliced into thin rings

2 eggs

4 boneless, skinless chicken breast halves (about 1½–2 lbs. total),
   cut into bite-sized pieces

1½ cups Italian-style bread crumbs

1 tablespoon olive oil

In a medium-sized heavy skillet, melt the butter. Add the onions, coating them with butter. Cover the pan and turn the heat to medium-low. Stir it every 10 minutes until the onions are golden brown and soft, 20 to 30 minutes.

In a large bowl, lightly beat the eggs. Add the chicken pieces and stir them to coat them well. Drain any excess liquid and add the bread crumbs. Toss the chicken to coat it thoroughly.

In a nonstick skillet, heat the oil over medium heat. Add the chicken and brown it on all sides until it is just cooked through, about 5 to 8 minutes. (Remove some chicken for very picky eaters.) Add the onions to the chicken and stir it until it is warmed through.

This is a good alternative to rice and beans. Quinoa is a delicate and quick-cooking grain that is much higher in calcium, magnesium, phosphorous, and potassium than white rice. If you can't locate quinoa in your market, use brown or white rice instead. The cilantro is important for the flavor, so don't skip it. Serve this dish with steamed green beans.

quinoa and black bean burritos

Prep + Cook = 30 minutes

8 servings

Nutritional Information per serving:

Calories 430, Total Fat 8g, 113%, Saturated Fat 1.5g, 8%, Cholesterol 0mg, 0%, Sodium 790mg, 33%, Total Carbohydrate 74g, 25%, Dietary Fiber 11g, 44%, Protein 15g, Sugar 7g

- 1 teaspoon olive oil
- 1 onion, diced
- 1½ teaspoons chopped garlic (about 3 cloves)
- 1 cup frozen corn kernels
- ¾ cup uncooked quinoa
- 1½ cups vegetable or chicken broth
- 1 teaspoon ground cumin
- 2 cans (15 ounces each) black beans, drained
- ½ cup chopped fresh cilantro
- 8 large flour or whole wheat tortillas
- salsa for serving

In a medium saucepan, heat the oil over medium heat. Add the onion and garlic and sauté them until they are lightly browned, about 5 minutes. While the onion and garlic are cooking, take the corn out of the freezer and thoroughly rinse the quinoa under cold water.

Add the quinoa, broth, and cumin to the saucepan. Bring the mixture to a boil. Cover it, reduce the heat, and simmer it for 20 minutes.

Stir the corn, beans, and cilantro into the saucepan and simmer the filling until it is heated through.

Serve it wrapped in warm tortillas topped with salsa.

cilantro: it's all good When cooking with cilantro, you can chop and add the flavorful stems in addition to the leaves.

Crab cakes are a Maryland staple, so after living in the Free State for nine years I thought it was time I learned how to make them. If you don't eat shellfish, you can get good results using canned salmon or tuna in place of the crab. Serve this dish with cocktail sauce (you can buy a jar or make your own by combining ketchup, horseradish or Chinese mustard, and lemon juice), corn on the cob, and English muffins.

maryland crab cakes

Prep + Cook =
30 minutes +

Makes about 12
small patties

Nutritional
Information per
crab cake:

Calories 90, Total Fat
5g, 8%, Saturated Fat
1.5g, 8%, Cholesterol
50mg, 17%, Sodium
170mg, 7%, Total
Carbohydrate 2g, 1%,
Dietary Fiber 0g, 0%,
Protein 7g, Sugar
<1g

1 egg

¼ cup light mayonnaise

1 tablespoon Worcestershire sauce

1 tablespoon Old Bay seasoning

1 tablespoon lemon juice (about ¼ lemon)

2 tablespoons minced chives (or use scallions)

1 pound fresh lump crab meat

1 cup crushed stoned wheat crackers (about 12 crackers) or bread crumbs

2–3 tablespoons olive oil

1–2 tablespoons butter

In a large bowl, whisk together the egg, the mayonnaise, the Worcestershire sauce, the Old Bay, the lemon juice, and the chives. Fold in the crab meat and ½ cup of the crushed crackers and combine them thoroughly.

Line a baking sheet with waxed paper and with wet hands, form the crab mixture into cakes about 2 inches across and ½ inch high. Press them together firmly, but don't mash the cakes. Using your hands, sprinkle and press the remaining crackers into the cakes to form a crust. Refrigerate them for 30 minutes to 2 hours, if time allows.

When you are ready to cook them, heat 2 tablespoons of oil and 1 tablespoon of butter in a large nonstick skillet over medium heat. When the butter starts to bubble, add the crab cakes and cook them on each side until they are well browned, about 3 to 5 minutes per side. Add the remaining oil and butter to the pan, if necessary. Remove the cakes to a plate lined with a paper towel to drain them.

Serve the crab cakes hot (keep them warm in an oven preheated to 300 degrees, if necessary).

TIP: Your kids may enjoy smashing the crackers with a mallet. Put the crackers in a resealable bag to minimize the mess.

One of my favorite appetizers is baked artichoke dip. This casserole turns those delicious flavors and that creamy consistency into a wonderful meal. The casserole only uses half a box of pasta, but you may want to make the whole package to serve some to picky eaters. Serve this dish with roasted baby carrots (see p. 299).

baked artichoke pasta

Prep (20 minutes) + Cook (30 minutes)

6 servings

Nutritional Information per serving:

Calories 390, Total Fat 19g, 29%, Saturated Fat 5g, 25%, Cholesterol 15mg, 5%, Sodium 560mg, 23%, Total Carbohydrate 41g, 14%, Dietary Fiber 4g, 16%, Protein 13g, Sugar 1g

1 can (14 ounces) quartered artichoke hearts, drained

1 jar (6 ounces) quartered and marinated artichoke hearts with their liquid

2 teaspoons chopped garlic (about 4 cloves)

1 cup shredded Parmesan cheese

½ cup light mayonnaise

¼ cup pine nuts

2 tablespoons bread crumbs

Preheat the oven to 400 degrees. Spray a 2-quart casserole dish with nonstick cooking spray.

Cook the pasta according to the package directions until it is al dente and drain it.

In a food processor or blender, coarsely blend the artichokes, marinated artichokes with their liquid, garlic, Parmesan cheese (reserving 1 tablespoon for topping), mayonnaise, and pine nuts.

In a large bowl, mix the pasta with the artichoke mixture. Transfer it to the casserole dish and smooth the top with a spatula.

In a small bowl, mix together the reserved Parmesan cheese and the bread crumbs. Sprinkle this topping on the casserole.

Bake the casserole, uncovered, for 30 minutes until the top is browned. Serve it hot.

tiny treasures Delicious pine nuts are a good source of dietary fiber, protein, and iron. If you store them in the freezer, they will taste fresh for months. They also make a great snack or addition to salads or grains.

This hearty and flavorful salad is a treat for Andrew and me. For our kids, who are not big salad eaters, I serve extra hard-boiled eggs, plain bacon, and sliced oranges, with a loaf of French bread for all of us.

cobb salad

Prep + Cook =
25 minutes

6 servings

Nutritional
Information per
serving:

Calories 190, Total
Fat 13g, 20%, Satu-
rated Fat 4.5g, 23%,
Cholesterol 90mg,
30%, Sodium 380mg,
16%, Total Carbohy-
drate 10g, 3%, Di-
etary Fiber 4g, 16%,
Protein 9g, Sugar 6g

8–10 slices bacon (turkey, pork, or vegetarian)

2 hard-boiled eggs, sliced

1 small head romaine lettuce, washed and chopped

2 tomatoes, chopped

1 ripe avocado, chopped

½ cup crumbled blue cheese

⅓ cup (or to taste) balsamic vinaigrette dressing

Cook the bacon over medium heat in a nonstick skillet, turning it occasionally, until it is crisp, about 8 minutes. Remove it to a paper towel to drain. Chop or crumble it into small pieces.

Combine all the ingredients in a large bowl and toss them thoroughly.

hard-boiled There are many different methods for cooking hard-boiled eggs, and each cook seems to feel passionately that his or her method is best. Here is my favorite: Immerse raw eggs in cool water in a pan just large enough to hold them in one layer. Bring the water to a low boil and cook the eggs at a very low boil, uncovered, for 12 minutes, then run the eggs under cold water and refrigerate them until you're ready to use them, up to 1 week.

Your family will enjoy this delicious cross between taco night and chili night. This is a quick and versatile recipe—top it with Cheddar cheese and tortilla chips or wrap it in a tortilla. Serve it on its own or over rice with chopped mango on the side.

taco chili with cilantro sour cream

Prep + Cook = 20 minutes

8 servings

Nutritional Information per serving:

Calories 230, Total Fat 5g, 8%, Saturated Fat 2g, 10%, Cholesterol 25mg, 9%, Sodium 640mg, 27%, Total Carbohydrate 27g, 9%, Dietary Fiber 6g, 24%, Protein 19g, Sugar 8g

1 pound ground beef, turkey, chicken, or vegetarian ground "meat"

1 teaspoon chopped garlic (about 2 cloves)

1 tablespoon chili powder

1 teaspoon cinnamon

1 can (15 ounces) kidney beans with their liquid

1 can (15 ounces) unsweetened corn kernels, drained

1 can (15 ounces) Italian-style stewed tomatoes, drained

1 teaspoon salt (or less to taste)

1 cup low-fat sour cream

1 tablespoon lime juice (about ¼ lime)

2 tablespoons minced cilantro

In a large pot, brown the meat over medium heat. While it is cooking, add the garlic, chili powder, and cinnamon. When the meat is almost cooked through, add the beans, corn, tomatoes, and salt. Simmer the chili for 10 minutes, or more if time allows.

In a small bowl, mix together the sour cream, lime juice, and cilantro.

Serve the chili with a dollop of the cilantro sour cream on top.

spice of life In recent scientific studies, cinnamon has shown great promise as a powerful tool for fighting diabetes and lowering cholesterol. That gives us one more excuse to use this fragrant and delicious spice in more recipes.

I love making a lasagna with ravioli, which eliminates several steps in making a traditional lasagna. You can substitute your favorite vegetables, such as mushrooms or spinach, for those I have suggested, or add a layer of turkey sausage for a heartier dish. Serve it with steamed green beans sprinkled with lemon juice and salt.

ravioli lasagna

Prep (15 minutes) + Cook (1 hour)

8 servings

Nutritional Information per serving:

Calories 270, Total Fat 10g, 15%, Saturated Fat 5g, 25%, Cholesterol 50mg, 17%, Sodium 800mg, 33%, Total Carbohydrate 32g, 11%, Dietary Fiber 3g, 12%, Protein 14g, Sugar 8g

1 jar (26 ounces) red pasta sauce

1 family-sized package (20 ounces) refrigerated cheese or meat ravioli

1½ cups shredded reduced-fat mozzarella cheese

½ red bell pepper, diced

1 cup shredded carrots

1 cup thinly sliced cooked turkey sausage (optional)

Preheat the oven to 375 degrees. Coat a 9-inch square baking dish and one side of a foil sheet with nonstick cooking spray.

Spread a few spoonfuls of the pasta sauce in the bottom of the dish. Top it with 1 layer of ravioli (let their edges touch but not overlap). Top the ravioli with half of the veggies and half of the cheese as well as the turkey sausage (optional). Repeat the layers once more, ending with the cheese. (You will probably have some leftover ravioli, which you can cook separately for pickier eaters.)

Cover the lasagna tightly with the foil, sprayed side down. Cook it for 1 hour, and remove the foil for the last 5 minutes of baking.

TIP: If you are making the Tangy Flank Steak tomorrow, don't forget to marinate it tonight.

Flank steak is a great cut of meat to make if you're in a hurry, as it is thin and cooks quickly. This combination of mustard and herbs gives the meat a savory flavor. You can also cook this steak on the grill. If you don't eat red meat, try this recipe with chicken, firm white fish, or firm sliced tofu. Serve it with Creamy Mashed Potatoes (see p. 300).

tangy flank steak

Prep + Cook= 20 minutes + Marinate

6 Servings

Nutritional Information per serving:

Calories 370, Total Fat 17g, 26%, Saturated Fat 7g, 35%, Cholesterol 80mg, 27%, Sodium 500mg, 21%, Total Carbohydrate 3g, 1%, Dietary Fiber 0g, 0%, Protein 50g, Sugar 0g

2 pounds flank steak

1 bottle (8 ounces) vinaigrette salad dressing

⅓ cup Dijon mustard

1 tablespoon dried thyme

Place the steak in a resealable plastic bag or a flat container with a lid. Pour the dressing over the steak and marinate it for at least 1 hour and up to 24 hours. Remove the steak from the bag (discard the marinade!) and place it on a broiling pan lined with foil.

Preheat the broiler and place the shelf about 3 inches from the heating element. Cover one side of the meat with half the Dijon mustard and half the thyme. Broil the steak for 6 to 8 minutes (depending on desired doneness). Flip the steak, coat the second side with the rest of the mustard and thyme, and cook it for 6 to 8 minutes more until it is tender and no longer pink in the middle.

Slice the steak into strips and serve it.

This is a very flavorful topping to liven up fish fillets, suggested by my friend Kirsten Thistle. After baking it, we scraped the topping off the kids' portions for a simpler flavor for their less mature taste buds. Serve it with rice pilaf and roasted asparagus (see p. 299).

zesty baked salmon

Prep + Cook = 30 minutes

5 servings

Nutritional Information per serving:

Calories 390, Total Fat 24g, 37%, Saturated Fat 5g, 25%, Cholesterol 90mg, 30%, Sodium 540mg, 23%, Total Carbohydrate 9g, 3%, Fiber 0g, 0%, Protein 33g, Sugar <1g

- 1½ pounds thin salmon fillet (preferably wild Alaskan)
- ½ cup chopped pitted green olives
- 1 teaspoon minced garlic (about 2 cloves)
- 2 tablespoons minced fresh parsley
- 1 tablespoon plus 1 teaspoon olive oil
- 1 tablespoon Dijon mustard
- ½ cup bread crumbs

Preheat the oven to 400 degrees. Place a sheet of foil on top of a baking sheet and spray it with nonstick cooking spray. Place the salmon on the foil.

In a small bowl, combine the olives, garlic, parsley, 1 tablespoon oil, mustard, and bread crumbs. Press the mixture evenly on top of the fish. Drizzle 1 tsp. oil evenly over the topping.

Bake it until the salmon is cooked through and flakes easily in the center and the topping is browned, about 15 to 20 minutes, depending on the thickness of the fish.

Serve immediately.

TIP: For this recipe, you can use any kind of pitted or stuffed green olives, or even store-bought olive tapenade. If you do the latter, you can skip the garlic, parsley, oil, and mustard, and just press the bread crumbs on top of the olive tapenade.

Omelets make great dinners—who has time to make them most mornings? They are also a good way to use up the leftover cheeses and veggies in your fridge! This recipe makes 4 omelets. Cut them in half and serve them with Hash Browns (see p. 300).

spinach and mushroom omelets

Prep + Cook =
15 minutes

4 servings

Nutritional Information per serving:

Calories 500, Total Fat 20g, 32%, Saturated Fat 12g, 64%, Cholesterol 60 mg, 22%, Sodium 740 mg, 30%, Total Carbohydrate 54g, 18%, Dietary Fiber 4g, 14%, Protein 26g, Sugar 10g

1 tablespoon olive oil

1 pound sliced mushrooms

1 bag (6 ounces) fresh spinach

12 eggs (3 eggs per omelet)

½ cup milk

salt and pepper to taste

4 tablespoons butter

1 cup shredded Cheddar cheese

Other Filling Ideas

sautéed red bell peppers, onions, and feta cheese

chopped tomatoes, basil, and mozzarella cheese

crumbled goat cheese, boiled potatoes, and rosemary

smoked salmon and capers.

In a nonstick pan, heat the oil over medium heat and sauté the mushrooms and spinach until the mushrooms shrink and the spinach is wilted, about 5 minutes.

Note: The following instructions are for cooking 1 omelet at a time. In a small bowl, beat 3 eggs lightly, add ¼ of the milk, and season with salt and pepper.

In a medium skillet (preferably nonstick), melt 1 tablespoon of butter over medium-low heat to coat the pan's surface. Add the 3 eggs and turn the pan to evenly distribute them in a circular shape. Cook the eggs until the surface starts to get firm. Add ¼ of the spinach and mushrooms and ¼ cup of the cheese and cook the omelet until the eggs are firm. Fold the omelet and serve it.

TIP: With practice, you can get a couple of omelets going on the stove at once while singing to the baby and answering the phone.

This flavorful chicken is slightly sweet and smells and tastes wonderful. Scramble recipe tester Debbie Firestone and her family rated this recipe a 10 out of 10! Serve it with couscous and baked sweet potatoes (see p. 300).

moroccan chicken

Prep + Cook =
30 minutes

4 servings

Nutritional
Information per
serving:

Calories 330, Total
Fat 6g, 9%, Saturated
Fat 1g, 5%, Choles-
terol 100mg, 33%,
Sodium 790mg, 33%,
Total Carbohydrate
25g, 8%, Dietary
Fiber 3g, 12%, Pro-
tein 42g, Sugar 17g

¼ cup currants or raisins

¼ cup currant jelly (or use apricot jelly or jam)

¼ cup white wine

2 tablespoons soy sauce

1 teaspoon curry powder

¼ teaspoon cinnamon

1 tablespoon olive oil

1½ pounds boneless, skinless chicken breasts or thighs cut into 1-inch pieces

1 red bell pepper, chopped

1 cup carrot chips (carrots cut in ridges) or sliced carrots

In a small bowl, combine the currants, jelly, wine, soy sauce, curry powder, and cinnamon. Set this sauce aside.

In a large heavy skillet, heat the olive oil over medium heat. Add the chicken, peppers, and carrots and cook them until the chicken is fully cooked, about 8 minutes. Stir in the sauce mixture and cook it for about 2 more minutes until the sauce is slightly thickened. Serve the chicken hot.

{

right on, raisins Raisins are a great source of antioxidants and fiber, and are actually good for your teeth, contrary to earlier belief, because they contain acids that eliminate the bacteria that cause cavities!

This wonderful pasta comes from Scramble contributor Sherry Ettleson. To give it an extra kick, add some red pepper flakes. Serve it with sautéed zucchini, tomatoes, and garlic—and some hearty bread to scoop up the sauce.

fettuccine with chickpea sauce

Prep + Cook =
30 minutes

8 servings

Nutritional
Information per
serving:

Calories 360, Total
Fat 11g, 16%, Saturated Fat 1.5g, 8%,
Cholesterol 0 mg,
0%, Sodium 180 mg,
7%, Total Carbohydrate 56g, 19%, Dietary Fiber 5g, 19%,
Protein 11g, Sugar 6g

1 package (16 ounces) fettuccine

⅓ cup olive oil

1 teaspoon chopped garlic (about 2 cloves)

1 medium onion, chopped

1½ teaspoons dried oregano

12 fresh basil leaves, chopped, or 1 tablespoon dried

2 bay leaves

1 can (15 ounces) chickpeas, drained and rinsed

2 medium tomatoes, diced

½ teaspoon kosher salt

grated Parmesan cheese for serving

Cook the fettuccine according to the package directions until it is al dente. Before it is done, remove about ¾ cup of the cooking water and set it aside.

In a large skillet, heat the oil over medium heat. Add the garlic and cook it for 1 minute. Add the onion, oregano, basil, and bay leaves and cook it for 5 more minutes.

In a shallow bowl, mash ¼ cup of the chickpeas (or use a food processor to puree them).

Add the mashed and whole chickpeas, tomatoes, and salt to the onions. Cover it, lower the heat, and cook it for 15 minutes, stirring occasionally. Remove the bay leaves.

Drain the pasta and stir it into the sauce. Add at least ½ cup of the reserved pasta water to thin the sauce. Serve the pasta hot, topped with Parmesan cheese.

This light and delicate fish is great with rice and green beans sautéed with a little butter and garlic.

breaded tilapia with garlic-lime sauce

Prep + Cook =
15 minutes

6 servings

Nutritional
Information per
serving:

Calories 120, Total
Fat 3.5g, 6%, Satu-
rated Fat 1g, 4%,
Cholesterol 55 mg,
18%, Sodium 50 mg,
2%, Total Carbohy-
drate 1g, 0%, Dietary
Fiber 0g, 0%, Protein
21g, Sugar 0g

- 1½ pounds tilapia fillets
- ½ teaspoon chopped garlic (about 1 clove)
- ½ cup dry white wine
- 1 tablespoon lime juice (about ¼ lime)
- 1 tablespoon olive oil
- ½ cup flour
- salt and pepper to taste
- 1 teaspoon butter
- 2 scallions, chopped

Rinse the fish and pat it dry.

In a small bowl, combine the garlic, wine, and lime juice. Set it aside.

In a large nonstick skillet, heat the oil over medium-high heat.

Put the flour on a shallow plate and season it with salt and pepper. Dredge the fil-lets in the flour and add them to the skillet. Cook them for about 3 minutes per side until they are lightly browned. Transfer them to a clean plate and cover them to keep them warm.

In the skillet that held the fish, melt the butter over low heat. Add the wine mixture to the skillet and cook it at a low boil until it is reduced by half, 2 to 3 minutes. Stir in the scallions and heat them for about 30 seconds.

Serve the fish warm with the sauce spooned over it (you may want to leave some fish plain for younger kids).

Usually, Eggplant Parmesan is fried, so it tastes good but is very high in fat. This recipe avoids excess fat by broiling the eggplant instead. It tastes so good that you won't miss the extra calories! Serve it over spaghetti with a green salad.

baked eggplant parmesan

Prep (20 min.) +
Cook (25 min.)

6 servings

Nutritional Information per serving:

Calories 260, Total Fat 10g, 16%, Saturated Fat 6g, 28%, Cholesterol 60mg, 20%, Sodium 780mg, 33%, Total Carbohydrate 27g, 9%, Dietary Fiber 4g, 17%, Protein 17g, Sugar 12g

1 egg

1½ cups bread crumbs

½ cup flour

1 medium eggplant, cut in ½-inch slices

1 jar (26 ounces) red pasta sauce

2 cups shredded part-skim mozzarella cheese

2 tablespoons grated Parmesan cheese

Preheat the broiler. Line a baking sheet with foil. In a shallow bowl, beat the egg. In another shallow bowl, mix the bread crumbs and flour.

Dip the eggplant slices in the egg, then in the bread crumb mixture (coating both sides), and place them on the baking sheet.

Broil the eggplant on both sides until it is well browned, 3 to 5 minutes per side. (Be sure to set a timer in case you get distracted!)

Preheat the oven to 375 degrees. Spray a 9 × 13-inch baking dish with nonstick cooking spray.

Layer the bottom of the dish with eggplant slices. Cover the eggplant with the sauce. Sprinkle mozzarella cheese on top, then Parmesan. (Alternatively, you can layer eggplant, sauce, and cheese like a lasagna in a smaller pan.)

Bake it for 20 to 30 minutes until the cheeses are melted and slightly browned.

TIP: If you're making the Wild Rice and Corn Casserole tomorrow, cook the wild rice tonight while the Eggplant Parmesan bakes.

My college roommate, Vicki Botnick, gave me the recipe for this soothing casserole. It's easy to prepare if you cook the rice in advance (even the night before) and is full of healthy and flavorful ingredients. It's great topped with a spoonful of fire-roasted salsa and with sliced kiwi on the side.

wild rice and corn casserole

Prep (15 minutes) +
Cook (1 hour +)

8 servings

Nutritional
Information per
serving:

Calories 250, Total
Fat 10g, 16%, Saturated Fat 6g, 30%,
Cholesterol 30mg,
10%, Sodium 610 mg,
25%, Total Carbohydrate 27g, 9%, Dietary Fiber 3g, 12%,
Protein 12g, Sugar 7g

3 cups cooked wild rice (about 1 cup dry rice)

1 can (15 ounces) corn kernels, drained (or use 1½ cups frozen corn kernels)

1 cup finely chopped onion (about ½ medium onion)

1 can (4 ounces) chopped green chilies

2 cups shredded Cheddar cheese

1 cup skim milk

¼ teaspoon salt

1 tablespoon chili powder

½ teaspoon cumin

mild fire-roasted salsa for serving

Cook the rice according to package directions. (I use 1 cup wild rice, 2 cups water, and 1 tablespoon olive oil.) Remove it from the heat and allow it to cool for a few minutes. (You can do this anytime during the day or the day before.)

Preheat the oven to 350 degrees. Spray a 2-quart casserole dish with nonstick cooking spray.

In a large bowl, combine all the ingredients, reserving ½ cup of the cheese.

Pour the mixture into the casserole dish and top it with the remaining cheese. Bake it for 1 hour. Let it cool for about 10 minutes.

Serve the casserole topped with salsa.

dinner on the double Some women I know have discovered a way to pair up and take a night off from cooking each week, while still enjoying a delicious home-cooked meal. Once a week, each of them makes double of whatever she is cooking and delivers it to the other's home. They each pick a night in advance so they know when they'll have to cook or can take a night off to enjoy each other's delivery. It's easy to make twice the normal amount of dinner, and it's wonderful to try somebody else's cooking.

spring

week 1

Chicken Tikka

Cool Rice Pilaf Salad

Classic Tuna Casserole

Sweet Potato Pancakes
(or Burgers)

Cuban Black Beans and Rice

week 2

Baked Turkey Breast with
Roasted Potatoes

Wild Mushroom Risotto with
Shrimp and Peas

Baked Penne with Sausage,
Spinach, and Tomatoes

Sweet and Crunchy
Chinese Salad

Classic Meatloaf

week 3

Chicken and Broccoli
Casserole

Rotini with Chunky Red Clam
(or Vegetable) Sauce

Ratatouille with Fresh Basil

Veggie Delight Sandwiches

Saffron Bean Salad

week 4

Lemon Feta Chicken

Pan-Browned Sausage and
Potatoes

Spinach Burritos

Thai Fried Rice with Shrimp
or Chicken

Sweet and Creamy Red Beet
Pasta

week 5

Steak with Soy-Lime
Marinade

Sweet and Sour Sole

Ziti with Roasted Eggplant
and Peppers

Grilled Balsamic Chicken
Salad

Chili con Barley

week 6

Chicken Sticks

Sloppy Joes

Polenta-Tomatillo Casserole

Creamy Wild Rice and
Vegetable Soup

Penne Pesto with Radicchio
and Olives

week 7

Grilled Steak Mojito

Rigatoni with Lima Beans,
Artichokes, and Spinach

Shrimp and Broccoli Stir-Fry

Crispy Bean Quesadillas

Caesar Salad with Chicken

week 8

Roast Chicken with Vegetables

Pasta with Herbed Butter

Red Snapper with Stewed Tomatoes

Grilled Cheese Sandwiches with Brie and Baby Spinach

One-Pot Italian Rice and Beans

week 9

Grilled Honey Mustard Chicken

Three-Cheese Spinach Orzo Bake

Black Bean, Fennel, and Tomato Stew

Hot Reuben Sandwiches

Curly Noodle Delight

week 10

Sautéed Mini Chicken Burgers

Tacos del Mar

Lentil Stew with Honey-Ginger Yogurt

Quick Couscous Paella with Crumbled Bacon

Fresh Tomato and Basil Quiche

week 11

Penne with Smoked Sausage and Peppers

Drew's Crunchy Crispix-Coated Chicken Cutlets

Crustless Spinach Pie

Spicy Sausage and Kale Soup

Baked Halibut with Pesto

week 12

Chinese Lasagna

Honey-Glazed Salmon

Mediterranean Vegetable Stew

The Big Guy's Baked Chicken

Zesty Pasta Salad

week 13

Turkey and Spinach Enchiladas

Tuna with Citrus Sauce

No-Bake Chicken Parmesan

Peanut Butter Stew (and Couscous, Too!)

Ravioli with Creamy Tomato Sauce

Subscriber and friend Karen Murray shared this delicious recipe with me. The yogurt marinade makes the chicken very moist and flavorful. To make the Indian feast complete, serve it with prepared Indian-flavored basmati rice from a box, mixed with plain white rice to reduce the intensity of the flavor (and the sodium) for the kids. We enjoy it with chutney (a fruity Indian condiment) and steamed carrots.

chicken tikka

Prep (15 minutes) +
Cook (20 minutes)
+ Marinate

6 servings

Nutritional
Information per
serving:

Calories 280, Total
Fat 9g, 14%, Satu-
rated Fat 3g, 16%,
Cholesterol 125mg,
42%, Sodium 125 mg,
5%, Total Carbohy-
drate 3g, 1%, Dietary
Fiber 0g, 0%, Protein
45g, Sugar 2g

1¼ cup (10 ounces) plain reduced-fat yogurt

1 teaspoon chopped garlic (about 2 cloves)

1 chunk (1 inch) ginger root, peeled and minced

1 teaspoon cumin

2 teaspoons curry powder

2 tablespoons lime juice (about ½ lime)

1 tablespoon plus 1 teaspoon peanut oil

4–5 boneless, skinless chicken breast halves (1½–2 pounds total)

1 tablespoon butter

In a food processor or blender or by hand, mix together the yogurt, garlic, ginger, cumin, curry powder, and lime juice and 1 tablespoon of the peanut oil until the mixture is smooth. Reserve ½ cup of this yogurt mixture in a small bowl and refrigerate it to serve with the cooked chicken later.

Place the remaining yogurt mixture in a wide shallow container. Add the chicken breasts and turn them to coat them well. Cover the bowl and refrigerate it for at least 4 hours and up to 24 hours.

When you are ready to cook, remove the chicken from the marinade to a plate, scraping off and discarding the excess yogurt mixture along with the rest of the marinade from the dish.

In a large nonstick skillet, heat the butter and remaining 1 teaspoon of the peanut oil over medium to medium-low heat. When the butter has melted, add the chicken breasts in a single layer. Sauté them, turning them once or twice, until the chicken starts to brown on its surface and is no longer pink in the center, about 20 minutes. (If the outside is cooking much faster than the inside, reduce the heat slightly and cover the pan.) The pan will get juicy because of the marinade, but there is no need to drain the juice.

When the chicken is cooked through, remove it from the pan to a cutting board and slice it crosswise into strips. Serve it with the yogurt mixture from the refrigerator.

I invented this salad out of necessity on the first really warm day of spring. I had invited friends to come to dinner after Solomon's baseball game but forgot that our supermarket closes early on Sundays. The resulting dinner, made from things we already had in the house, was a welcome surprise. This salad would also be a hit at a picnic or as a side dish for meat or fish. Serve it with warm pita bread and hummus dip.

cool rice pilaf salad

Prep + Cook =
25 minutes

8 servings

Nutritional
Information per
serving:

Calories 200, Total Fat 5g, 8%, Saturated Fat 0.5g, 3%, Cholesterol 0mg, 0%, Sodium 870mg, 36%, Total Carbohydrate 36g, 12%, Dietary Fiber 2g, 8%, Protein 5g, Sugar <1g

2 boxes (6 ounces each) Near East or similar brand rice pilaf mix

4 stalks hearts of palm

10 sundried tomatoes, marinated in oil

20 pitted kalamata olives

2 plum tomatoes

2 scallions

1 cup diced cooked chicken (optional)

2 tablespoons olive oil

2 tablespoons red wine vinegar

Prepare the rice pilaf according to the package directions, using the spice pack and omitting oil or butter.

While the rice is cooking, chop the hearts of palm, sundried tomatoes, olives, plum tomatoes, and scallions into small pieces and put them in a large bowl.

When the rice pilaf is finished cooking, uncover it, remove it from the heat, and let it cool for several minutes. Add it to the vegetables in the bowl. Add the chicken (optional), oil, and vinegar and toss the salad.

Serve the salad at room temperature.

My sister-in-law, Soozy Miller, shared this recipe with me after her guests devoured it at a recent gathering in Atlanta. It's healthy comfort food that your family will likely polish off, too. Serve it with a crisp lettuce salad with shredded carrots, chopped hearts of palm, and grated Parmesan cheese.

classic tuna casserole

Prep (25 minutes) +
Cook (30 minutes)

8 servings

Nutritional
Information per
serving:

Calories 200, Total
Fat 6g, 9%, Saturated
Fat 2g, 10%, Cholesterol 85mg, 28%,
Sodium 800mg, 33%,
Total Carbohydrate
23g, 8%, Dietary
Fiber 3g, 12%, Protein 16g, Sugar 4g

6 ounces wide egg noodles

1 can (13 ounces) sliced mushrooms, drained

1 can (7 ounces) chunk light tuna in water, drained

1 cup peas

1 can (10 ounces) reduced-fat cream of celery soup

1 cup shredded carrots (make your own or buy matchstick carrots)

¾ cup shredded Cheddar cheese

2 eggs, lightly beaten

¾ cup Italian-style bread crumbs

Preheat the oven to 350 degrees. Spray a large round casserole dish with nonstick cooking spray.

Prepare the egg noodles according to the package instructions.

While the noodles are cooking, combine all the other ingredients, except ¼ cup of the bread crumbs, in a bowl and mix them. When the noodles are cooked, drain them and quickly add them to the tuna mixture and mix them in thoroughly.

Transfer the mixture to the casserole dish and sprinkle the reserved bread crumbs on top.

Bake the casserole, uncovered, for 30 minutes until lightly browned on top.

TIP: Cook the whole bag of egg noodles and toss the extras with butter or olive oil for picky eaters.

These potato pancakes have a terrific blend of flavors and a nice crunchy texture. I found that with just a little oil and a nonstick skillet they came out nicely browned. If you make the batter ahead of time, refrigerate it until you're ready to cook, and drain the excess liquid from the bowl before frying. Serve the pancakes with sour cream and/or applesauce for dipping, plus a salad topped with shredded carrots, sunflower seeds, and Gorgonzola cheese. You can also eat them like a burger on an English muffin or roll.

sweet potato pancakes (or burgers)

Prep (20 minutes) + Cook (20 minutes)

16 pancakes (8 servings)

Nutritional Information per serving:

Calories 150, Total Fat 8g, 13%, Saturated Fat 1g, 5%, Cholesterol 55mg, 18%, Sodium 310mg, 13%, Total Carbohydrate 16g, 5%, Dietary Fiber 2g, 6%, Protein 3g, Sugar 4g

1 large sweet potato

1 large white potato

1 medium onion

2 eggs, beaten

½ cup flour

1 teaspoon salt

¼ teaspoon cayenne pepper (optional)

6 tablespoons vegetable oil

Using a hand grater (a great arm workout!), or a food processor with a grating blade, coarsely grate the sweet potato and white potato and finely dice or grate the onion. Drain the vegetables then wrap them in a clean dish towel for a minute or two to get the remaining water out.

Transfer the grated vegetables to a large bowl. Stir in the beaten eggs. Thoroughly mix in the flour, salt, and cayenne (optional).

Preheat the oven to 250 degrees and line a baking sheet with foil.

In a large nonstick skillet, heat 2 tablespoons of the oil over medium heat. When the oil is hot, scoop in spoonfuls of the potato mixture and flatten them with the spoon or a spatula.

Cook the pancakes for several minutes per side until they are well browned. After each batch, add a tablespoon or two of oil to the pan to keep the pancakes browning nicely. If they start to get too browned on the outside before the middle is cooked, reduce the heat.

Transfer the cooked pancakes to the baking sheet to keep them warm in the oven while the rest of the pancakes cook.

This is a healthy, inexpensive, and satisfying meal from Sherry Ettleson. Serve it with a sliced mango for a true Cuban feast. If your store doesn't carry leeks, you can substitute half of an onion for the leek. If you like spicier food, you can heat this up with some cayenne pepper.

cuban black beans and rice

Prep + Cook =
30 minutes

6–8 servings

Nutritional
Information per
serving:

Calories 260, Total
Fat 3.5g, 5%, Satu-
rated Fat 2g, 10%,
Cholesterol 10mg,
3%, Sodium 420mg,
18%, Total Carbohy-
drate 48g, 16%, Di-
etary Fiber 8g, 32%,
Protein 9g, Sugar 1g

- 1½ cups dry white or brown rice
- 1 medium leek, chopped (use white part and about ½ inch of green part)
- 2 tablespoons butter
- 2 teaspoons minced garlic (about 4 cloves)
- 1 red bell pepper, chopped
- 1 stalk celery, chopped
- 1 teaspoon cumin
- ½ teaspoon thyme
- ½ teaspoon pepper
- 2 teaspoons lemon juice (about ¼ lemon)
- ½ cup vegetable or chicken broth
- 2 cans (15 ounces each) black beans with their liquid
- sour cream or plain yogurt for serving

In a medium stockpot with a tight-fitting lid, prepare the rice according to the package directions. Soak the chopped leek in cold water for a few minutes to clean it thoroughly.

Meanwhile, in another stockpot or a large skillet, melt the butter over medium heat. Add the garlic, leek, bell pepper, celery, cumin, thyme, pepper, lemon juice, and broth. Bring it to a boil, then lower the heat, cover the pot, and simmer it for 10 minutes. Add the beans and stir it until it is heated through.

Serve the beans over the rice, topped with sour cream or yogurt.

have ten minutes? start an herb garden

With everything blooming and the kids playing outside, spring is the ideal time to plant an herb garden. It may sound daunting, but it takes about ten minutes to transfer a few basic herbs from their temporary garden-store containers to pots or soil in your backyard or on your deck.

Pick a sunny spot for your herb garden. My back deck is my favorite place because it's easy to step out there while I'm preparing dinner and snip the evening's herbs. Also, the ravenous deer in our neighborhood haven't yet mastered the steps.

I plant lots of basil (at least three pots) and one pot each of rosemary, thyme, mint, sage, and oregano. I have also had success with hot peppers and tomatoes. Make sure to get potting soil, larger pots for the herbs, and water catchers to go under the pots.

The hardest part of maintaining the herbs is keeping the pots watered throughout the summer so the roots don't dry out. If your kids are old enough, it's a perfect opportunity for them to help and lets them observe how plants grow. I get such a thrill out of bringing in fresh ingredients each night from my own garden. As obvious as it may be to you seasoned gardeners, the joys and culinary rewards of using ingredients from my garden far outweigh the small effort it takes to maintain it.

My mom served this delicious turkey breast to my family over spring break. It reminds me of Thanksgiving dinner but only takes twenty minutes to prepare. If you can't find a turkey breast at your market, you can use a whole chicken for this recipe instead. Serve it with stuffing and cranberry sauce (mix one can of cranberry sauce with chopped celery and walnuts for a delicious and easy twist on tradition).

baked turkey breast with roasted potatoes

Prep (20 minutes) +
Cook (1½–2 hours)

8 servings

Nutritional
Information per
serving:

Calories 270, Total
Fat 4g, 6%, Saturated
Fat 1.5g, 6%, Cholesterol 80mg, 26%,
Sodium 290mg, 12%,
Total Carbohydrate
21g, 7%, Dietary
Fiber 2g, 6%, Protein
36g, Sugar 10g

1 bone-in, skin-on turkey breast, about 2½ pounds (sometimes sold frozen)

½ cup orange juice

1 cup chicken or vegetable broth

½ cup marsala or white wine

3 tablespoons Kitchen Bouquet (a meat-browning sauce) or soy sauce

½ teaspoon garlic powder

½ teaspoon paprika

1 sweet potato, cut into ½-inch chunks

1 white potato, cut into ½-inch chunks

1 red apple, cored and sliced in wedges

¼ cup red currant jelly (or use apricot jelly)

Preheat the oven to 350 degrees. Defrost the turkey breast, if necessary, and put it in a large roasting pan.

In a medium bowl, mix together the orange juice, broth, marsala or wine, and Kitchen Bouquet or soy sauce and pour the mixture over the turkey. Sprinkle the turkey with the garlic powder and paprika. Spread the potatoes and apple chunks around the turkey.

Bake the turkey breast for 1½ to 2 hours, basting it twice, until a meat thermometer inserted into the thickest part of the meat registers 170 degrees.

About half an hour before the turkey is fully cooked (set a timer to remind yourself to do this), melt the jelly for about 45 seconds in the microwave or briefly on the stovetop to thin it. Remove the turkey from the oven and spread the jelly on top. Return it to the oven for the last 30 minutes of cooking. For a browner top, put the turkey breast under the broiler for the final 5 minutes of cooking.

My friend Jessica Honigberg invented this pumped-up risotto recently. Preparing the risotto mix in the microwave saves the thirty minutes or more of tending the stove for a traditional risotto, but the flavor is still rich and delicious. Serve it with a Tropical Fruit Salad (see p. 297).

wild mushroom risotto with shrimp and peas

Prep + Cook = 30 minutes

8 servings

Nutritional Information per serving:

Calories 230, Total Fat 2.5g, 4%, Saturated Fat 0g, 0%, Cholesterol 85mg, 28%, Sodium 530mg, 22%, Total Carbohydrate 33g, 11%, Dietary Fiber 2g, 8%, Protein 16g, Sugar 2g

2 boxes (5.45 ounces each) wild mushroom risotto mix (try to get a brand with microwave directions)

1 pound medium shrimp, peeled and deveined

1 tablespoon olive oil

1½ cups frozen peas

Remove the peas and shrimp (if you are using frozen varieties) from the freezer. In a large microwave-safe bowl, prepare both boxes of risotto in the microwave according to package directions. (If your package doesn't have microwave directions, prepare the risotto on the stovetop.)

In a large nonstick skillet over medium heat, sauté the shrimp in the oil until it is pink, about 3 minutes. When the shrimp is cooked, remove it from the heat and add the peas to the skillet, and sauté them for about 2 minutes.

When the risotto is tender and all the broth is absorbed, toss it immediately with the peas and shrimp. Cover it until you're ready to serve.

This fabulous baked dish is great for company. You can prepare it ahead of time and bake it when friends arrive. Serve it with bread and Green Beans Parmesan (see p. 298).

baked penne with sausage, spinach, and tomatoes

Prep (25 minutes) +
Bake (30 minutes)

8 servings

Nutritional
Information per
serving:

Calories 520, Total
Fat 23g, 35%, Satu-
rated Fat 9g, 45%,
Cholesterol 55mg,
18%, Sodium 1280mg,
53%, Total Carbohy-
drate 47g, 16%, Di-
etary Fiber 4g, 16%,
Protein 30g, Sugar 6g

- **12 ounces penne pasta (or any medium tube-shaped pasta)**
- **1 pound hot Italian sausage (turkey, pork, or beef)**
- **1 medium onion, chopped**
- **1½ teaspoons minced garlic (about 3 cloves)**
- **1 can (28 ounces) diced peeled tomatoes with their juice**
- **1 container (7 ounces) refrigerated prepared pesto sauce**
- **1 bag (6–9 ounces) baby spinach**
- **8 ounces shredded mozzarella cheese**
- **1 cup grated Parmesan cheese**
- **¼ teaspoon red pepper flakes (optional)**

Cook the pasta according to the package directions and drain it.

Meanwhile, heat a large heavy saucepan over medium-high heat. Add the sausage, onion, and garlic, and sauté them using a wooden spoon to break up the sausage, until the sausage is cooked through, about 10 minutes.

Add the tomatoes with their juice to the pan. Simmer the sauce until it thickens slightly, stirring it occasionally, about 10 minutes. Stir in the pesto and red pepper flakes (optional).

Preheat the oven to 375 degrees. Spray a 9 × 13-inch baking dish with nonstick cooking spray. Combine the pasta, spinach and mozzarella cheese, and ⅓ cup of the Parmesan cheese in the baking dish. Gently stir in the tomato sauce. Sprinkle the remaining ⅔ cup Parmesan cheese over the casserole.

Bake the penne until the sauce bubbles and the cheeses melt, about 30 minutes.

This salad is very hearty and filling, so you can get by serving it for dinner with a side of Chinese dumplings. It's also a great salad to bring to a party, as it's a crowd-pleaser.

sweet and crunchy chinese salad

Prep + Cook =
30 minutes

8 servings

Nutritional
Information per
serving:

Calories 310, Total
Fat 19g, 30%, Saturated Fat 3g, 15%,
Cholesterol 35mg,
12%, Sodium 460mg,
19%, Total Carbohydrate 18g, 6%, Dietary Fiber 3g, 12%,
Protein 18g, Sugar 9g

- ½ cup red wine vinegar
- ¼ cup vegetable oil
- ¼ cup water
- 1 tablespoon soy sauce
- 2 tablespoons sugar (use superfine sugar if you have it)
- ¼ cup butter
- 2 packages (3 ounces each) Top Ramen brand Oodles of Noodles, any flavor
- ½ cup slivered almonds
- 1 head bok choy (Chinese cabbage) or romaine lettuce, or a combination of both
- 4 scallions, green and white parts, finely chopped
- ½ cup dried cranberries (or use 1 can mandarin oranges)
- ¾ pound cooked chicken, chopped (optional)

In a medium jar with a lid, combine the vinegar, oil, water, soy sauce, and sugar. Shake it thoroughly to combine the ingredients and refrigerate the dressing until you're ready to use it.

In a large skillet, melt the butter over medium heat. Discard the flavoring packet from the ramen noodles. Break the noodles into small pieces. Add the noodles and almonds to the skillet and sauté them, stirring frequently, until they are golden brown. Drain them on paper towels. (For a lower-fat dish, you can simply brown the noodles and the almonds in your toaster oven or conventional oven at 350 degrees.)

Thoroughly chop the bok choy or lettuce and combine it with the scallions and dried cranberries in a large bowl. Toss this with the dressing (you probably won't need all of it), noodles, nuts, and chicken just before serving.

super food Bok Choy is a good source of dietary fiber, protein, numerous vitamins, folate, calcium, iron, magnesium, potassium, and manganese. Not bad for a humble leaf!

This meatloaf is a winner with or without the tomato sauce for a simple, satisfying meal. Serve it with oven-roasted potatoes (see p. 300), English muffins (for making sandwiches), and ketchup.

classic meatloaf

Prep (10 minutes) +
Cook (1 hour)

8 servings

Nutritional
Information per
serving:

Calories 280, Total
Fat 12g, 18%, Satu-
rated Fat 4.5g, 22%,
Cholesterol 70mg,
23%, Sodium 820mg,
34%, Total Carbohy-
drate 15g, 5%, Di-
etary Fiber 1g, 5%,
Protein 27g, Sugar 5g

2 pounds ground beef, chicken, or turkey

1 egg

1 cup milk

1 cup Italian-style bread crumbs

½ teaspoon salt

¼ teaspoon pepper

½ teaspoon garlic powder

1 can (15 ounces) tomato sauce (optional)

Preheat the oven to 350 degrees. Spray a loaf pan with nonstick cooking spray.

In a large bowl, thoroughly mix together all the ingredients except the tomato sauce. You can do this by hand or with a fork.

Put the mixture in the loaf pan and smooth it into a loaf shape. Bake it for 1 hour. After 45 minutes, pour the tomato sauce over the loaf (optional) and return it to the oven for the final 15 minutes of cooking.

drink your milk!!! Children who do not drink milk or do not get enough calcium have an increased risk of bone fractures. Other good sources of calcium include yogurt, cheese, canned salmon, fortified cereals and juice, dark green leafy vegetables, and tofu.

This casserole, from friend and subscriber Jolynn Childers Dellinger, is healthy and light and tastes great. If you don't want to cook the chicken, you can buy precooked chicken at the supermarket. I wouldn't recommend using frozen chopped broccoli, as fresh has a better consistency for this dish. Serve the casserole with chopped cantaloupe and angel hair pasta tossed with olive oil or butter and garnished with fresh parsley.

chicken and broccoli casserole

Prep (25 minutes) +
Cook (25 minutes)

6 servings

Nutritional
Information per
Serving

Calories 220, Total Fat 8g, 12%, Saturated Fat 3.5g, 18%, Cholesterol 60mg, 20%, Sodium 500mg, 21%, Total Carbohydrate 14g, 5%, Dietary Fiber 3g, 13%, Protein 25g, Sugar 4g

2 chicken breast halves (about 1 pound total) (or use 2 cups cooked chicken), cut into strips

1 large head broccoli, chopped

1 can (10¾ ounces) condensed cream of chicken, mushroom, or Cheddar soup

½ cup plain yogurt

1 tablespoon lemon juice (about ¼ lemon)

1 teaspoon curry powder

½ cup (or more to taste) shredded Cheddar cheese

¼ cup Italian-style bread crumbs

Preheat the oven to 350 degrees.

In a nonstick skillet, cook the chicken over medium-high heat until it is no longer pink, about 6 to 8 minutes. Once the chicken is cooked, transfer it to a cutting board and chop it into ½-inch pieces.

While the chicken is cooking, cut the broccoli into stalks and microwave it with ½ cup water in a covered dish for 5 minutes, until it is slightly tender. When the broccoli is cooked, transfer it to a cutting board and chop it into smaller pieces.

Combine the chicken and broccoli in a large casserole dish.

In a small bowl, mix together the soup, yogurt, lemon juice, and curry powder. Pour the sauce over the chicken and broccoli.

In a measuring cup, mix together the cheese and bread crumbs. Sprinkle the mixture over the casserole.

Bake the casserole, uncovered, for 25 minutes, until it is slightly browned on top.

This is a satisfying and nutritious chunky spaghetti sauce for the whole family, inspired by a recipe from subscriber Rhonda Summerlin. The sauce takes on a sweetness that kids love. Scramble recipe tester Margaret Mattocks said, "My grandson ate so much I thought he was going to pop." Top it with grated Parmesan cheese, if desired. For a spicier option, sprinkle it with Tabasco sauce at the table. Serve it with a green salad with diced carrots and red or green bell peppers (use the extra from the sauce) and Parmesan cheese.

rotini with chunky red clam (or vegetable) sauce

Prep + Cook = 30 minutes

8 servings

Nutritional Information per serving:

Calories 300, Total Fat 3.5g, 5%, Saturated Fat 0g, 0%, Cholesterol 15mg, 5%, Sodium 500mg, 21%, Total Carbohydrate 53g, 18%, Dietary Fiber 4g, 16%, Protein 15g, Sugar 8g

- 1 package (16 ounces) rotini or other pasta
- 1 tablespoon olive oil
- ½ red or green bell pepper, diced
- ½ yellow onion, diced
- 1 cup diced carrots (1–2 carrots)
- 2 teaspoons chopped garlic (4 cloves) or ½ teaspoon garlic powder
- 1 can (28 ounces) crushed or diced tomatoes
- 1 teaspoon dried basil
- ½ teaspoon dried oregano
- ¼ teaspoon salt
- 2 teaspoons sugar
- 1 can (6.5 ounces) chopped clams (optional)

Cook the pasta according to the package directions and drain it when it is done.

Meanwhile, in a large heavy skillet, heat the oil over medium-high heat. Add the peppers, onions, carrots, and garlic and sauté them until the onions and peppers are softened, about 5 minutes.

Add the tomatoes, basil, oregano, salt, and sugar to the skillet and bring the mixture to a boil. Simmer it, partially covered, for about 20 minutes.

Stir in the clams (optional) for the final 2 to 3 minutes of cooking the sauce.

This is a quick and fresh version of the classic French vegetable stew. Serve it with rice pilaf and with whole grain bread to soak up the sauce.

ratatouille with fresh basil

Prep (20 minutes) +
Cook (20 minutes)

6 servings

Nutritional
Information per
serving:

Calories 100, Total
Fat 5g, 8%, Saturated
Fat 0.5g, 3%, Choles-
terol 0mg, 0%,
Sodium 440mg, 18%,
Total Carbohydrate
14g, 5%, Dietary
Fiber 5g, 20%, Pro-
tein 2g, Sugar 7g

2 tablespoons olive oil

1 large onion, halved and thinly sliced

4 garlic cloves, peeled and sliced

½ teaspoon dried thyme or 1½ teaspoons fresh thyme

1 small eggplant, cut into ½-inch cubes

1 zucchini, halved lengthwise and cut into thin slices

1 red bell pepper, seeded and cut into 1-inch strips

1 can (15 ounces) diced tomatoes with their liquid

1 teaspoon kosher salt

pepper to taste

1 cup (or more) fresh basil leaves, torn or shredded

In a large skillet, heat the oil over medium heat. Add the onion, garlic, and thyme and stir it occasionally while the onion softens, about 5 minutes.

While the onion cooks, chop the other vegetables and add them as you go, stirring the veggies with each addition. Stir in the tomatoes with their liquid, the salt, and pepper to taste. Cover the pan, reduce the heat, and simmer it until the vegetables are very tender, about 20 more minutes. Stir in the basil and serve the ratatouille.

wash. wash. wash. To avoid disease and foodborne illnesses:

Wash your hands before cooking or eating.

Wash fruits and vegetables (even those without edible skins) before eating them to avoid introducing whatever is on the outside of the food into the edible portion you feed your family.

Rinse cans before opening them. A significant amount of dust and dirt can accumulate on top of cans while they're sitting in the store and on your pantry shelf.

When Andrew and I worked as legislative interns in Washington, D.C., we sometimes used our meager wages to treat ourselves at a nearby deli to these delicious sandwiches for lunch (when we weren't eating ramen noodles). I re-created them for a picnic recently, and they were just as good as we remembered. We prefer them without tomatoes, but try them both ways (or even with sliced avocado) for variety. Serve them with scrambled eggs for a heartier dinner.

veggie delight sandwiches

Prep = 10 minutes

4–6 servings

Nutritional Information per serving:

Calories 260, Total Fat 6g, 9%, Saturated Fat 3.5g, 18%, Cholesterol 15mg, 5%, Sodium 450mg, 19%, Total Carbohydrate 40g, 13%, Dietary Fiber 2g, 8%, Protein 8g, Sugar 3g

4–6 sesame bagels (or use wheat bread)
1 small container veggie cream cheese
½ cucumber, peeled and thinly sliced
alfalfa sprouts
1 tomato, thinly sliced (optional)

Slice the bagels in half and toast them lightly. Spread cream cheese on the bottom half of each bagel and top it with a layer of cucumber, sprouts, and tomato (optional). Press the top half of the bagel on top and slice the sandwiches in half crosswise. Wrap the sandwiches tightly in foil if you are taking them to a picnic.

{ **fluffy scrambled eggs** Combine 6 eggs with 1 heaping tablespoon of plain yogurt and 1 heaping tablespoon of cottage cheese. Cook the eggs in a nonstick skillet, stirring them occasionally, over medium heat until they are just firm. Season them with salt.

This stand-by dish tastes divine and is so colorful that it brightens up any meal. A meal in itself, it's also great served with chicken or shrimp or wrapped in a tortilla and topped with salsa or sour cream. We have found that this is a popular dish at showers, potlucks, and picnics.

saffron bean salad

Prep + Cook = 30 minutes

8 servings

Nutritional Information per serving:

Calories 140, Total Fat 3.5g, 5%, Saturated Fat 0.5g, 3%, Cholesterol 0mg, 0%, Sodium 290mg, 12%, Total Carbohydrate 23g, 8%, Dietary Fiber 4g, 16%, Protein 5g, Sugar 3g

- 1 package (10 ounces) saffron-flavored yellow rice
- 1 can (15 ounces) black beans, drained and rinsed
- 6 plum tomatoes (or 4 regular tomatoes), diced
- 1 small red onion, finely chopped
- ⅛ cup balsamic vinegar, or more to taste
- ⅛ cup olive oil, or more to taste
- ½ cup fresh cilantro leaves, chopped

Cook the rice according to the package directions. While the rice cooks, put the beans, tomatoes, and onions in a large serving bowl. Add the warm rice to the bowl and top it with the vinegar, oil, and cilantro. Toss it thoroughly.

TIP: You can make this salad up to a day ahead of when you plan to eat it.

cutting boards Designate a separate board for onions and garlic so they won't accidentally flavor your fruits and vegetables. Any board (and utensils) used for cutting raw meat or chicken should be washed with plenty of soap and hot water after each use.

good nutrition *can* come out of cans, bags, and boxes

When you dump the bag of frozen mixed vegetables into your stir-fry, you may wonder if anything this easy can really be good for your family. Likewise, when you prepare a pot of chili, you may question whether your family would have been better served, healthwise, if you had soaked the beans overnight yourself, and then gently simmered them for a few more hours, rather than spend twenty seconds prying the lids off the cans of pre-cooked beans. In other words, when we take cooking shortcuts, such as using frozen and canned vegetables, beans, and fruits, are we short-changing our families' health?

The answer is a qualified no. Usually, fresh and canned foods are comparable in nutrition to fresh. Frozen and canned vegetables and fruits are often picked at their peak and immediately frozen or canned, thereby sealing their nutrients in before they can be depleted by age. An abundance of research shows that using these convenient foods can be a healthy alternative to buying "fresh" produce, which isn't always very fresh, and is a much better alternative to not using fruits and vegetables at all. An added bonus is that packaged fruits and vegetables are often cheaper than fresh.

There are, of course, exceptions. Some frozen and canned foods are packaged with unhealthy additives or sauces (such as cream and cheese sauces) or have a lot of added salt or sugar. Try to steer toward the varieties with few or no additives. When you cook or prepare them at home, you will probably use a lighter hand with seasonings and oils.

Nothing could prevent me from buying fresh fruits and vegetables altogether, especially when they are fresh, affordable, and in season. When I can find them locally grown and organic, even better, but, short of stopping at the farm stand to buy fruit, feeding my family fruits and vegetables from a package is a fast, affordable, and healthy substitute.

This chicken is tangy and succulent and unbelievably quick to prepare. Serve it with couscous and steamed baby carrots (or leave the carrots uncooked and serve them with dip).

lemon feta chicken

Prep (5 minutes) + Cook (30–40 minutes)

8 servings

Nutritional Information per serving:

Calories 320, Total Fat 9g, 14%, Saturated Fat 4g, 19%, Cholesterol 155mg, 52%, Sodium 280mg, 12%, Total Carbohydrate 1g, 0%, Dietary Fiber 0g, 0%, Protein 55g, Sugar 1g

- **6 boneless, skinless chicken breast halves (2½–3 pounds)**
- **2 tablespoons fresh lemon juice (about ½ lemon)**
- **2 teaspoons chopped fresh oregano or ½ teaspoon dried**
- **¼ teaspoon pepper**
- **4 ounces feta cheese, crumbled**

Preheat the oven to 350 degrees.

Place the chicken in a baking dish. Drizzle it with 1 tablespoon of the lemon juice. Sprinkle it with the oregano and pepper. Top it with the feta, then the remaining lemon juice.

Bake the chicken for 30 to 40 minutes or until it is just cooked through in the thickest part. (Check it with a meat thermometer or sharp knife. The chicken should have an internal temperature of 160 degrees and no longer be pink inside.) Do not flip the chicken while cooking it.

This homey meal really satisfies, but when I told my British-born friend, Deb Ford, what I was going to call it, she assured me this is *not* Bangers and Mash (a British mainstay of boiled sausage and mashed potatoes)! For the sausage, I use precooked chicken andouille sausage, which is low in fat and very flavorful, and our kids don't mind the spiciness. If you prefer, use sweet Italian sausage or your favorite variety. Serve it with a spinach salad with diced avocado, dried cranberries, and Parmesan cheese.

pan-browned sausage and potatoes

Prep + Cook =
30 minutes

6 servings

Nutritional
Information per
serving:
Calories 240, Total
Fat 11g, 17%, Saturated Fat 3.5g, 18%,
Cholesterol 50mg,
17%, Sodium 660mg,
28%, Total Carbohydrate 18g, 6%, Dietary Fiber 2g, 8%,
Protein 16g, Sugar 3g

- 1½ **pounds small red potatoes**
- **salt to taste (about ¾ teaspoon)**
- 1 **tablespoon butter**
- 1 **tablespoon olive oil**
- 2 **Vidalia or other yellow onions, sliced into half rings**
- 1½ **pounds andouille chicken sausage, halved lengthwise (or use mild or meatless sausage)**

Cover the potatoes with water, add the salt, and bring the water to a boil. Cook the potatoes until they are fork tender, 15 to 20 minutes, and drain them. Toss them immediately with the butter.

Meanwhile, in a large heavy-duty skillet, heat the oil over medium heat and cook the onions for about 5 minutes until they are translucent. Top the onions with the sausages and cook them, flipping occasionally, until the sausages and onions are well browned, about 15 to 20 minutes, or until the potatoes are ready.

While still warm, serve the cooked potatoes on the plate with the sausage and onions.

TIP: When buying potatoes, look for potatoes that are smooth, and firm. Avoid potatoes with large cuts, cracks, bruises, dark or green spots. Also, look for potatoes that are uniform in size for even cooking.

Burritos make such a simple and satisfying meal that I can hardly make enough variations for my family. These are reminiscent of my favorite burritos from Burrito Brothers in Washington, D.C. Serve them with tortilla chips, salsa, and guacamole.

spinach burritos

Prep + Cook = 15 minutes

6 servings

Nutritional Information per serving:

Calories 400, Total Fat 10g, 16%, Saturated Fat 3g, 15%, Cholesterol 5mg, 2%, Sodium 850mg, 35%, Total Carbohydrate 62g, 21%, Dietary Fiber 9g, 34%, Protein 14g, Sugar 3g

1 tablespoon olive oil

2 cans (15 ounces each) pinto beans, drained and rinsed

½ cup mild salsa, plus additional for serving

9 ounces baby spinach

½ cup shredded Cheddar or Monterey Jack cheese

6 large flour or whole wheat tortillas

guacamole (optional, see p. 298)

In a large skillet, heat the oil over medium heat. Add the beans and salsa and cook them for several minutes, stirring them occasionally.

In a loosely covered bowl, wilt the spinach in the microwave, about 2 minutes.

Add the spinach to the beans and salsa and stir it gently (you can also keep it separate if anyone in your house is afraid of green food). Remove the bean mixture from the heat and add the cheese. Stir it gently until the cheese is melted.

Warm the tortillas in the microwave (about 1 minute on high).

Put a scoop of the bean-spinach mixture in the lower middle of each tortilla. Add additional salsa and guacamole (optional), if desired. Fold half the tortilla up over the beans and roll it up to secure it.

{ **guacamole to go** You can now purchase very fresh-tasting all-natural guacamole in the refrigerator or freezer cases of some supermarkets and warehouse stores. We have found that they taste almost as good as homemade.

Your kids will probably love this sweet and savory dish as much as you will. Serve it with Sesame Stir-fried Green Beans (see p. 299).

thai fried rice with shrimp or chicken

Prep + Cook = 30 minutes

8 servings

Nutritional Information per serving:

Calories 380, Total Fat 10g, 16%, Saturated Fat 1.5g, 8%, Cholesterol 35mg, 12%, Sodium 370mg, 15%, Total Carbohydrate 51g, 17%, Dietary Fiber 5g, 21%, Protein 21g, Sugar 10g

- 2 cups dry white or brown rice (6–8 cups cooked)
- ½ cup peanuts (optional)
- 1 pound shrimp, peeled and deveined, or boneless, skinless chicken breasts, diced
- 2 tablespoons peanut or vegetable oil
- 1 teaspoon chopped garlic (about 2 cloves)
- 1 tablespoon peeled and minced fresh ginger
- 4 scallions, sliced
- 1½ cups frozen peas
- 2 cups drained pineapple chunks (save the juice for tomorrow's Waldorf Salad)
- ¼ cup soy sauce (or more to taste)
- ¼ teaspoon pepper

Cook the rice according to the package directions. Remove the saucepan from the heat, uncover it, and fluff the rice.

While the rice is cooking, prepare the remaining ingredients for the stir-fry. Toast the peanuts (optional) in a toaster oven on a light setting or in a 300-degree preheated oven for about 2 minutes, being careful not to let them burn.

When the rice is about 10 minutes from done, in a large heavy-duty skillet, heat the oil over medium-high heat. Add the garlic and ginger and sauté them for 1 to 2 minutes until they are fragrant and just starting to brown. Add the scallions and stir-fry them for 1 minute. Add the peas and pineapple and cook the vegetables for another minute or two.

Push the vegetables to one side of the skillet and add the shrimp or chicken to the other side. Cook it for about 2 minutes until the shrimp or chicken is almost cooked through (shrimp will turn pink and chicken will no longer be pink). Combine the shrimp or chicken with the vegetables and continue to cook the mixture for a few more minutes until the shrimp or chicken is fully cooked.

Stir in the cooked rice, soy sauce, and pepper and toss it until it is heated through. Top the rice with the peanuts (optional).

3 steps to prevent kitchen burns

Kitchen burns are still a major source of injuries for children, especially toddlers. Most of these painful and dangerous accidents can be prevented by following these recommendations:

1. Use the back burners to cook or heat water or food whenever possible.

2. Turn pot handles toward the back of the stove (so little hands can't easily grab and upend pots and pans).

3. Keep hot liquids away from the counter and table edges.

If your child does receive a minor burn, run his or her hand under cold water for several minutes to ease the pain. Do not use ice, butter, or grease, which can make burns worse. For a serious burn, seek medical attention immediately.

Beets are nutritional powerhouses, high in potassium, folic acid, and fiber. They also have a remarkably kid-friendly taste, color, and texture. In this colorful pasta, the beets are sweet and mild, and the goat cheese gives everything a slightly creamy texture. Serve it with a Waldorf Salad (see p. 297).

sweet and creamy red beet pasta

Prep + Cook = 30 minutes

8 servings

Nutritional Information per serving:

Calories 300, Total Fat 9g, 14%, Saturated Fat 3g, 15%, Cholesterol 5mg, 2%, Sodium 470mg, 20%, Total Carbohydrate 44g, 15%, Dietary Fiber 3g, 11%, Protein 11g, Sugar 5g

- 1 package (16 ounces) radiatorre or spiral-shaped pasta
- 1 can (14 ounces) sliced beets
- 4 tablespoons olive oil
- 1½ teaspoons chopped garlic (about 3 cloves)
- ½ teaspoon salt
- ¼ teaspoon pepper
- 5 fresh basil leaves
- 5 fresh mint leaves (or use extra basil)
- 4 ounces soft goat cheese (chèvre)

In a large stockpot cook the pasta according to the package directions. Drain the beets in a colander and cover them with a paper towel to absorb extra water.

When you put the pasta into the boiling water, heat the oil and garlic in a large skillet over medium heat. Cut each sliced beet into several ¼-inch slices. When the garlic just begins to brown (1 minute), add the beets, salt, pepper, basil, and mint. Stir it gently for several minutes.

When the pasta is nearly done, remove ½ cup of the pasta's cooking water and set it aside. Drain the pasta and add it to the skillet while it is still warm. Toss it with the beets and herbs and stir in the cheese. If the mixture needs some added creaminess, add the reserved cooking water from the pasta. Stir it well and serve the dish warm.

This marinade, which uses some of my favorite flavors, also works well for chicken or fish fillets. This is definitely a Scramble subscriber favorite! Serve the steak with Baked Potato Chips (see p. 300) and a spinach salad with grated Parmesan cheese, pecans, and diced avocado.

steak with soy-lime marinade

Prep + Cook = 20 minutes + Marinate

6 servings

Nutritional Information per serving:

Calories 280, Total Fat 10g, 15%, Saturated Fat 4g, 20%, Cholesterol 90mg, 30%, Sodium 780mg, 33%, Total Carbohydrate 3g, 1%, Dietary Fiber 0g, 1%, Protein 44g, Sugar 2g

4 rib eye, New York strip, or similar steaks, 1 inch thick (2½ pounds total)

¼ cup soy sauce

2 tablespoons lime juice (about ½ lime)

1 teaspoon minced garlic (about 2 cloves)

1 teaspoon minced fresh ginger or ¼ teaspoon ground

1 tablespoon brown sugar or honey

Lay the steaks flat in a large dish with sides just big enough to hold them in a single layer. In a measuring cup, mix together the remaining ingredients and pour them over the steaks. Flip the steaks once or twice to soak them in the marinade.

If time allows, refrigerate the steaks in the marinade for at least 15 minutes and up to 24 hours.

When you're ready to cook, heat a large heavy skillet over medium-high heat. Add the steaks and remaining marinade to the skillet. Cook the steaks 4 to 5 minutes per side until they are browned and cooked through to the desired doneness. Slice the steaks into strips to serve them. (Alternatively, grill them on a preheated grill for 8 to 12 minutes over medium-high heat.)

avocado awareness Let hard avocados ripen on the counter for a few days after you buy them, until they're just soft to the touch. Then refrigerate them until you're ready to use them.

To chop an avocado, cut it in half, remove the pit, and use a large spoon to scoop out the flesh in one piece. Put it flat side down on a cutting board and cut it into slices, then dice those slices.

This delicious fish is updated from my great-grandmother Celia's recipe. Her unusual secret ingredient? Gingersnaps! You can also use this preparation for tofu or boneless chicken (which may require a little longer cooking time). Serve it with gnocchi to absorb the delicious sauce and with roasted asparagus (see p. 299).

sweet and sour sole

Prep + Cook =
15 minutes

4 servings

Nutritional Information per serving:

Calories 210, Total Fat 2.5g, 4%, Saturated Fat .5g, 3%, Cholesterol 80mg, 27%, Sodium 260mg, 11%, Total Carbohydrate 18g, 6%, Dietary Fiber <1g, 4%, Protein 29g, Sugar 12g

- 1 small onion, halved and thinly sliced
- 4 tablespoons lemon juice (about 1 lemon)
- 4 gingersnap cookies
- ¼ cup white vinegar
- ¼ cup brown sugar
- ¼ cup tomato sauce or red pasta sauce
- ¾ cup water
- 1–1½ pounds sole fillets (or use flounder or tilapia)

In a large heavy frying pan, over medium to medium-high heat, bring all the ingredients except the fish to a boil. Stir it thoroughly, mashing the ginger snaps.

When the ginger snaps have dissolved into the sauce, put the fillets on top of the sauce. Reduce the heat, cover the pan, and simmer the mixture for about 5 minutes until the fillets are cooked through and flake easily.

TIP: Your family may enjoy ginger snaps with vanilla frozen yogurt for dessert.

This is a fabulous, flavorful pasta that our friend Sara Emley recently served to our book club to rave reviews (the book was good, too). It takes longer than Scramble pasta dishes usually do because you need to roast the vegetables, but it's so good that you may want to serve it to company. Serve this recipe with fresh strawberries and warm pita bread.

ziti with roasted eggplant and peppers

Prep (30 minutes) +
Cook (30 minutes)

8 servings

Nutritional
Information per
serving:

Calories 290, Total
Fat 5g, 8%, Saturated
Fat 3g, 15%, Choles-
terol 15mg, 5%,
Sodium 480mg, 20%,
Total Carbohydrate
50g, 17%, Dietary
Fiber 4g, 16%, Pro-
tein 11g, Sugar 4g

1 small (about 1 pound) eggplant, diced

1 yellow bell pepper, diced

1 red onion, peeled and diced

1 teaspoon minced garlic (about 2 cloves)

½ cup olive oil

1 teaspoon kosher salt

¼ teaspoon black pepper

1 pkg. (16 ounces) ziti or other short pasta

¼ cup lemon juice (about 1 lemon)

6 ounces feta cheese, finely diced (not crumbled)

15 fresh basil leaves, chopped

1 tablespoon fresh oregano leaves (optional)

Preheat the oven to 450 degrees. In a roasting pan or on a baking sheet, toss the diced eggplant, the bell pepper, the onion, and the garlic with ¼ cup oil and salt and pepper. Roast it for 30 to 40 minutes, turning it once, until it is lightly browned and softened.

Meanwhile, cook the pasta according to the package directions until it is al dente. Drain it and transfer it to a large serving bowl.

Combine the lemon juice and the remaining ¼ cup of oil in a measuring cup and toss it with the pasta in the bowl. Add the roasted vegetables, cheese, and fresh herbs and toss it thoroughly. Serve it warm or at room temperature.

TIP: To chop basil leaves, stack washed and dried leaves on top of each other and cut them into strips, then cut the strips crosswise into smaller pieces.

Your whole family can enjoy this wonderful meal, made almost entirely on the grill. Serve non-salad-eaters the grilled chicken and roasted peppers with the corn while the adults enjoy the salad. You can prepare the dressing and marinate the chicken the night before and grill it just before dinner. Serve it with grilled corn on the cob (see p. 299).

grilled balsamic chicken salad

Prep + Cook = 30 minutes + Marinate

4 servings

Nutritional Information per serving:

Calories 260, Total Fat 12g, 18%, Saturated Fat 3g, 15%, Cholesterol 70mg, 23%, Sodium 580mg, 24%, Total Carbohydrate 7g, 2%, Dietary Fiber 2g, 8%, Protein 30g, Sugar 2g

- **1 pound boneless, skinless chicken breasts**
- **½ cup light balsamic vinaigrette dressing, or make your own (see the Tip below)**
- **1 yellow bell pepper, cut in 4 large pieces, seeds and ribs removed**
- **1 tablespoon olive oil**
- **1 bag (about 7 ounces) prewashed mixed salad greens**
- **¼ cup crumbled blue cheese**
- **¼ cup glazed walnuts or plain chopped walnuts**
- **1 Roma tomato, diced**

Lay the chicken breasts in a single layer in a dish with sides. Pour ¼ cup of the dressing on them, flip them several times to coat them, and refrigerate them for 10 minutes or up to 24 hours. Reserve the remaining dressing for the salad.

Preheat the grill to high heat and remove the remaining dressing from the refrigerator. Brush both sides of the peppers with the oil. Grill the chicken and peppers over direct heat for 4 to 5 minutes per side, flipping them once, until they are lightly browned on the outside and the chicken is no longer pink in the center. After flipping the chicken, brush it with the marinade from the dish.

Meanwhile, put the salad greens, cheese, walnuts, and tomato in a large bowl.

Slice the grilled chicken and peppers into thin strips and cut the strips into 1-inch pieces. Add them to the salad in the bowl. Top the salad with the remaining ¼ cup of the dressing (or to taste) and toss it thoroughly.

TIP: To make orange balsamic vinaigrette, in a large measuring cup, thoroughly whisk together ¼ cup olive oil, ⅛ cup orange juice, ⅛ cup balsamic vinegar, and 1 tablespoon Dijon mustard.

TIP: If you're making Chili con Barley tomorrow night, soak the barley tonight so it will cook more quickly.

I loved this new version of chili so much I made it twice in one week. I've found that the key to faster cooking is to soak the barley overnight, which takes about two minutes to do but lops about an hour off the cooking time. Serve the chili with biscuits and top it with shredded Cheddar cheese.

chili con barley

Prep (20 minutes) +
Cook (30–40
minutes)

8 servings

Nutritional
Information per
serving:

Calories 280, Total
Fat 5g, 8%, Saturated
Fat 5g, 3%, Choles-
terol 0, 0%, Sodium
410mg, 17%, Total
Carbohydrate 52g,
17%, Dietary Fiber
12g, 50%, Protein 9g,
Sugar 10g

- 1 cup barley, soaked overnight in 3 cups water (or use quick-cooking barley)
- 2 tablespoons olive oil
- 2 large onions, chopped
- 2 large carrots, chopped
- 2 teaspoons chopped garlic (about 4 cloves)
- 2 stalks celery, chopped
- 1 tablespoon cumin
- 1 tablespoon chili powder
- 1 tablespoon dried basil
- 1 can (15 ounces) red or black beans with their liquid
- 1 can (15 ounces) chickpeas with their liquid
- 1 can (15 ounces) tomato sauce
- 2 tablespoons lemon juice (about ½ lemon)
- shredded Cheddar cheese for serving

In a medium container with a lid, soak the barley in the water overnight. When you are ready to make dinner, drain the barley in a colander.

In a large stockpot, heat the oil over medium heat. Add the onions, carrots, garlic, and celery and sauté them for about 5 minutes. Add the spices and the barley and cook them for about 2 more minutes. Add the beans, tomato sauce, and lemon juice and simmer the chili for about 30 to 40 more minutes, stirring it often, until the barley is tender to the bite. If you like a thinner chili, add water, chicken broth, or vegetable broth to thin it.

Serve the chili in bowls topped with Cheddar cheese.

These chicken strips have a great crunchy coating, suggested by our friend Christina McHenry. Our kids love to eat them off the stick. Serve them with fruit kabobs (kids enjoy making these) arranged on toothpicks or small skewers and with ketchup, honey mustard, or barbecue sauce as a dipping sauce for the chicken.

chicken sticks

Prep + Cook =
25 minutes

8 servings

Nutritional
Information per
serving:

Calories 240, Total Fat 11g, 17%, Saturated Fat 4g, 19%, Cholesterol 105mg, 34%, Sodium 200mg, 8%, Total Carbohydrate 5g, 2%, Dietary Fiber> 1g, 3%, Protein 29g, Sugar 0g

1 egg

1 cup crushed stoned wheat crackers (about 15 crackers)

⅓ cup grated Parmesan cheese

2 pounds chicken tenderloins (or use boneless, skinless chicken breasts cut into 1-inch strips)

2 tablespoons butter

2 tablespoons olive oil

8 wooden skewers (optional)

In a shallow bowl, beat the egg. In a second shallow bowl, combine the crushed crackers and the cheese. Dip each tenderloin in the egg (allowing the extra to drip back into the bowl) and then coat it with the cracker mixture. Set the coated tenderloins aside on a plate.

In a large skillet, melt 1 tablespoon of the butter into 1 tablespoon of the oil over medium heat. Add only as many tenderloins as will fit in a single layer and cook them for about 4 minutes per side until they are nicely browned. Continue until you have cooked all the tenderloins, adding the additional butter and oil to the pan if needed. Put the cooked tenderloins on a clean plate.

Push the skewers (optional) into some or all of the chicken tenderloins. Be sure to push them all the way through so the kids won't accidentally bite down on the ends.

I have great memories of eating these messy sandwiches as a kid. I've updated my mom's version by adding some healthy veggies to the meat sauce. You can even make this completely meatless. The finer you dice the carrots and peppers, the less likely your kids will be to detect them in the mix. Some kids like to eat the Sloppy Joes in a taco shell instead of on a bun! Serve them with an Italian Salad with sliced tomatoes, fresh mozzarella, and basil leaves (see p. 298).

sloppy joes

Prep + Cook = 25 minutes

8 servings

Nutritional Information per serving:

Calories 280, Total Fat 13g, 20%, Saturated Fat 5g, 25%, Cholesterol 50mg, 17%, Sodium 550mg, 23%, Total Carbohydrate 24g, 8%, Dietary Fiber 4g, 16%, Protein 17g, Sugar 5g

- **1 pound ground beef, turkey, or vegetarian ground "meat"**
- **½ yellow onion, diced**
- **1 red bell pepper, finely diced**
- **1 large carrot or 5–6 baby carrots, finely diced**
- **1 can (15 ounces) tomato sauce**
- **2 tablespoons Worcestershire sauce**
- **2 tablespoons ketchup**
- **1 tablespoon brown sugar**
- **8 whole wheat buns**

In a large skillet over medium heat, brown the beef or turkey in its own juices until it is almost cooked through. (If you're using vegetarian ground "meat," add it after the tomato sauce instead.) Drain off the excess liquid and add the diced vegetables to the skillet. Sauté the mixture for 2 more minutes and add all the remaining ingredients except the buns. Bring it to a boil, reduce the heat, cover the skillet, and simmer it for 15 to 20 minutes until the vegetables are tender.

To serve the sandwiches, toast the buns and fill each one with a large spoonful of the meat mixture.

TIP: To avoid soggy bread, serve the Sloppy Joes with a slotted spoon or spatula so the excess juices stay behind.

This healthy combination of ingredients makes for an easy one-dish meal that has received rave reviews from Scramble subscribers. If you are feeling ambitious, you could even make your own polenta, but I have found the prepared variety sold in tubes to be quite good. Serve this dish with steamed carrots.

polenta-tomatillo casserole

Prep (10 minutes) +
Cook (30 minutes)

10 servings

Nutritional
Information per
serving:

Calories 170, Total
Fat 7g, 11%, Satu-
rated Fat 3.5g, 18%,
Cholesterol 15mg,
5%, Sodium 630mg,
26%, Total Carbohy-
drate 20g, 7%, Di-
etary Fiber 0g, 0%,
Protein 8g, Sugar 5g

1 tube (18–24 ounces) prepared polenta (sold with grains)

1 can (15 ounces) pinto or black beans, drained

1 can (15 ounces) unsweetened corn kernels, drained

1 cup shredded Monterey Jack cheese

1½ cups mild tomatillo green salsa

2 tablespoons chopped fresh cilantro

½ cup half and half

1 cup blue corn tortilla chips, crumbled (optional)

Preheat the oven to 375 degrees.

Cut the polenta into ½-inch cubes. Put the polenta cubes into the bottom of a 9 × 13-inch baking dish. Top them with the beans and corn, then half of the cheese.

In a medium bowl or measuring cup, combine the salsa, cilantro, and half and half. Pour the mixture over the ingredients in the baking dish. Top it with the remaining cheese.

Cover the pan and bake the casserole for 25 to 30 minutes. Let it stand for a few minutes before serving.

When you serve the casserole, you can mash the softened polenta with a fork and top it with crumbled tortilla chips, if desired.

TIP: Use leftover half and half in your morning coffee for a rich treat.

{ **polenta: italian for grits?** Polenta is an Italian cornmeal mixture, a bit like a cross between cornbread and grits. Many prepared brands are fat free, and are delicious when baked or broiled with flavorful toppings.

This is a rich and creamy soup that I have made many times for guests. It takes longer than thirty minutes but doesn't involve much more than about twenty minutes of actual work time. Serve it with bread and a spinach salad with diced oranges, walnuts, and blue cheese.

creamy wild rice and vegetable soup

Prep (20 minutes) +
Cook (45 minutes)

8 servings

Nutritional
Information per
serving:

Calories 200, Total
Fat 8g, 12%, Saturated Fat 4.5g, 23%,
Cholesterol 20mg,
7%, Sodium 180mg,
8%, Total Carbohydrate 24g, 8%, Dietary Fiber 2g, 8%,
Protein 8g, Sugar 4g

2 tablespoons butter

3 carrots, peeled and finely diced

2 leeks, thoroughly washed, white and light green parts only, finely diced (about 2½ cups)

2 celery stalks, finely diced

¼ cup all-purpose flour

8 cups chicken broth

¾ cup wild rice

¾ cup half and half

3 tablespoons dry sherry

Salt to taste

In a large stockpot over medium heat, melt the butter. Add the carrots, leeks, and celery and cook them, stirring them occasionally, until they are softened, about 5 minutes.

Reduce the heat to low, add the flour, and cook the mixture, stirring it constantly, for about 3 minutes until most of the flour is absorbed.

Slowly add the broth, whisking it well to eliminate flour lumps. Bring the soup to a simmer.

Add the rice, return the soup to a simmer, and cook it, stirring it frequently, until the rice is tender but still somewhat chewy, about 45 minutes.

Warm the half and half in the microwave on high for about 30 seconds and stir it and the sherry into the soup. Season the soup with salt to taste (it may not need any).

TIP: If you have a food processor, use it to finely dice the carrots, leeks, and celery. If not, start chopping.

My husband, Andrew, couldn't get enough of this flavorful pasta, and the kids didn't mind it either. If your kids are picky, you may want to leave some pasta plain just in case. Radicchio is an Italian leafy vegetable with a purple color. If your market doesn't carry it, you can use arugula or spinach leaves instead. Serve the pasta with a green salad mixed with the remaining radicchio and some fresh mint leaves.

penne pesto with radicchio and olives

Prep + Cook =
25 minutes

8 servings

Nutritional Information per serving:

Calories 380, Total Fat 16g, 24%, Saturated Fat 4g, 21%, Cholesterol 10mg, 4%, Sodium 400mg, 17%, Total Carbohydrate 46g, 15%, Dietary Fiber 3g, 13%, Protein 14g, Sugar 3g

1 package (16 ounces) penne or other short pasta

1 container (7 ounces) prepared refrigerated pesto (or use homemade, see p. 214)

¼ cup pitted kalamata olives

¼ cup marinated sundried tomatoes

1–2 cups (to taste) finely chopped radicchio

¼ cup shredded Parmesan cheese

Cook the pasta according to the package directions.

Put the pesto, olives, and tomatoes in a large metal bowl. When the pasta is cooked, drain it and toss it with the ingredients in the bowl. Add the radicchio and Parmesan cheese and toss it again.

Serve the pasta hot or at room temperature.

quinoa and barley: a hot new pop duo? No, but they are two healthy and delicious whole grains that can make your dinners sing! According to the American Dietetic Association, "Whole-grain foods give nutritional benefits of the *entire* grain—vitamins, minerals, dietary fiber, and other natural plant compounds called phytochemicals." Using whole wheat bread and buns also gives you the health advantages of whole grains. In contrast, refined grains, such as white rice and all-purpose flour, contain only the center of the grains and thus don't have all the health benefits of whole grains. Because they are denser, whole grains often take longer to cook. You can often reduce their cooking time by soaking the grains overnight.

cooking with kids

One night my son, Solomon, was feeling grumpy and out of sorts. I invited him to help me make dinner, which, to my surprise, he was willing to do. It had been a while since Solomon, who was eight, cooked with me. By the time dinner was ready, Solomon was back to his bouncy self and said, "Mom, cooking with you got rid of my blues." He got such a thrill out of opening cans by himself, slicing olives (with a plastic serrated knife), and mixing the sauce that he's volunteered to help us make dinner many times since.

From the time our kids were babies, we have tried to welcome them in the kitchen. Before they were walking, they'd bounce in their jumpers in the kitchen doorway or spin in their ExerSaucers while I made dinner. Atop our sturdy stepladder when they were toddlers, they "washed dishes" in the sudsy kitchen sink while I cooked, or made their own "dinner" out of flour, food coloring, water, and soap. Six-year-old Celia still likes to make "Daddy's Speshl Sup" out of the ickiest things she can find in the kitchen and garden and surprise Andrew with it at the table.

Now Solomon and Celia are old enough to help make dinner and set the table. It takes extra patience to let the kids help in the kitchen, and sometimes I am in too much of a hurry to relinquish much control. When they do help, I try to find tasks that they can do all by themselves, and I try to hold my tongue if cheese isn't sprinkled evenly or peeled carrots retain some skin. I also make sure to keep sharp objects far away and to teach the kids to keep their hands away from the stove and oven. When time and patience allow, cooking dinner is a great way for us to spend time together during busy weeknights.

Like the chic Cuban mojito cocktail, these steaks get their extra hint of flavor from mint, lime, and sugar. Though I don't cook steak often, my family thoroughly enjoys the occasions when I do. Of course, the kids like their steak dipped in ketchup. You can grill stalks of asparagus and sweet potatoes while the steak is cooking (see p. 299).

grilled steak mojito

Prep + Cook =
30 minutes

4 servings

Nutritional
Information per
serving:

Calories 250, Total
Fat 11g, 17%, Satu-
rated Fat 3.5g, 18%,
Cholesterol 75mg,
25%, Sodium 250mg,
10%, Total Carbohy-
drate 2g, 1%, Dietary
Fiber 0g, 0%, Protein
35g, Sugar 2g

2 pounds boneless New York strip or Delmonico steaks (2 or 3 steaks)

3–4 tablespoons fresh lime juice (about 1 lime)

5 fresh mint leaves

½ teaspoon kosher salt

1 tablespoon sugar

1 teaspoon unsweetened cocoa powder (optional)

1 tablespoon olive oil

Put the steaks in a flat container with sides, one just large enough to hold them in a single layer. Combine all the other ingredients together in the blender and pour the marinade over the steaks. Flip the steaks in it several times.

Preheat the grill to high heat. Cook the steaks on the preheated grill with the lid closed to the desired doneness, about 4 to 5 minutes on each side for medium rare.

Remove the cooked steaks to a plate or cutting board and slice them into strips.

This unusual combination makes a delicious and hearty pasta dinner. Serve it with chopped cantaloupe.

rigatoni with lima beans, artichokes, and spinach

Prep + Cook = 30 minutes

8 servings

Nutritional Information per serving:

Calories 330, Total Fat 4.5g, 7%, Saturated Fat 0.5g, 3%, Cholesterol 0mg, 0%, Sodium 170mg, 7%, Total Carbohydrate 59g, 20%, Dietary Fiber 8g, 32%, Protein 13g, Sugar 4g

1 package (10 ounces) frozen lima beans

1 package (16 ounces) rigatoni (tubes) or pasta shells

2 tablespoons olive oil

1 medium onion, chopped

1 teaspoon minced garlic (about 2 cloves)

1 can (15 ounces) diced tomatoes with Italian seasoning

½ teaspoon brown sugar

salt and pepper to taste

1 package (6 ounces) fresh baby spinach

1 can (14 ounces) artichoke hearts in water, drained and quartered

grated Parmesan cheese to taste

Remove the lima beans from the freezer and set them aside. Cook the pasta according to the package directions.

Meanwhile, in a large saucepan, heat the oil over medium heat. Add the onion and garlic and cook them, stirring them occasionally, until they are softened, about 5 minutes.

Add the tomatoes, the sugar, and salt and pepper to taste. Bring the sauce to a boil, then partially cover it and simmer it for 10 minutes.

Add the lima beans to the sauce and return it to a boil. Reduce the heat, replace the lid, and simmer it for 3 more minutes.

Add the spinach to the sauce. Replace the lid and cook the sauce until the spinach is wilted, about 3 more minutes.

When the pasta is finished cooking, drain it and add it to the sauce, along with the artichoke hearts. Top with Parmesan cheese to taste.

This is a mild, family-friendly stir-fry recipe. You can substitute diced chicken breasts or extra-firm tofu for the shrimp. Serve the stir-fry with frozen egg rolls heated according to the package directions.

shrimp and broccoli stir-fry

Prep + Cook =
30 minutes

6 servings

Nutritional
Information per
serving:

Calories 360, Total
Fat 4.5g, 7%, Satu-
rated Fat 0.5g, 3%,
Cholesterol 115mg,
38%, Sodium 650mg,
27%, Total Carbohy-
drate 57g, 19%, Di-
etary Fiber 4g, 16%,
Protein 23g, Sugar 7g

1½ cups dry rice, cooked according to package directions

2 heads broccoli florets (about 4 cups)

3 tablespoons soy sauce

2 tablespoons rice vinegar

1½ tablespoons brown sugar

1 tablespoon peeled and chopped fresh ginger, or ½ teaspoon ground ginger

1 tablespoon sesame or peanut oil

4 scallions, thinly sliced

1 can (15 ounces) corn kernels (use a kind without added sugar, if possible, or use 2 cups frozen kernels)

1 pound large shrimp, peeled and deveined

Cook the rice according to the package directions.

While the rice is cooking, steam the broccoli in ½ cup boiling water, covered, until it is just tender, about 4 minutes. Drain it.

Meanwhile, in a measuring cup, whisk together the soy sauce, vinegar, brown sugar, and ginger until the sugar dissolves.

In a wok or large nonstick skillet, heat the oil over high heat. Add the scallions, corn, and shrimp. Stir-fry it for 2 to 3 minutes or until the shrimp are pink.

Add the broccoli and the soy mixture and stir-fry it until all the ingredients are coated with the sauce and heated through.

Serve the stir-fry over the rice.

move over, knife! There are lots of great uses for kitchen scissors. When little ones need a pizza or a quesadilla or piece of chicken cut up into bite-sized pieces, try using kitchen scissors. Scissors are also great for snipping fresh herbs or scallions, and a heavy-duty pair can be slipped into the dishwasher and will last for years.

You can make these quesadillas on the stovetop, if you prefer, by browning each side in a skillet over medium heat. The quesadillas are delicious with just beans and cheese, but they're also quite good if you add your family's favorite fillings or whatever you have left over in the refrigerator from the week's meals. Serve them with Lemony-Garlic Spinach (see p. 298).

crispy bean quesadillas

Prep + Cook =
20 minutes

6 servings

Nutritional
Information per
serving:

Calories 390, Total
Fat 15g, 24%, Saturated Fat 8g, 38%,
Cholesterol 35mg,
11%, Sodium 1090mg,
45%, Total Carbohydrate 46g, 15%, Dietary Fiber 6g, 25%,
Protein 19g, Sugar 8g

6 soft-taco-sized flour or whole wheat tortillas

1 can (15 ounces) vegetarian refried beans

2 cups shredded sharp Monterey Jack cheese

toppings (optional): 1½–2 cups total, chopped, of 1 or more of the following:
olives; fresh tomatoes; corn kernels; avocado; baby spinach; cooked ham,
steak, or chicken

salsa for serving

guacamole for serving (see p. 298)

Preheat the oven to 375 degrees. Spray a large cookie sheet with nonstick cooking spray.

On half of each tortilla, spread 1 large spoonful of beans and a handful each of cheese and toppings (optional). Fold the tortillas in half and place them on the pan.

Bake the quesadillas for 8 to 10 minutes until the tortillas are lightly browned and the cheese is melted.

Cut them into wedges with a sharp knife or pizza cutter for serving. Top them with salsa and guacamole as desired.

TIP: Vegetarian refried beans have a great flavor and are much lower in fat than traditional refried beans.

This recipe works for non-salad-eaters, too, as the chicken tastes great on its own. The recipe can also be adapted to how much cooking you want to do: You can buy the dressing and croutons or make your own with a little more effort. Vegetarians can use meatless "chicken" patties instead of the chicken breasts. Serve it with sourdough bread.

caesar salad with chicken

Prep + Cook =
30 minutes

6 servings

Nutritional
Information per
serving:

Calories 290, Total
Fat 13g, 20%, Satu-
rated Fat 3g, 15%,
Cholesterol 70mg,
23%, Sodium 410mg,
17%, Total Carbohy-
drate 13g, 4%, Di-
etary Fiber 3g, 12%,
Protein 31g, Sugar 2g

1–1½ **pounds boneless, skinless chicken breasts**

1 **tablespoon olive oil**

¼ **teaspoon salt**

⅛ **teaspoon garlic powder**

1 **small head romaine lettuce**

½ **cup grated Parmesan cheese**

croutons (or use store-bought)

2 **large slices sourdough bread, cut into ½-inch cubes**

1–2 **tablespoons olive oil**

¼ **teaspoon kosher salt**

dressing (or use 1 cup store-bought light Caesar dressing)

2 **tablespoons light mayonnaise**

2 **tablespoons olive oil**

½ **teaspoon chopped garlic (about 1 clove) or** ¼ **teaspoon garlic powder**

2 **tablespoons lemon juice (about ½ lemon)**

1 **teaspoon Worcestershire sauce**

½ **teaspoon anchovy paste**

Preheat the oven or toaster oven to 450 degrees if you are going to make the croutons.

Put the chicken breasts in a flat dish with sides. Drizzle them with the oil and sprinkle them with the salt and garlic powder. Flip the chicken several times to coat it. Heat a large nonstick skillet over medium heat. Add the chicken breasts and cook them until both sides are browned and the chicken is no longer pink in the center, about 10 to 12 minutes. (If the outside gets too browned before the inside cooks, cover the pan and reduce the heat or finish cooking the chicken in the microwave on high for 2 minutes.) Slice the cooked chicken into thin strips. (Set some chicken aside for non-salad-eaters, if necessary.)

Wash the lettuce, dry it thoroughly, and chop or rip it into bite-sized pieces.

To make the croutons, in a medium bowl, toss the bread cubes with the oil and the salt. Place them on a baking sheet in a single layer and bake them in the preheated oven for 3 to 5 minutes until they are slightly crisp and browned. Watch them carefully so they don't burn.

To make the dressing, thoroughly whisk together all the ingredients.

Just before serving, vigorously toss the lettuce, chicken, cheese, croutons, and dressing (you won't necessarily need all of it) in a large salad bowl.

kids and calcium
how much is enough?

Juice boxes, sports drinks, vitamin water, and pink lemonade—with all these tempting sugary drinks, it can be hard for us to get enough plain old milk into our kids' bellies. When I was a kid, we had our share of Tang and Kool-Aid, but I also remember guzzling a lot of milk with meals. Now that I'm a parent, I want to make sure our two are getting enough calcium to make their bones strong and healthy.

According to the current recommendation of the USDA, which sets nutritional guidelines for Americans, adults and children should have two to three servings of milk, yogurt, or cheese each day. What counts as a serving? One cup (8 ounces) of milk or yogurt or $1^1/_2$ ounces of cheese (about $^1/_4$ cup of shredded cheese). Tofu, broccoli, chickpeas, lentils, canned sardines, salmon, and other fish with bones are also good sources of calcium, according to the American Academy of Pediatrics, which recommends three servings per day, or at least 800 mg., of calcium for four- through eight-year-olds and four servings, or 1,300 mg, for nine- through eighteen-year-olds.

The best way to make sure your kids get enough calcium is to make calcium-rich foods a daily habit. In our house, milk is the only drink option for the kids at dinner. The kids also get yogurt and cheese in their lunches, and they sometimes have cereal with milk for a snack. Some families routinely drink calcium-fortified fruit juices or soy milk, especially if their kids don't like or can't tolerate regular milk. Many doctors and dietitians, believing that the health benefits of drinking milk outweigh the downside of the extra sugar, also recommend adding chocolate or other flavoring to milk if kids won't drink it plain. If your kids don't like any of these options, consult a dietitian about other healthy choices, so they don't miss out on this important nutrient.

This recipe is a complete all-in-one-dish meal. You can use chicken pieces instead of a whole chicken if you prefer, which will cut the cooking time to about an hour. Serve it with couscous or bulgur wheat.

roast chicken with vegetables

Prep (10 minutes) +
Cook (90 minutes)

8 servings

Nutritional
Information per
serving:

Calories 320, Total
Fat 16g, 25%, Saturated Fat 4g, 20%,
Cholesterol 140mg,
47%, Sodium 410mg,
17%, Total Carbohydrate 8g, 3%, Dietary
Fiber 2g, 8%, Protein
36g, Sugar 4g

1 bag (16 ounces) baby carrots

1 large onion, peeled, halved, and sliced into half rings

4 potatoes (Yukon Gold or red), chopped into bite-sized pieces

1 whole chicken (about 4 pounds) (or use 8–10 chicken pieces)

¾ cup water or chicken broth

¼ cup olive oil

¾ teaspoon garlic powder

¾ teaspoon paprika

½ teaspoon dried rosemary

¾ teaspoon kosher salt

¼ teaspoon pepper

Preheat the oven to 400 degrees. Put the vegetables in a large roasting or baking pan and put the chicken on top. Pour the water or chicken broth around the vegetables. Pour the oil evenly over the chicken and sprinkle the spices on top of the chicken.

Bake the chicken for a total of about 1½ hours, covered for the first 45 minutes. Chicken is done when juices at the base of the thigh run clear or an instant-read thermometer inserted in the thigh measures 170 degrees. After the first 45 minutes, uncover the pan and baste the chicken and stir the vegetables. If time allows, let the chicken rest for 10 to 15 minutes after removing it from the oven.

clean bill of health It is not necessary to wash chicken before cooking it. In fact, a recent study suggests doing so can more easily spread the bacteria in your kitchen.

This is a light and lovely pasta to welcome in the warmer weather. Our six-year-old, Celia, said it was the best thing I've ever made! Serve it with steamed broccoli.

pasta with herbed butter

Prep + Cook =
20 minutes

6 servings

Nutritional
Information per
serving:

Calories 370, Total
Fat 10g, 15%, Satu-
rated Fat 4g, 20%,
Cholesterol 15mg,
5%, Sodium 150mg,
6%, Total Carbohy-
drate 58g, 9%, Di-
etary Fiber 2g, 8%,
Protein 12g, Sugar 2g

- 1 package (16 ounces) gemilli or other spiral-shaped pasta
- 1 cup chopped fresh basil (or try a mixture of mostly basil and some sage)
- 2 tablespoons butter
- 1 tablespoon olive oil
- 1 teaspoon minced garlic (about 2 cloves)
- 2 tablespoons pine nuts (optional)
- ¼ teaspoon salt
- ¼ –½ cup grated Parmesan cheese

Cook the pasta according to the package directions until it is al dente. Meanwhile, chop the herbs.

Five minutes before the pasta is done, melt the butter in a large heavy skillet over medium heat. Add the oil, garlic, and pine nuts (optional) and cook the mixture for about 2 minutes, stirring it occasionally.

Before draining the pasta, use a ladle to scoop out about ½ cup of the pasta's cook-ing water into a measuring cup.

To the skillet with the butter and garlic, add the drained pasta, reserved cooking liquid, herbs, salt, and Parmesan cheese and toss it over low heat for 1 to 2 minutes until it is warmed through and the cheese is melted. Serve it hot.

{ **edgewise** A very sharp chef's knife works well for chopping herbs.

This Mexican-style baked fish goes perfectly with yellow rice and asparagus. You can bake the asparagus, tossed with a little olive oil, salt, and pepper, in a smaller dish while the fish cooks.

red snapper with stewed tomatoes

Prep (10 minutes) +
Cook (25 minutes)

6 servings

Nutritional
Information per
serving:

Calories 140, Total
Fat 3.5g, 5%, Saturated Fat 0.5g, 3%,
Cholesterol 30mg,
10%, Sodium 290mg,
12%, Total Carbohydrate 5g, 2%, Dietary
Fiber <1g, 4%, Protein 23g, Sugar 3g

1 package (10 ounces) yellow rice

1½ pounds red snapper fillets

1 can (14 ounces) Mexican-style stewed tomatoes with their liquid

¼ cup capers (or use ½ cup pitted olives, any variety)

1 tablespoon olive oil

Preheat the oven to 325 degrees. Cook the rice according to the package directions.

In a large glass baking dish, combine the tomatoes and their liquid with the capers. Top the tomatoes with the fish fillets and drizzle the oil over the fish.

Bake the fish, uncovered, for 15 minutes. Spoon some of the tomato mixture over the fish and bake it for 10 to 15 more minutes, until the fish flakes easily with a fork. Serve it hot, spooning the sauce over the fish and rice.

This gourmet twist on grilled cheese is a treat. Opt for mustard or jam, depending on your preference for savory or sweet. If your kids aren't very adventurous, make traditional grilled cheese for them with Cheddar or American cheese and serve spinach on the side. Serve the sandwiches with tomato soup.

grilled cheese sandwiches with brie and baby spinach

Prep + Cook = 15 minutes

4 servings

Nutritional Information per serving:

Calories 390, Total Fat 23g, 36%, Saturated Fat 14g, 69%, Cholesterol 70mg, 24%, Sodium 660mg, 28%, Total Carbohydrate 26g, 9%, Dietary Fiber 3g, 11%, Protein 16g, Sugar 2g

2–3 tablespoons butter

1 teaspoon minced garlic (about 2 cloves)

1 bag (6 or 9 ounces) baby spinach

8 medium slices firm whole-grain or sourdough bread

2 tablespoons Dijon mustard or apricot jam

8 ounces Brie cheese, cut into $\frac{1}{8}$-inch slices

In a large skillet, melt 1 tablespoon of the butter over medium heat. Add the garlic and cook it for 30 seconds. Add the spinach and toss it until it begins to wilt. Transfer it to a bowl and set it aside.

With a paper towel, wipe the skillet clean. To build the sandwiches, spread 4 slices of the bread with mustard or jam. Divide the cheese slices among the 4 slices of bread. Top them with the spinach mixture. Cover them with the remaining bread slices. Lightly spread the outsides with the remaining butter.

In the skillet, cook the sandwiches over medium-low heat until they are browned, turning them once and then pressing them down with a spatula. Slice the sandwiches in half and serve them.

This is one of those great weeknight recipes that doesn't win any points for looks but is really satisfying and yummy. If your market does not carry quick-cooking brown rice, substitute regular (not instant) white rice instead. Serve this dish with a green salad topped with shredded carrots and red cabbage and blue cheese.

one-pot italian rice and beans

Prep (10 minutes) +
Cook (30 minutes)

6 servings

Nutritional
Information per
serving:

Calories 240, Total
Fat 6g, 9%, Saturated
Fat 2g, 10%, Choles-
terol 5mg, 2%,
Sodium 810mg, 34%,
Total Carbohydrate
36g, 12%, Dietary
Fiber 8g, 32%, Pro-
tein 13g, Sugar 5g

1 package (10 ounces) frozen green beans

1 can (15 ounces) red kidney beans (preferably unsweetened), drained

1 can (15 ounces) diced tomatoes with their liquid

1 cup red pasta sauce or tomato sauce

1 cup pitted black olives (strong or mild varieties) plus ½ cup of their juice

1 cup quick-cooking brown rice

1 teaspoon dried basil

shredded mozzarella cheese for serving

In a microwave or on the stovetop, partially defrost the green beans. Drain off the excess liquid.

In a medium stockpot with a tight-fitting lid, combine all the remaining ingredients except the cheese. Bring it to a boil, cover it, reduce the heat, and simmer it for 30 minutes until the rice is tender.

Serve each portion topped with cheese to taste.

This simple recipe for grilled chicken, a favorite in the home of our friends Kathryn and Mark Spindel, is a big hit with kids. If you don't have a grill or the weather is not cooperating, you can use a preheated broiler, with the rack positioned four or five inches from the heating element, so the chicken doesn't get too brown on the outside before the inside is cooked. Or grill it ahead of time and warm it up or serve it cold. Serve it with coleslaw (see p. 298).

grilled honey mustard chicken

Prep + Cook = 25 minutes + Marinate

6 servings

Nutritional Information per serving:

Calories 210, Total Fat 6g, 9%, Saturated Fat 1.5g, 8%, Cholesterol 120mg, 40%, Sodium 250mg, 10%, Total Carbohydrate 7g, 2%, Dietary Fiber 0g, 0%, Protein 31g, Sugar 6g

5 tablespoons honey

5 tablespoons Dijon mustard

1 pack (4–5 pounds) chicken thighs and drumsticks (about 12 pieces)

In a small bowl, mix together the honey and mustard.

Put the chicken in a large plastic dish with a cover. Pour or brush the marinade mixture over the chicken and shake it thoroughly. Marinate it in the refrigerator at least 1 hour or preferably overnight.

Grill the chicken on a preheated grill (or broil it in a preheated broiler) for about 8 to 10 minutes per side (or 5 to 6 minutes per side if you are using boneless thighs), basting it once with the marinade, until it is cooked through and slightly browned.

Serve the chicken warm or cold.

This easy casserole goes well with a Cucumber Salad (see p. 297).

(see p. 297)

three-cheese spinach orzo bake

Prep (20 minutes) +
Cook (30 minutes)

6 servings

Nutritional
Information per
serving:

Calories 220, Total
Fat 8g, 12%, Satu-
rated Fat 3.5g, 18%,
Cholesterol 85mg,
28%, Sodium 580mg,
24%, Total Carbohy-
drate 23g, 8%, Di-
etary Fiber 3g, 12%,
Protein 14g, Sugar 5g

- ¾–1 cup uncooked orzo (to make 1½ cups cooked)
- 1 box (10 ounces) frozen chopped spinach
- 1½ cups red pasta sauce
- ½ cup grated Parmesan cheese
- 2 eggs, lightly beaten
- ½ cup low-fat ricotta cheese
- ¼ teaspoon nutmeg
- ½ cup shredded mozzarella cheese

Preheat the oven to 375 degrees. Spray a 9-inch glass pie pan with nonstick cooking spray.

Cook the orzo (boil it for 8 minutes or follow the package directions) and drain it.

Thaw the spinach in the microwave (about 4 minutes on high) and drain it if necessary.

In a medium bowl, combine the orzo, ½ cup of the red sauce, and the Parmesan cheese. Spread the mixture over the bottom of the pie pan.

In a medium bowl, mix the spinach, eggs, ricotta, and nutmeg. Spoon the mixture over the pasta and spread it evenly. Spread the remaining ½ cup of the red sauce over the spinach mixture. Sprinkle it with mozzarella cheese.

Bake the casserole, uncovered, for 30 minutes. Serve it hot.

This luscious stew smells super, and the soft vegetables and rice melt in your mouth. It's a great sensory experience. Serve it with a good bread for soaking up the broth.

black bean, fennel, and tomato stew

Prep (20 minutes) +
Cook (40 minutes)

6 servings

Nutritional
Information per
serving:

Calories 190, Total
Fat 4g, 7%, Saturated
Fat 1.5g, 7%, Choles-
terol 5mg, 1%,
Sodium 560mg, 23%,
Total Carbohydrate
32g, 11%, Dietary
Fiber 9g, 36%, Pro-
tein 9g, Sugar 11g

1 tablespoon olive oil

1 bulb fennel (use the bulb only), chopped

1 medium onion, chopped

1 teaspoon minced garlic (about 2 cloves)

1 can (28 ounces) diced tomatoes

½ teaspoon dried oregano

3 cups water

1 tablespoon brown sugar

½ cup uncooked brown rice

½ teaspoon pepper, or less to taste

1 can (15 ounces) black beans with their liquid

grated Parmesan cheese for serving

In a stockpot, heat the oil over medium-high heat. Add the fennel, onion, and garlic and sauté them for 5 minutes.

Add the tomatoes, oregano, water, and brown sugar. Raise the heat and bring it to a boil. Add the rice, reduce the heat to medium-low, cover the pot, and simmer the stew for 40 minutes.

Stir in the pepper and black beans and cook it for a few more minutes.

Serve the stew hot, topped with plenty of Parmesan cheese.

My favorite deli sandwich is also a quick and satisfying treat for dinner. If you can't find corned beef in your supermarket's deli section, substitute sliced roast beef, ham, or turkey. If you like a sweeter taste, you can substitute coleslaw for the sauerkraut. Serve the sandwiches with potato chips (look for a variety with lower fat and sodium, or make Baked Potato Chips: see p. 300) and dill pickles.

hot reuben sandwiches

Prep + Cook =
15 minutes

4 servings

Nutritional
Information per
serving:

Calories 430, Total
Fat 16g, 25%, Saturated Fat 6g, 30%,
Cholesterol 85mg,
28%, Sodium 1790mg,
75%, Total Carbohydrate 37g, 12%, Dietary Fiber 5g, 20%,
Protein 31g, Sugar 4g

¼ cup ketchup

2 tablespoons mayonnaise

8 slices rye or pumpernickel bread

1 tablespoon margarine or butter

1 pound sliced corned beef (or use sliced roast beef, ham, turkey,
    or vegetarian sliced "meat")

4 slices Swiss cheese

1 cup sauerkraut

In a small bowl or measuring cup, combine the ketchup and mayonnaise.

On one side of each piece of bread, spread a thin layer of margarine or butter. On the nonbuttered sides of 4 slices of the bread, layer about 6 slices of corned beef, 1 slice of Swiss cheese, 1 large spoonful of sauerkraut, and about 1 tablespoon of the dressing. Press the top half of each sandwich on so the buttered sides of both pieces of bread are on the outside.

Heat a large nonstick skillet over medium heat. Cook the sandwiches on both sides, pressing them down with a spatula, until the outsides are nicely browned, about 3 to 5 minutes per side. Remove them from the pan and slice them on the diagonal for serving.

TIP: If you prefer, use ⅓ cup Thousand Islands dressing instead of the ketchup and mayonnaise.

My neighbor Christina McHenry shared this kid-pleasing recipe for stir-fried noodles. Serve it with a Japanese Salad (see p. 298).

curly noodle delight

Serve it with a Japanese Salad (see p. 298).

Prep + Cook =
15 minutes

8 servings

Nutritional
Information per
serving:

Calories 170, Total
Fat 5g, 8%, Saturated
Fat 1g, 5%, Choles-
terol 0mg, 0%,
Sodium 1120mg, 47%,
Total Carbohydrate
27g, 9%, Dietary
Fiber 3g, 12%, Pro-
tein 5g, Sugar 7g

- 1 package (16 ounces) mixed deluxe frozen vegetables
- 1 teaspoon sesame or vegetable oil
- 1 package (8 ounces) sliced mushrooms
- 1 can (8 ounces) diced water chestnuts
- ¼ cup oyster sauce (available with Asian foods) (or use stir-fry sauce)
- 2 tablespoons soy sauce
- 1 tablespoon honey
- 4 packages (3 ounces each) ramen noodles (discard flavor packets) or 12 ounces curly noodles

In a microwave-safe bowl or on the stove-top, partially defrost the frozen vegetables (about 3 minutes on high). In a medium stockpot, boil water to cook the ramen noodles.

Meanwhile, in a large skillet or a wok, heat the oil over medium heat. Add the mushrooms and water chestnuts and sauté them for 3–5 minutes until the mushrooms start to shrink.

In a small bowl or measuring cup, combine the oyster sauce, soy sauce, and honey.

When the water starts to boil for the noodles, add the mixed vegetables to the skillet (drain them first if necessary) with the mushrooms and water chestnuts and toss the mixture occasionally. Cook the noodles for 3 minutes and drain them thoroughly.

Add the cooked noodles and sauce to the vegetables, and toss the mixture thoroughly to coat the noodles. Keep it warm until you're ready to serve it.

ten tips for safe and easy barbecues

Our whole family loves the smoky taste of steak, chicken, and salmon cooked on the grill—we even like grilled vegetables and corn. A few years ago, Andrew and I swapped our charcoal barbecue for a gas grill because it's easier to start and heats up faster. Some purists say the flavor isn't true barbecue, but we've been very happy with our gas grill, and we now cook out more often. I wanted to share a few of our tips for easy and safe outdoor grilling:

1. Teach the kids to steer clear of the grill at all times, as they can't tell by looking whether it's hot.

2. Before turning it on, clean the grill with a scraper, and coat the grates with nonstick cooking spray or a little cooking oil, so food doesn't stick to them.

3. Stock extra-long matches to light the burner or the coals, so you don't burn your fingertips.

4. Preheat gas grills for about ten minutes on high with the cover closed, and preheat charcoal grills for thirty minutes. Grills should be very hot before you start to cook.

5. Both gas and charcoal grills cook more efficiently with the cover closed.

6. Many vegetables, thinner fish fillets, and even slices of bread can be cooked on the grill, as long as the pieces are big enough not to fall through the grates or you use some aluminum foil and/or a vegetable and fish tray to hold them.

7. To keep meat juicy, don't press down on it with a spatula while it's cooking.

8. Be sure not to put cooked meat back on the dish the uncooked meat was on, with its raw juices and potentially harmful bacteria.

9. Scrape and turn off the grill as soon as you're through cooking, before you forget.

10. Finally, Andrew discovered that it's often easier and more relaxing to grill in advance for a crowd and either serve the food cold or heat it up in the oven or on the grill when guests are ready to eat. This way we can actually enjoy the company, rather than sweat over the grill.

Our kids gobbled up these delicious patties suggested by our friend Mark Spindel. They're so versatile—the basic recipe is delicious, or you can give them an Indian flavor by adding curry powder or an Asian flavor by adding a little ginger and soy or teriyaki sauce. Serve them with Baked French Fries (p. 300) and ketchup for dipping.

sautéed mini chicken burgers with herbs

Prep + Cook = 20 minutes

8 servings

Nutritional Information per serving:

Calories 220, Total Fat 4.5g, 7%, Saturated Fat 1g, 6%, Cholesterol 95mg, 32%, Sodium 140mg, 6%, Total Carbohydrate 6g, 2%, Dietary Fiber 0g, 0%, Protein 36g, Sugar 0g

2 pounds ground chicken

1 ½ teaspoons minced garlic (about 3 cloves)

½ cup minced fresh parsley (or more to taste)

½ teaspoon dried oregano

½ teaspoon dried basil

2 tablespoons lemon juice (about ½ lemon)

salt and pepper to taste

½ cup bread crumbs

1–2 tablespoons olive oil

In a large bowl, combine the chicken, garlic, parsley, oregano, basil, and lemon juice. Season the mixture with salt and pepper.

Put the bread crumbs on a small shallow dish.

Form the chicken mixture into small patties, about 2 inches in diameter. Press the patties into the bread crumbs to coat each side and set them aside on a plate. You should have about 15 patties.

In a large nonstick skillet, heat the oil over medium heat. Cook the patties until they are browned on each side and cooked through, about 10 minutes total. If they are cooking too fast on the outside, reduce the heat and cover the pan for a few minutes. Serve them hot.

Scramble recipe contributor Sherry Ettleson says these tacos remind her of Mexican border towns, where you can get a variety of fresh fish tacos any time of day or night at a taqueria stand. We served this as make-your-own-tacos, putting all the fixings in bowls on the table and letting people fill their taco shells or tortillas their own way. Serve them with your favorite taco garnishes, such as guacamole, shredded Cheddar cheese, sour cream, or chopped lettuce. This fish tastes so good, it is great on its own over rice. Serve the tacos with yellow rice.

tacos del mar

Prep + Cook =
30 minutes

8 servings

Nutritional
Information per
serving:

Calories 150, Total
Fat 5g, 8%, Saturated
Fat 0.5g, 3%, Choles-
terol 25mg, 8%,
Sodium 200mg, 8%,
Total Carbohydrate
14g, 5%, Dietary
Fiber 2g, 8%, Protein
12g, Sugar 3g

1 tablespoon olive oil

1 red bell pepper, diced

1 small onion, diced

1 teaspoon minced garlic (about 2 cloves)

1 can (15 ounces) diced tomatoes with their liquid

½ teaspoon cumin

1 pound cod fillets (or other white fish fillets)

3–4 tablespoons lime juice (about 1 lime)

⅛ teaspoon salt (or more to taste)

⅛ teaspoon pepper

8 taco shells or soft-taco-sized flour or whole wheat tortillas

In a large heavy skillet, heat the oil over medium heat. Add the peppers, onions, and garlic and sauté them until they are tender and just starting to brown, 5 to 8 minutes.

Stir in the tomatoes with their liquid and the cumin and bring the mixture to a low boil. Place the fish on top of the mixture, sprinkle it with the lime juice, and season it with the salt and pepper.

Cover, reducing the heat enough to keep the sauce simmering, and cook it for 15 minutes, until the fish is opaque and flakes very easily. Pull the fish apart into chunks and serve, using a slotted spoon, so the tacos don't get too drippy.

TIP: If you plan to make the Lentil Stew with Honey-Ginger Yogurt tomorrow night, get a head start tonight by soaking the lentils.

This is a great stew with an Indian flair. If you soak the lentils the night before making this stew, they will cook in about half the time. Serve the stew with steamed asparagus, which also tastes good topped with the yogurt sauce.

lentil stew with honey-ginger yogurt

Prep (10 minutes) +
Cook (40 minutes)

8 servings

Nutritional
Information per
serving:

Calories 290, Total
Fat 8g, 13%, Saturated Fat 1.5g, 7%,
Cholesterol 5mg, 1%,
Sodium 340mg, 14%,
Total Carbohydrate
40g, 13%, Dietary
Fiber 16g, 66%, Protein 17g, Sugar 12g

2 tablespoons olive oil

1 large onion, chopped

2 teaspoons chopped garlic (about 4 cloves)

1½ tablespoons curry powder

4 cups chicken or vegetable broth (or two 15-ounces cans + 3 ounces water)

2 cups dried lentils, rinsed

1 can (15 ounces) diced tomatoes

1½ cups nonfat or low-fat plain yogurt

1½ tablespoons minced fresh ginger or 1 teaspoon ground ginger

1 tablespoon honey

1 package pita bread

In a heavy saucepan, heat the oil over medium-high heat. Add the onion and sauté it until it starts to brown, about 5 minutes. Add the garlic and curry powder and cook it, stirring, for 1 more minute. Add the broth and lentils and bring the liquid to a boil. Reduce the heat to medium-low, cover the pan, and simmer the lentils until they are tender and most of the liquid is absorbed, about 40 minutes (or about 20 minutes if the lentils have soaked overnight). Stir in the tomatoes.

While the lentils are cooking, combine the yogurt, ginger, and honey in a medium bowl. Wrap the pita bread in aluminum foil and warm it in the oven at 300 degrees for 10 to 15 minutes. Serve the lentils topped with the yogurt sauce, using the pita to scoop up the mixture.

ginger at the ready Have fresh ginger handy anytime you may need it for grating and chopping by simply slipping it into a freezer bag and into your freezer. When fresh grated or chopped ginger is called for in a recipe, just peel the outside skin with a knife or carrot peeler and grate or chop it at will. Refreeze the remaining section of ginger immediately.

I love paella but until this one I had not found a recipe that's quick and easy enough for a weeknight dinner. This version uses couscous instead of rice, greatly reducing the cooking time. You can stir in cooked sausage, shrimp, tofu, or chicken instead of the bacon, but I like the combination of these flavors. Serve it with a spinach salad with diced oranges and slivered red onion.

quick couscous paella with crumbled bacon

Prep + Cook = 20 minutes

6 servings

Nutritional Information per serving:

Calories 220, Total Fat 6g, 9%, Saturated Fat 1g, 4%, Cholesterol 0mg, 0%, Sodium 260mg, 11%, Total Carbohydrate 32g, 11%, Dietary Fiber 4g, 17%, Protein 8g, Sugar 4g

6 strips bacon (turkey, pork, or vegetarian)

2 tablespoons olive oil

1 medium red bell pepper, diced

4 scallions, chopped

1 teaspoon minced garlic (about 2 cloves)

1 teaspoon curry powder

¼ teaspoon dry mustard

2 cups hot vegetable or chicken broth (or use one 15-ounce can broth plus 1½ ounces water)

1 cup frozen peas

1 cup uncooked plain couscous

Cook the bacon according to the package directions until it is very crisp. Chop or break the cooked bacon into small pieces and set it aside.

Meanwhile, in a medium stockpot with a tight-fitting lid, heat the oil over medium heat. Add the peppers, scallions, garlic, curry powder, and dry mustard and sauté them for about 5 minutes, stirring the mixture occasionally, until the peppers are softened.

Stir in the heated broth and bring it to a low boil. Stir in the peas and couscous. Cover the pan, remove it from heat, and let it stand for 5 minutes until the couscous has absorbed the broth.

Stir in the bacon just before you serve the paella.

This quiche has become a favorite of my friend Stephanie Lowet. The yogurt makes for light and healthy dinnertime or brunch fare. Serve it with corn bread and a green salad with thinly sliced red onion, chopped dates, and grated Parmesan cheese.

fresh tomato and basil quiche

Prep (20 minutes)+
Cook (45 minutes)

8 servings

Nutritional
Information per
serving:

Calories 240, Total
Fat 14g, 22%, Satu-
rated Fat 4.5g, 23%,
Cholesterol 165mg,
55%, Sodium 380mg,
16%, Total Carbohy-
drate 16g, 5%, Di-
etary Fiber 1g, 4%,
Protein 11g, Sugar 4g

1 (9-inch) unbaked pie crust, completely thawed if frozen

6 eggs

1 cup plain nonfat or low fat yogurt

½ cup fresh chopped basil, divided

½ teaspoon salt

½ teaspoon pepper

½ cup shredded Swiss cheese (or use Parmesan or mozzarella)

2–3 large fresh tomatoes, cut into ½ inch pieces (about 2 cups total)

2 tablespoons Parmesan cheese

Preheat the oven to 375 degrees. Press the crust into a tart or pie pan and trim the excess from the edges. Bake it for 10 to 15 minutes until very lightly browned. Remove it from the oven.

In a large bowl, whisk together the eggs, yogurt, ¼ cup of the basil, the salt, pepper and Swiss cheese. Pour the mixture into the pie shell. Top it evenly with the tomatoes and remaining basil. Sprinkle the Parmesan cheese on top and bake it for 40 to 45 minutes or until firm and lightly browned.

Cut it into wedges and serve it warm.

This easy, hearty pasta recipe is a good one to experiment with and adapt to your own taste—try adding corn kernels or olives, for example. A flavorful sausage is the key to making this a great dish. Serve it with fresh bread and corn.

penne with smoked sausage and peppers

Prep + Cook =
25 minutes

8 servings

Nutritional
Information per
serving:

Calories 320, Total
Fat 6g, 9%, Saturated
Fat 1.5g, 8%, Choles-
terol 15mg, 5%,
Sodium 490mg, 20%,
Total Carbohydrate
51g, 17%, Dietary
Fiber 3g, 12%, Pro-
tein 14g, Sugar 7g

1 package (16 ounces) penne or other short pasta

1½ tablespoons olive oil

½ large yellow onion, sliced into half rings

2 green bell peppers, sliced into half rings

½ teaspoon garlic powder or 1 teaspoon minced garlic (about 2 cloves)

8–10 ounces precooked smoked chicken or turkey sausage,
    sliced and halved or quartered

3 cans (15 ounces each) Italian-style diced tomatoes

grated Parmesan cheese to taste

Cook the pasta according to the package directions and drain it.

Meanwhile, in a large frying pan, heat the oil over medium heat. Add the onions, peppers, and garlic and sauté them until they are softened, 5 to 8 minutes. Add the sausage and sauté the mixture for 3 to 5 more minutes. Add the tomatoes and simmer the sauce for 10 to 15 minutes.

In a large metal bowl, mix the pasta with the sauce. Top it with Parmesan cheese.

shape up The pasta shapes in these recipes are merely suggestions and can usually be swapped for your favorites. Little ones in your house may enjoy choosing the shape of the evening's pasta.

My cooking assistants, ages eight and six, tested ten-year-old Drew Thieme's chicken and gave it four stars (out of four) for ease of preparation and taste. If you prefer, bread the chicken instead with smashed Cheerios, Corn Flakes, Chex, or your favorite unsweetened cereal. Serve with Creamy Mashed Potatoes (see p. 300) and ketchup.

drew's crunchy crispix-coated chicken cutlets

Prep + Cook =
20 minutes

4 servings

Nutritional Information per serving:

Calories 250, Total Fat 8g, 12%, Saturated Fat 1g, 5%, Cholesterol 65mg, 22%, Sodium 210mg, 9%, Total Carbohydrate 14g, 5%, Dietary Fiber 0g, 0%, Protein 28g, Sugar 3g

2 cups Crispix cereal, crushed

½ cup nonfat buttermilk, or use 1 large beaten egg

1–1½ pound thinly sliced chicken cutlets, or boneless, skinless breasts, pounded thin

1 teaspoon Old Bay seasoning or salt and black pepper

2 tablespoons canola oil

Put the cereal in a resealable bag and smash it with a mallet until it is crushed, but not pulverized.

Put the cereal in a shallow bowl. Put the buttermilk (or egg) in a separate shallow bowl. Coat each chicken cutlet in the buttermilk, then the cereal, and put it aside on a plate. Season the breaded chicken with Old Bay or salt and pepper.

In a large nonstick skillet, heat the oil over medium heat. Cook the chicken until it is browned and cooked through, turning it once, about 3 to 4 minutes per side for thin cutlets.

the best oils for health The best oils to use in cooking are the ones that have the least amount of saturated fats: canola oil, olive oil, peanut oil, safflower oil, sesame oil, sunflower oil, and avocado oil.

This recipe for crustless spinach pie was suggested by Claudia Ades. It is simple, elegant, and delicious and tastes great the next day, too. Serve it with vanilla yogurt, pineapple chunks, and whole-grain bread.

crustless spinach pie

Prep (20 minutes) + Cook (30–35 minutes)

8 servings

Nutritional Information per serving:
Calories 130, Total Fat 7g, 11%, Saturated Fat 3.5g, 19%, Cholesterol 120mg, 41%, Sodium 240mg, 10%, Total Carbohydrate 5g, 2%, Dietary Fiber 1g, 5%, Protein 11g, Sugar 1g

- 1 package (10 ounces) frozen chopped spinach
- 4 eggs
- 1 cup part-skim ricotta cheese
- ¾ cup grated Parmesan cheese
- ¾ cup chopped portobello or conventional mushrooms
- ½ cup finely chopped scallions (about 4 large scallions)
- ½ teaspoon dried oregano
- ½ teaspoon dried basil or 1 tablespoon fresh
- salt and pepper to taste

Preheat the oven to 375 degrees. Spray a 9-inch pie pan with nonstick cooking spray.

Defrost the spinach and drain it thoroughly, pressing it to squeeze out excess water.

In a large bowl, combine all the ingredients. Pour the mixture into the pie pan.

Bake the pie for 30 to 35 minutes until it is lightly browned and set. Let it cool slightly before cutting and serving it.

I first enjoyed this soup in the kitchen of my friend Nachama Wilker, who is a wonderful cook. I've modified it to meet the time constraints of the harried chef. It's still delicious and provides great leftovers. Save time by adding the ingredients as you go and chopping the next addition while the soup simmers. Serve it with fresh bread and grapes.

spicy sausage and kale soup

Prep + Cook =
30 minutes

12 servings

Nutritional
Information per
serving:

Calories 170, Total
Fat 4.5g, 7%, Saturated Fat 1g, 5%,
Cholesterol 20mg,
7%, Sodium 470mg,
20%, Total Carbohydrate 0g, 0%, Dietary
Fiber 23g, 8%, Protein 11g, Sugar 2g

1 pound spicy sausage (use mild sausage if your family prefers it, or flavored meatless sausage)

1 large yellow onion, quartered and thinly sliced

1 tablespoon minced garlic (6 cloves)

2 boxes (32 ounces each) chicken broth

4 cups water

12 ounces kale, chopped

6 red potatoes, halved and thinly sliced

2 cans kidney or pinto beans with their liquid

Remove the casings from the sausage (or dice precooked sausage) and cook the sausage over medium heat in a large stockpot for a few minutes until it is slightly browned.

Add the onion and garlic and cook the mixture, stirring it occasionally, for about 5 minutes.

One at a time, add the chicken broth, water, kale, and potatoes, covering the pan and bringing it to a simmer between additions.

Cover the soup and simmer it for 10 more minutes.

Add the beans with their liquid and stir the soup until it is heated through.

This pretty dish is mild enough for the kids. The white fish against the contrast of the green pesto sauce provides a touch of style. Serve it with bulgur wheat and steamed carrots.

baked halibut with pesto

Prep + Cook =
30 minutes

6 servings

Nutritional
Information per
serving:

Calories 250, Total
Fat 12g, 18%, Satu-
rated Fat 4g, 21%,
Cholesterol 60mg,
21%, Sodium 160mg,
7%, Total Carbohy-
drate 1g, 0%, Dietary
Fiber 0g, 0%, Protein
33g, Sugar 0g

2 pounds halibut fillets (with or without skin) or other thick white fish

2 tablespoons butter

¼ cup pesto sauce (store-bought or homemade: see recipe below)

Preheat the oven to 400 degrees.

Put the butter in a casserole dish and place it in the oven until it is melted. Remove the dish from the oven, add the fish, and coat both sides of the fillets with butter by turning them once. Brush the pesto sauce on top.

Bake the fish for 15 to 20 minutes, depending on its thickness, until it is just cooked through.

presto pesto To make delicious fresh pesto: In a blender or food processor, combine 2 cups tightly packed fresh basil leaves, 2 chopped garlic cloves, 2 tablespoons pine nuts, $1/2$ cup olive oil, and $1/2$ cup grated Parmesan cheese. Process or blend the mixture until it is coarsely chopped.

My friend Kirsten Thistle gave me this recipe for a great twist on lasagna. Egg roll wrappers, found in the refrigerated section of many grocery stores, are even easier to use and more tender than no-bake lasagna noodles. Serve it with Coleslaw (see p. 298).

chinese lasagna

Prep (20 minutes) +
Cook (30 minutes)

8 servings

Nutritional
Information per
serving:

Calories 510, Total
Fat 19g, 29%, Saturated Fat 7g, 35%,
Cholesterol 100mg,
33%, Sodium 1100mg,
46%, Total Carbohydrate 48g, 16%, Dietary Fiber 4g, 16%,
Protein 36g, Sugar
10g

1 pound ground beef or turkey (or vegetarian ground "meat")

16 ounces part-skim or nonfat ricotta cheese

1 egg, lightly beaten

1 package (10 ounces) frozen chopped spinach

2 tablespoons grated Parmesan cheese

4 cups red pasta sauce (or use a 26-ounce jar mixed with
        6 ounces tomato sauce or water)

1 package (16 ounces) egg roll wrappers

2 cups shredded mozzarella cheese

Preheat the oven to 375 degrees.

In a nonstick skillet, brown the meat over medium heat until it is no longer pink, about 5 minutes.

In a medium bowl, mix the ricotta, egg, spinach, and Parmesan cheese together.

In a 9 × 13-inch baking dish, layer the lasagna in the following order: (1) one cup of red sauce; (2) a layer of egg roll wrappers (to cover the sauce); (3) all of the meat; (4) a third of the mozzarella cheese; (5) one cup of red sauce; (6) another layer of egg roll wrappers; (7) all of the ricotta mixture; (8) a third of the mozzarella; (9) one cup of red sauce; (10) the final layer of egg roll wrappers; (11) the final cup of red sauce; (12) the final third of the mozzarella.

Bake the lasagna, uncovered, for 25 to 30 minutes until it is browned and bubbly.

TIP: The lasagna will be easier to cut if you allow it to cool for 10 minutes before taking a knife to it.

My friend Lisa Flaxman taught me this simple, tasty method for preparing salmon. It's great for kids and popular with adults, too. Serve it with mini corn muffins and peas.

honey-glazed salmon

Prep + Cook =
25 minutes

4 servings

Nutritional
Information per
serving:

Calories 480, Total
Fat 24g, 37%, Saturated Fat 7g, 34%,
Cholesterol 165 mg,
54%, Sodium 170 mg,
7%, Total Carbohydrate 17g, 6%, Dietary Fiber 0g, 0%,
Protein 47g, Sugar
17g

2 tablespoons butter

¼ cup honey

1½–2 pounds salmon fillet, cut in 4 servings

Preheat the oven to 350 degrees. Spray a 9 × 13-inch baking dish with nonstick cooking spray or line a cookie sheet with foil.

In a small saucepan, melt the butter in the honey over low heat. With a pastry brush, generously paint the butter-honey mixture over the fish.

Place the salmon in the baking dish or on the cookie sheet skin side down. Bake it for 15 to 20 minutes until it flakes easily in the thickest part and is cooked through. Do not flip the fish while cooking it.

This is a rich and hearty stew that's quick to prepare. Serve it over couscous with pita bread. If you suspect that your kids won't eat this stew all mixed together, leave aside some chickpeas and spinach for them to eat separately (you can even spoon a little sauce over their couscous).

mediterranean vegetable stew

Prep + Cook = 30 minutes

8 servings

Nutritional Information per serving:

Calories 220, Total Fat 9g, 13%, Saturated Fat 1g, 6%, Cholesterol 0 mg, 0%, Sodium 390 mg, 16%, Total Carbohydrate 29g, 10%, Dietary Fiber 7g, 29%, Protein 7g, Sugar 9g

- ¼ cup olive oil
- 1 red onion, chopped
- 1 medium eggplant, peeled and chopped into 1-inch cubes
- 1 can (15 ounces) chickpeas (garbanzo beans), drained
- 1 teaspoon minced garlic (about 2 cloves)
- 1 teaspoon cumin
- 15 fresh mint leaves, coarsely chopped (or use basil)
- ½ teaspoon kosher salt
- 1 can (28 ounces) crushed tomatoes
- 2–3 cups baby spinach

In a large skillet or saucepan, heat the oil over medium heat. Add the onion and sauté it until it is soft, about 5 minutes.

Add the eggplant and sauté the vegetables for 5 more minutes, stirring them frequently so the eggplant does not stick to the bottom of the pan.

Add the chickpeas, garlic, cumin, mint, and salt and sauté the mixture for 1 more minute. Add the tomatoes. Bring the stew to a boil and simmer it gently for about 15 minutes, until the eggplant is very tender. Add the spinach and stir the stew until the spinach is wilted, about 2 minutes.

No, not that Big Guy—this is the fabulous chicken recipe of my father-in-law, Mark Goldfarb. He makes it slightly different each time, but I was able to pin down some exact measurements when I re-created it at home. This can be prepared up to a day ahead and baked before dinner. Serve it with a Japanese salad (see p. 298) and a loaf of bread.

the big guy's baked chicken

Prep (15 minutes) +
Cook (40 minutes)

6 servings

Nutritional
Information per
serving:

Calories 260, Total
Fat 8g, 13%, Satu-
rated Fat 2.5g, 12%,
Cholesterol 100 mg,
34%, Sodium 1440
mg, 60%, Total Car-
bohydrate 9g, 3%, Di-
etary Fiber <1g, 2%,
Protein 36g, Sugar 7g

- **1 whole chicken, cut up (add extra pieces for bigger families)**
- **½ cup soy sauce**
- **¼ cup white wine**
- **2 tablespoons honey**
- **1 teaspoon chopped garlic (about 2 cloves)**
- **¼ teaspoon ginger powder or 1 teaspoon fresh grated ginger**
- **1 small onion, diced**
- **1 tomato, diced**

Preheat the oven to 350 degrees. Line a deep baking pan with heavy-duty foil. Place the chicken skin side down in the pan.

In a large measuring cup, mix together the soy sauce, wine, honey, garlic, and ginger. Pour the sauce over the chicken and flip the chicken a couple of times to coat it with the sauce. Sprinkle the onion and tomato over the chicken.

Bake the chicken, uncovered, for 40 minutes. Heat the broiler and broil the chicken for about 5 minutes per side until both sides are nicely browned. Serve the chicken with the sauce spooned over it.

This is a great dish to bring to a picnic or party. Try variations of this pasta salad with your favorite spices, cheeses, and vegetables. If your family does not eat meat, you can leave the sausage out or use meatless sausage alternatives. Serve the salad with steamed broccoli tossed with grated Parmesan cheese.

zesty pasta salad

Prep + Cook =
25 minutes

8 servings

Nutritional
Information per
serving:

Calories 220, Total Fat 10g, 16%, Saturated Fat 4g, 20%, Cholesterol 25 mg, 8%, Sodium 410 mg, 17%, Total Carbohydrate 22g, 7%, Dietary Fiber 1g, 5%, Protein 11g, Sugar 4g

1 package (16 ounces) pasta spirals

8 ounces smoked turkey (or meatless) sausage, diced into ¼–½-inch pieces

2½ tablespoons olive oil

2½ tablespoons balsamic vinegar

½ teaspoon salt

⅛ teaspoon pepper

¼ teaspoon garlic powder

¼ teaspoon dried thyme or 1 teaspoon fresh

1 teaspoon dried basil or 1 tablespoon fresh

2 fresh tomatoes, seeded and diced

4 ounces sharp Cheddar cheese, cubed (about 1 cup)

Cook the pasta according to the package directions and drain it.

Meanwhile, in a medium nonstick skillet, brown the sausage over medium heat.

In a small bowl or measuring cup, make a dressing by whisking together the oil, the vinegar, and all of the spices.

In a large serving bowl, combine the pasta, sausage, tomatoes, and cheese.

Pour the dressing over the pasta mixture and toss them together. Serve the pasta salad warm or at room temperature.

This is probably the dish my husband requests most often, and it is also very popular with the Six O'Clock Scramble newsletter subscribers. I love making it, since it's so easy to prepare. Serve the enchiladas with chips, salsa, and guacamole.

turkey and spinach enchiladas

Prep + Cook =
30 minutes

8 servings

Nutritional
Information per
serving:

Calories 320, Total
Fat 14g, 22%, Saturated Fat 5g, 25%,
Cholesterol 70mg,
23%, Sodium 620mg,
26%, Total Carbohydrate 28g, 9%, Dietary Fiber 3g, 12%,
Protein 21g, Sugar 2g

1–1¼ pounds ground turkey (or use beef)

1 package (10 ounces) frozen chopped spinach

1 tablespoon chili powder

1 teaspoon cumin

1¼ cups mild salsa

1 cup shredded Cheddar cheese

8 soft-taco-sized flour tortillas

Preheat the oven to 350 degrees. Spray a 9 × 13-inch baking dish with nonstick cooking spray.

In a large nonstick skillet, brown the turkey over medium heat. While the meat is browning, thaw the spinach in the microwave or on the stove top and squeeze out the excess water. If the turkey is browned before the spinach is ready, remove it from the heat until you are ready to add the spinach, so it doesn't get overcooked.

Pour off any excess liquid from the turkey and add the spinach, chili powder, cumin, and salsa. Cook it until it is heated through. Remove it from the heat and stir in ¾ cup of the cheese.

Divide the mixture among the tortillas, spooning it down the center of each tortilla. Roll the tortillas and transfer them to the baking dish. Sprinkle the remaining cheese on top. Cover the dish with aluminum foil and bake the enchiladas until they are warmed through, about 15 minutes. Remove the foil for the last 5 minutes of baking.

This is a delicious and easy marinade for firm fish such as tuna or halibut. Since both types of fish are expensive, I save money by using only one pound of the fish, slicing it thinly, and serving it with filling side dishes. Serve it with rice pilaf and a green salad with diced Gouda cheese and apples, and a balsamic vinaigrette.

tuna with citrus sauce

Prep + Cook =
30 minutes

4 servings

Nutritional
Information per
serving:

Calories 130, Total
Fat 1.5g, 2%, Saturated Fat 0g, 0%,
Cholesterol 50mg,
17%, Sodium 300mg,
13%, Total Carbohydrate 1g, 0%, Dietary
Fiber 0g, 0%, Protein
27g, Sugar 0g

- ¼ cup soy sauce
- ¼ cup freshly squeezed orange juice (from 1 small orange)
- ¼ cup fresh lime juice (about 1 lime)
- 1 teaspoon sesame oil
- 2 tuna steaks (about ½ pound each)
- lime wedges for serving

In a measuring cup, whisk together the soy sauce, orange and lime juices, and sesame oil. Reserve about a quarter of this marinade in a small bowl for later.

Place the tuna steaks in a small flat dish, cover them with the marinade, and turn them to coat both sides. Set the tuna aside to marinate for 5 to 30 minutes.

Preheat the grill or place a medium nonstick skillet over medium-high heat. Transfer the tuna to the grill or skillet, discarding the marinade. Cook it for 2 minutes. Turn it and cook it to the desired degree of doneness, about 3 minutes for medium rare (our favorite) or up to 7 minutes for well done.

Transfer the tuna to a cutting board and slice it thinly. Serve it with the reserved sauce and wedges of lime.

TIP: While the fish marinates, make the rice pilaf and the salad.

Chicken Parmesan is always popular with both adults and kids. It's quick and filling with a side of egg noodles and steamed asparagus.

no-bake chicken parmesan

Prep + Cook = 20 minutes

6 servings

Nutritional Information per serving:

Calories 300, Total Fat 10g, 15%, Saturated Fat 3.5g, 18%, Cholesterol 130mg, 43%, Sodium 550mg, 23%, Total Carbohydrate 8g, 3%, Dietary Fiber 1g, 4%, Protein 43g, Sugar 4g

- 4–6 boneless, skinless chicken breast halves (2–2½ pounds)
- 2 eggs, beaten
- ½ cup bread crumbs
- 1 tablespoon olive oil
- 1½ cups red pasta sauce
- 1 cup shredded (or more to taste) or 8–10 slices mozzarella cheese

Pound the chicken breasts firmly with a mallet to make them uniform in thickness.

Put the beaten eggs and bread crumbs in separate shallow bowls. Dip the breasts in the egg, then in the bread crumbs, and set them aside on a plate.

In a large skillet over medium-high heat, sauté the breasts on each side in the oil until they are lightly browned and about three-quarters of the way cooked, approximately 4 minutes per side.

With a spoon, spread a generous layer of pasta sauce on top of the chicken breasts, followed by a layer of the sliced or shredded mozzarella cheese.

Cover the pan, turn the heat down to medium, and sauté the breasts until they are cooked through and the cheese is completely melted, about 5 minutes.

Though it may sound like a strange combination of ingredients, this West African–inspired stew is so flavorful and colorful that it gets rave reviews from nearly all who try it. In fact, Lisa Flaxman and I named our first cookbook after it. Serve the stew over couscous with slices of mango on the side.

peanut butter stew (and couscous, too!)

Prep (25 minutes) + Cook (20 minutes)

8 servings

Nutritional Information per serving:

Calories 210, Total Fat 10g, 15%, Saturated Fat 1.5g, 8%, Cholesterol 0mg, 0%, Sodium 610mg, 25%, Total Carbohydrate 25g, 8%, Dietary Fiber 3g, 12%, Protein 7g, Sugar 12g

- 2 tablespoons peanut oil
- 1 large onion, chopped
- 1 teaspoon minced garlic (about 2 cloves)
- 2 cups chopped cabbage (about ¼ green cabbage)
- 1 large sweet potato, scrubbed and cut into ½-inch cubes
- 3 cups tomato juice
- 1 cup apricot or apple juice
- 1 teaspoon salt
- 1 teaspoon grated, peeled fresh ginger root or ¼ teaspoon ground ginger
- 2 chopped tomatoes or 1 can (15 ounces) diced tomatoes, drained (you can use some of the sauce from the tomatoes in place of the tomato juice above)
- ½ cup smooth natural peanut butter

In a large pot, heat the oil over medium-high heat. Add the onions and sauté them until they are softened, about 5 minutes. Add the garlic, cabbage, and sweet potatoes and sauté the mixture, covered, for 5 minutes.

Add the juices, salt, ginger, and tomatoes. Bring the mixture to a boil, reduce the heat, cover the pan, and simmer the stew for 15 to 20 minutes until the potatoes are tender.

Add the peanut butter, stirring it in thoroughly so it doesn't clump. Simmer the stew gently until you're ready to serve it.

sweet potatoes or plain? Everybody knows that the sweet potato is sweeter than its plain cousin, but did you know that it contains more than twice the fiber and more beta-carotene? No matter which flavor you prefer, you are getting almost no fats and lots of nutrients with both potatoes.

This pasta, from Sue Brodsky Burnett, is quick to prepare and appeals to the taste buds of adults and kids alike. Serve it with a loaf of bread and Ambrosia Fruit Salad (see p. 298).

ravioli with creamy tomato sauce

Prep + Cook =
15 minutes

8 servings

Nutritional
Information per
serving:

Calories 310, Total
Fat 14g, 21%, Satu-
rated Fat 5g, 25%,
Cholesterol 30mg,
11%, Sodium 800mg,
33%, Total Carbohy-
drate 35g, 12%, Di-
etary Fiber 3g, 13%,
Protein 13g, Sugar 6g

- 2 packages (9 ounces each) reduced-fat cheese ravioli
- 1 tablespoon olive oil
- 1½ teaspoons minced garlic (about 3 garlic cloves)
- 3 cans (15 ounces each) diced tomatoes with their liquid
- 1 teaspoon sugar
- ½ cup dry white wine
- ½ cup half and half
- 10 fresh basil leaves
- ½ cup grated Parmesan cheese
- salt and pepper to taste

Cook the pasta according to the package directions and drain it.

Meanwhile in a large skillet, heat the oil over medium-high heat. Add the garlic and sauté it for 30 seconds, being careful not to let it burn.

Add the tomatoes with their juice, the sugar, and the wine and simmer the sauce for about 5 minutes.

Reduce the heat to medium-low, add the half and half and basil, and cook the sauce for about 2 more minutes, stirring often.

Add the Parmesan cheese and season the sauce with salt and pepper. Stir in the ravioli and serve it hot.

summer

week 1

Barbecue Chicken

Fusilli with Fresh Tomato Sauce

Pecan-Crusted Trout with Orange-Rosemary Sauce

Hot Meatball Subs

California Taco Salad

week 2

Orange Salmon

Lemon-Herbed Chicken Tenderloins

Pita Stuffed with Greek Salad

Solomon's Tortellini with Sneaky Tomato Sauce

Curry-Lime Pork Tenderloin

week 3

Thai Basil Chicken

Tuna Melts with Sliced Avocado and Tomato

Ravioli Soup with Grated Zucchini

Spinach and Feta Frittata

Holy Guacamole Tostadas

week 4

Grilled Sausage Kabobs with Summer Vegetables

Lime-Garlic Shrimp with Black Bean and Corn Salad

Rigatoni with Asparagus and Lemon

Celia's Honey Chicken

Japanese Eggplant and Green Beans in Garlic Sauce

week 5

Grilled Lime Chicken with Avocado Salsa

Smoked Salmon and Dill Sandwiches

Ziti with Tomato and Artichoke Sauce

Grilled Baby Back Ribs with Pineapple Glaze

Red Snapper V8

week 6

Grilled Steak with Garlic and Parmesan Crust

Pan-Fried Fish Sticks

Indian Spinach Curry (Saag Paneer)

Penne with Presto Pesto

Crispy Baked Drumsticks

week 7

Chicken Enchilada Casserole

Salad Licoise

Popeye Pie

Crunchy Rainbow Wraps

Chinese Barbecue Noodles

week 8

Baked Apricot Chicken

Tortellini Tossed with Fresh Mozzarella

Thai Rice Pot

Ginger-Soy Flank Steak

Warm Chicken Salad with Mixed Greens

week 9

Asian Turkey Burgers

Farfalle with Feta, Pine Nuts, and Tomatoes

Quick Tilapia with Lemon, Garlic, and Capers

Light Summer Minestrone

Peanut Beef (or Chicken or Tofu)

week 10

Spaghetti with Meat Sauce

Baked Zucchini Pie

Grilled Salmon with Herb Pesto

Creamy Tomato Soup

Terrific Tortilla Tower

week 11

Baked Macaroni and Cheese

Fiesta Chicken and Rice

Boca Burgers with Mushrooms, Onions, and Cheddar

Grilled Trout with Garlic and Rosemary

Veggie Chili

week 12

Make-Your-Own Tacos

Gnocchi with Artichokes and Sundried Tomatoes

Tuna Steaks in Pineapple-Ginger Marinade

Indonesian Curry Rice Salad

Frittata with Onions, Peppers, and Zucchini

week 13

Grilled Steak with Rosemary and Dijon

Barbecue Chicken with Yogurt Marinade

Broiled Zucchini Pasta with Cheese

Portobello Mushroom Pizzas

Mango-Salsa Shrimp or Chicken

This is a very popular dish among Scramble subscribers. The home-made sauce is such a breeze that you may never want to buy bottled sauce again! You can also use this sauce over grilled boneless chicken breasts, pork chops, fish, or grilled tofu and vegetables. If you don't want to turn on the grill, you can cook the chicken in the broiler instead. Serve it with colesaw (see p. 298) and watermelon wedges.

barbecue chicken

Prep (10 minutes) +
Cook (30 minutes)

8 servings

Nutritional
Information per
serving:

Calories 370, Total
Fat 15g, 24%, Satu-
rated Fat 4.5g, 22%,
Cholesterol 120 mg,
40%, Sodium 450 mg,
19%, Total Carbohy-
drate 14g, 5%, Di-
etary Fiber 0g, 0%,
Protein 42g, Sugar 9g

1 cup ketchup

¼ cup Worcestershire sauce

¼ cup red wine vinegar

¼ cup plus 1 tablespoon packed or granulated brown sugar

½ teaspoon garlic powder

2 teaspoons lemon juice (about ¼ lemon)

1 whole chicken, cut up (or use 10–12 drumsticks and thighs,
    if your family prefers them)

Preheat the grill (or broiler) to medium-high heat.

In a small saucepan over medium heat, combine the ketchup, Worcestershire sauce, vinegar, brown sugar, and garlic powder. Bring it to a low boil and simmer it until it is slightly thickened, about 5 minutes. Add the lemon juice and stir it until it is heated through. Remove it from the heat. Set aside half the sauce to serve on the side with the chicken.

Cook the chicken skin side down on the preheated grill, with the lid open, for about 2 minutes. Flip the chicken, brush it with the sauce, and cook it for about 10 minutes on that side. Flip the chicken, brush it with more sauce, and cook it for about 10 more minutes. Flip the chicken several more times, brushing it with more sauce each time, until it starts to get dark and crispy and is thoroughly coated with sauce. (Don't reuse this sauce for cooked chicken without bringing it to a boil first, as it may now have bacteria from the raw chicken.)

Check to make sure the breasts are cooked through before removing all the chicken from the grill. It takes about 30 minutes for all the chicken to be fully cooked. Serve it hot or cold with the reserved sauce.

This is a wonderful dish to highlight those juicy summer tomatoes. Serve it with corn on the cob.

fusilli with fresh tomato sauce

Prep + Cook = 20 minutes

8 servings

Nutritional Information per serving:

Calories 360, Total Fat 15g, 23%, Saturated Fat 2.5g, 13%, Cholesterol 0mg, 0%, Sodium 260mg, 11%, Total Carbohydrate 3g, 12%, Dietary Fiber 3g, 12%, Protein 9g, Sugar 4g

1 package (16 ounces) fusilli or other pasta

½ cup olive oil

¾ teaspoon salt

20 leaves fresh basil, chopped

2 pounds plum or Roma tomatoes, chopped

grated Parmesan cheese to taste

pepper to taste

Cook the pasta according to the package directions.

Meanwhile, in a large bowl, mix the tomatoes, oil, salt, and basil. Smash the tomatoes in the oil with a fork or potato masher and let the mixture stand.

When the pasta is cooked, drain it well and toss it with the tomato mixture. Top it with Parmesan cheese and pepper to taste.

This dish, from Shelley Schonberger, is wonderfully tasty and impressive for company, and you won't believe how easy it is to make. The recipe also works wonderfully with pounded boneless chicken breasts. Serve it with quinoa or rice and steamed asparagus.

pecan-crusted trout with orange-rosemary sauce

Prep + Cook = 20 minutes

4 servings

Nutritional Information per serving:

Calories 340, Total Fat 22g, 34%, Saturated Fat 8g, 39%, Cholesterol 100mg, 34%, Sodium 210mg, 9%, Total Carbohydrate 7g, 2%, Dietary Fiber 1g, 4%, Protein 28g, Sugar 5g

- 2 whole trout, boned and heads removed (have the fish market do this)
- ½ cup pecans
- 1 teaspoon flour
- ½ teaspoon salt
- 1 egg white, slightly beaten
- ¾ cup orange juice
- 1 teaspoon chopped rosemary
- 3 tablespoons butter

Wash the trout and pat it dry with paper towels. In a food processor, finely grind the pecans with the flour and salt. (If you do not have a food processor or don't want to dust it off, use a mallet to pulverize the nuts in a plastic bag, then shake them thoroughly with flour and salt.)

Brush the beaten egg white on the flesh side of the trout. Coat the trout by sprinkling the nut mixture onto the fish and pressing it firmly. (You can leave some of the fish without nuts if you don't think the kids will be that adventurous.)

In a small saucepan, bring the orange juice and rosemary to a boil over medium-high heat. Reduce the heat to medium and simmer the sauce for a few minutes until it is slightly reduced. Add 2 tablespoons of the butter and let them melt. Reduce the heat to low.

Meanwhile, in a large nonstick skillet, heat the remaining 1 tablespoon of the butter over medium-high heat. Add the trout, pecan side down. Cook it until the pecans are slightly browned, about 6 minutes. Transfer the trout to plates (cut them in half down the middle, if desired), pecan side up, and drizzle them with the orange-rosemary sauce.

I was thrilled by how easy it was to make authentic-tasting meatball subs, and my whole family enjoyed these hot sandwiches in various forms. Celia picked out the meatballs and ate the bread, cheese, and sauce separately. Solomon had fun trying to fit the whole sandwich in his mouth. And Andrew was delighted to devour one of his favorite childhood meals. Serve the subs with Baked French Fries (see p. 300).

hot meatball subs

Prep + Cook =
30 minutes

6 servings

Nutritional Information per serving (regular meatballs):

Calories 520, Total Fat 26g, 40%, Saturated Fat 12g, 60%, Cholesterol 60mg, 20%, Sodium 1760mg, 73%, Total Carbohydrate 48g, 16%, Dietary Fiber 7g, 28%, Protein 24g, Sugar 10g

Nutritional Information per serving (vegetarian meatballs):

Calories 390, Total Fat 13g, 20%, Saturated Fat 5g, 25%, Cholesterol 15mg, 5%, Sodium 1570mg, 65%, Total Carbohydrate 50g, 17%, Dietary Fiber 8g, 32%, Protein 22g, Sugar 9g

1 tablespoon olive oil

1 large onion, halved and sliced into half rings

1 large red bell pepper, sliced into rings

1 jar (26 ounces) red pasta sauce or 2 cans (15 ounces each) tomato sauce

1 pound frozen cooked meatballs (meatless or meat), or make fresh meatballs (see the Tip below)

6 small (about 6 inches) oblong French bread sandwich rolls

4 ounces provolone or mozzarella cheese, sliced or shredded

Preheat the broiler. Line a baking tray with foil.

In a large heavy skillet, heat the oil over medium heat. Add the onion and pepper and cook them, stirring them occasionally, until they are browned and soft, about 15 to 20 minutes.

Meanwhile, in a medium saucepan, heat the sauce. Add the meatballs and simmer them for 10 to 15 minutes.

Carefully cut each sandwich roll in half, trying to avoid slicing all the way through so the halves remain attached. Put several cooked meatballs and some sauce inside each roll and top it with peppers, onions, and cheese.

Put the sandwiches on the baking tray, with the fillings facing up, and broil them for 2 to 3 minutes until the cheese is melted and the rolls are slightly browned. Serve them hot.

TIP: To make fresh meatballs, in a medium bowl, mix together 1 pound ground meat, 1 egg, ½ cup bread crumbs, 2 tablespoons ketchup, and ¼ teaspoon garlic powder. Form the mixture into 1-inch meatballs. In a large frying pan, heat 1 to 2 tablespoons olive oil over medium-high heat. Cook the meatballs, turning them frequently, until they are browned on all sides, 5 to 8 minutes.

This salad is a crunchy alternative to taco night. You can get creative with ingredients. Consider adding cilantro, pistachios, diced sweet onion or diced red bell peppers. If you really want to get fancy, serve the salad in a taco-shell bowl, which some supermarkets carry. For picky eaters, serve the ingredients separately. Serve the salad with additional chips and salsa or warm tortillas.

california taco salad

Prep + Cook =
20 minutes

8 servings

Nutritional
Information per
serving:

Calories 280, Total
Fat 10g, 16%, Satu-
rated Fat 3g, 15%,
Cholesterol 55mg,
19%, Sodium 210mg,
9%, Total Carbohy-
drate 24g, 8%, Di-
etary Fiber 7g, 28%,
Protein 25g, Sugar 7g

- 1 small head iceberg or romaine lettuce, chopped (about 6–8 cups total)
- 1 can (15 ounces) black or red beans, drained and rinsed
- ½ cup (or more to taste) shredded Cheddar cheese
- 1 avocado, diced (see p. 177)
- 2 tomatoes or 1 mango, diced
- ½ cup sliced black olives, drained
- ½ pound cooked ground chicken or beef, or vegetarian ground "meat" seasoned with salt and chili powder (optional)
- 1 tablespoon lime juice (about ¼ lime)
- ½ cup (or to taste) bottled vinaigrette dressing
- 1 cup crushed tortilla chips or corn kernels
- sour cream for serving (optional)
- salsa for serving (optional)

In a large bowl, mix together the lettuce, beans, cheese, avocado, tomatoes or mango, olives, and meat (optional). Sprinkle the salad with the lime juice and dressing and toss it thoroughly. Top it with crumbled chips or corn kernels and a dollop of sour cream and salsa (optional). Serve the salad immediately.

the freshest flavors at the farmers' market

Some people leap out of bed on summer weekends to beat the crowds to a yard sale. Others are inspired to go running or take a bike ride before it gets too hot. Only one thing rouses me from my stupor on Saturday mornings, and that's the lure of the farmers' market.

On summer mornings by 7:50 I've got my shoes on, my teeth brushed, and my bed head concealed under a baseball cap so I can be among the first (how do those few scoundrels beat me each week?) to pick out the juiciest peaches, plumpest blueberries, crispiest green beans, and other goodies from my favorite vendors at the farmers' market at the old train station in Kensington, Maryland, which opens at 8:00 A.M. My haste is not exaggerated—I almost missed the last pint of cherry tomatoes at 8:15 one Saturday. Now that's pressure!

The produce at my supermarket is good, but no store-bought produce can compete with fruit and vegetables that have been picked that morning or the night before at local farms. For me, there's also something wonderful about being surrounded by other early risers who plan their weekend mornings (and week's menus) around fresh summer produce. We chat with the farmers, exchange recipes, and pat slobbering dogs while we ourselves drool over the week's selections.

Many farmers' markets have expanded their offerings beyond fruit and vegetables. In our local market, we can also buy fresh cut flowers, organic herbs and vegetables, homemade soaps, gourmet olive oils, fresh baked breads (with generous samples), and even fish flown in that morning from Maine. In my former hometown of Santa Barbara, California, the farmers' market is vast, filling several downtown blocks with exotic fruits, flavored honeys, and street performers.

Check your local papers to see where and when the nearest farmers' market is, and consider working at least occasional visits into your grocery-shopping trips. Your kids might enjoy going, too. Your family will surely taste the difference that farm-fresh fruit and vegetables make, and it feels good to support local farmers.

You can spend a few minutes preparing this recipe in the morning, and then just pop it in the oven at dinnertime. Serve the salmon with rice and peas (you can mix them together).

orange salmon

Prep + Cook =
30 minutes

4 servings

Nutritional
Information per
serving:

Calories 330, Total
Fat 18g, 28%, Satu-
rated Fat 3.5g, 18%,
Cholesterol 100mg,
33%, Sodium 360mg,
15%, Total Carbohy-
drate 4g, 1%, Dietary
Fiber 0g, 0%, Protein
34g, Sugar 3g

- 1½ **pounds salmon fillet**
- ½ **cup orange juice (preferably fresh, about 1 orange)**
- 1 **tablespoon soy sauce**
- ¾ **teaspoon peeled and grated or minced ginger root or ¼ teaspoon ginger powder**

Place the salmon skin side down in an oven-safe dish with sides. Use a dish just big enough to allow the salmon to lie flat.

In a measuring cup, mix together the orange juice, soy sauce, and ginger. Pour the marinade over the salmon.

If time allows, marinate the salmon in the refrigerator for up to 12 hours.

Preheat the oven to 400 degrees.

Bake the fish for 20 minutes until it flakes easily with a fork. Do not flip the fish while it is cooking.

This delicate dish can also be made using chicken breasts, if your market doesn't carry tenderloins. If you use breasts, pound them to an even thickness and cook them slightly longer, until they are no longer pink on the inside. Serve the chicken with couscous and Green Beans with Pesto (see p. 298).

lemon-herbed chicken tenderloins

Prep + Cook = 10 minutes + Marinate

4 servings

Nutritional Information per serving:

Calories 300, Total Fat 13g, 20%, Saturated Fat 2.5g, 12%, Cholesterol 110 mg, 36%, Sodium 470 mg, 20%, Total Carbohydrate 3g, 1%, Dietary Fiber 1g, 2%, Protein 41g, Sugar 1g

- 1½ pounds chicken tenderloins
- 2–3 tablespoons lemon juice (about ½ lemon)
- ¼ cup Dijon mustard
- ½ teaspoon dried rosemary or 1 teaspoon fresh
- ½ teaspoon dried thyme or 1½ teaspoon fresh
- ½ teaspoon dried parsley or 1 tablespoon fresh
- ½ teaspoon dried basil or 1 tablespoon fresh
- 2 tablespoons olive oil

Place the tenderloins in a flat dish with sides. In a small bowl, combine all the remaining ingredients except the olive oil and pour the marinade over the tenderloins. Marinate the chicken for 30 minutes and up to 12 hours, covered, in the refrigerator.

In a large nonstick frying pan, heat the oil over medium heat. Add the tenderloins and sauté them for 3 minutes on each side until they are just cooked through. Remove them from the heat immediately so they remain tender.

My family loves this light summer meal. (Of course, the kids like everything separate rather than mixed together.) If you prefer to make a salad rather than sandwiches, use store-bought pita chips instead of pita bread, making sure to add them at the last minute so they stay crispy. Serve the salad with a bowl of Greek olives and hummus and extra pita or pita chips.

pita stuffed with greek salad

Prep = 20 minutes

6 servings

Nutritional Information per serving:

Calories 360, Total Fat 17g, 27%, Saturated Fat 5g, 27%, Cholesterol 20 mg, 7%, Sodium 950 mg, 40%, Total Carbohydrate 42g, 14%, Dietary Fiber 3g, 12%, Protein 11g, Sugar 5g

- 1 cucumber
- 3 tablespoons olive oil
- 3 tablespoons red wine vinegar
- ¼ teaspoon salt
- 10–15 fresh mint leaves, chopped
- ¼ cup pitted kalamata olives, halved
- 3 cups (loosely packed) thinly sliced romaine lettuce
- 2 cups diced tomatoes (2–3 tomatoes)
- 1 cup crumbled feta cheese (about 4 ounces)
- 6 round pitas, cut in half

Peel the cucumber, cut it in half lengthwise, and seed it (use a serrated spoon to scrape out the seeds). Cut the halves in half again lengthwise and dice them.

Whisk the oil, vinegar, salt, and mint in the bottom of a large salad bowl to blend them. Add the olives, lettuce, tomatoes, and cheese and toss the salad. Carefully open the pitas at the cut end, stuff them with the salad, and serve them.

Our son rarely makes dinner requests, but one night when he was seven, he asked for tortellini with red sauce. I wanted to indulge him, but I also wanted to take the opportunity to make the sauce extra healthy without making it too chunky (he would balk at anything much lumpier than bottled sauce). I managed to slip a good portion of carrots into the already healthy sauce by dicing them finely and simmering them well. The resulting sauce got a big thumbs-up from our whole family and an eleven-year-old neighbor. Since this is Solomon's special request, serve it with a loaf of bread and his favorite fruit, strawberries.

solomon's tortellini with sneaky tomato sauce

Prep + Cook = 30 minutes

8 servings

Nutritional Information per serving:

Calories 230, Total Fat 9g, 14%, Saturated Fat 2.5g, 13%, Cholesterol 85 mg, 28%, Sodium 620 mg, 26%, Total Carbohydrate 29g, 10%, Dietary Fiber 4g, 15%, Protein 10g, Sugar 6g

- 2 packages (9 ounces each) cheese tortellini (or any variety)
- 2 tablespoons olive oil
- 1 small yellow onion (preferably Vidalia or a sweet onion), finely diced
- 10 baby carrots, finely diced
- 2 teaspoons minced garlic (about 4 cloves)
- 1 can (28 ounces) crushed tomatoes
- 1 can (15 ounces) tomato sauce
- 1–2 tablespoons brown sugar (to taste)
- Parmesan cheese for serving

Cook the tortellini according to the package directions.

In a large skillet, heat the oil over medium heat. Add the onions, carrots, and garlic and sauté them until they are slightly softened, about 5 minutes. Add the tomatoes, tomato sauce, and brown sugar and simmer the sauce gently for about 15 minutes until the tortellini is cooked.

Stir the tortellini into the sauce or serve them separately. Top the pasta with Parmesan cheese at the table.

This terrific recipe comes from Scramble subscriber Janet Krolman of Boston, Massachusetts. Serve the pork with grilled yellow squash (see p. 299) and sliced tomatoes sprinkled with balsamic vinegar and salt and pepper.

curry-lime pork tenderloin

Prep (10 minutes) + Cook (20–25 minutes) + Marinate

4 servings

Nutritional Information per serving:

Calories 240, Total Fat 9g, 14%, Saturated Fat 2.5g, 13%, Cholesterol 110mg, 37%, Sodium 230mg, 10%, Total Carbohydrate 4g, 1%, Dietary Fiber 0g, 0%, Protein 36g, Sugar 2g

- 1 pork tenderloin or 2 halves (about 1½–2 pounds)
- ½ teaspoon grated lime zest
- 3 tablespoons fresh lime juice (about 1 lime)
- 2 tablespoons fresh cilantro
- 1½ tablespoons brown sugar
- 1½ tablespoons vegetable oil
- 2 teaspoons curry powder
- ¼ teaspoon salt
- ¼ teaspoon pepper

Lay the tenderloin in a flat dish with sides. Use a dish just long enough to hold the meat in a single layer.

Zest the lime, making sure to get only the green part of the rind and not the white part beneath it. In a small bowl, whisk together all the ingredients, lime zest through pepper. Brush or pour the mixture over the tenderloin and flip the tenderloin several times to coat it. Marinate it in the refrigerator, covered, for at least 30 minutes and up to 24 hours if time allows.

On a grill preheated to medium-high, cook the tenderloin for 20 to 25 minutes, turning it occasionally, until it is nicely browned on the outside and just a tiny bit pink in the middle of the thickest part, or until it has an internal temperature of 170 degrees. (Alternatively, bake the tenderloin at 400 degrees for 20 minutes.)

Slice the tenderloin and serve it immediately.

healthy dessert Solomon and I concocted this delicious tropical smoothie that's a treat for dessert: Blend 1 cup frozen mango chunks, ²/₃ cup orange juice, 1 ripe banana, and ½ cup nonfat vanilla yogurt. Yum!

Traditionally, this dish, suggested by Kathryn Spindel, is spicy, but I toned it down for the kids at a recent gathering and they all asked for second helpings. If you want to spice things up, add a teaspoon of diced chili pepper or a little chili garlic paste. Serve the chicken with rice and steamed broccoli.

thai basil chicken

Prep + Cook =
20 minutes

6 servings

Nutritional
Information per
serving:

Calories 210, Total
Fat 6g, 9%, Saturated
Fat 1g, 5%, Choles-
terol 65mg, 22%,
Sodium 1260mg, 53%,
Total Carbohydrate
9g, 3%, Dietary Fiber
2g, 8%, Protein 28g,
Sugar 4g

- 2 tablespoons vegetable oil
- 2 tablespoons minced garlic (about 12 cloves)
- 1 large red onion, cut into 1-inch strips
- 1 medium red bell pepper, cut into thin strips
- 1½ pounds boneless, skinless chicken breasts, cut into 1-inch chunks
- 7–8 tablespoons soy sauce, to taste
- 1 tablespoon sugar
- 1½–2 cups fresh basil leaves, roughly chopped

In a large nonstick skillet, heat the oil over medium-high heat. Add the garlic, onion, and pepper and toss them for 2 minutes. Add the chicken and stir-fry it until it starts to brown on all sides but is not cooked through, about 3 to 5 minutes.

Add the soy sauce and sugar and cook the chicken, uncovered, tossing it occasionally, until it is just cooked through, about 2 to 3 more minutes.

Add the basil, toss it well, and remove the chicken from the heat. Cover it until ready to serve.

These open-faced sandwiches make a light, simple dinner or lunch. Of course, you can vary the ingredients in the tuna or try different cheeses, such as Swiss or Cheddar. Serve them with potato chips (look for one of the healthier varieties) and a Waldorf Salad (see p. 297).

tuna melts with sliced avocado and tomato

Prep + Cook =
15 minutes

4 servings

Nutritional
Information per
serving:

Calories 360, Total
Fat 18g, 28%, Satu-
rated Fat 6g, 30%,
Cholesterol 45mg,
15%, Sodium 660mg,
28%, Total Carbohy-
drate 31g, 10%, Di-
etary Fiber 5g, 20%,
Protein 20g, Sugar 1g

- 2 cans (6 ounces each) chunk light tuna
- 1–2 tablespoons light mayonnaise, to taste
- 1 stalk celery, finely diced
- 4 slices sourdough bread
- 1 ripe avocado, peeled and thinly sliced
- 1 ripe tomato, thinly sliced
- 4 slices Muenster cheese

Preheat the oven to 350 degrees. Line a baking sheet with aluminum foil. Drain the tuna.

In a small bowl, combine the tuna, mayonnaise, and celery and mix them thoroughly with a fork.

Lightly toast the bread. Spread 1 scoop of tuna on each piece of sourdough toast. Top it with slices of avocado and tomato and a thin slice of cheese. Transfer the sandwiches to the baking sheet and bake them for approximately 5 minutes until the cheese is melted.

Slice the sandwiches in half to serve them.

make-your-own ice cream sandwiches Top low fat cookies (such as graham crackers or chocolate wafers) with softened frozen yogurt or low fat ice cream to make your own ice cream sandwiches. Press a second cookie on top, then even the edges with a dull knife. Eat immediately, or wrap them in plastic wrap and freeze them until you are ready to serve.

This soup, suggested by Scramble newsletter subscriber Maggie Martin, is delicious and so easy that you may have time to let the kids help you make it. Celia got a kick out of grating the zucchini (though I finished the ends for her to protect her fingers). My husband declared this the best use of zucchini ever. The soup goes well with grilled cheese sandwiches.

ravioli soup with grated zucchini

Prep + Cook =
10 minutes

8 servings

Nutritional
Information per
serving:

Calories 220, Total
Fat 7g, 11%, Satu-
rated Fat 3.5g, 18%,
Cholesterol 30mg,
10%, Sodium 330mg,
14%, Total Carbohy-
drate 30g, 10%, Di-
etary Fiber 2g, 6%,
Protein 11g, Sugar 2g

1 box (32 ounces) chicken broth

2 packages (9 ounces each) refrigerated cheese ravioli (or tortellini)

2 large zucchini

shredded Parmesan cheese for serving

pepper for serving

In a stockpot, bring the broth to a boil. Add the ravioli and let it cook according to the package directions. Meanwhile, grate the zucchini with a cheese grater. When the tortellini is almost done, add the zucchini to the soup and cook it for 1 or 2 more minutes.

Season each bowl with Parmesan cheese and pepper to taste.

Even if you have never made a frittata before, this easy recipe can make you look like an expert. Customize your frittata by using similar quantities of your favorite veggies or cheese instead of the spinach and feta, if you prefer. Serve it with whole wheat toast and chopped cantaloupe.

spinach and feta frittata

Prep + Cook = 25 minutes

6 servings

Nutritional Information per serving:

Calories 170, Total Fat 12g, 18%, Saturated Fat 3.5g, 18%, Cholesterol 220mg, 73%, Sodium 370mg, 15%, Total Carbohydrate 6g, 2%, Dietary Fiber 2g, 20%, Protein 10g, Sugar 1g

1 bag (9 ounces) baby spinach or 1 box (10 ounces) frozen chopped spinach

1 tablespoon plus 2 teaspoons olive oil

½ large yellow onion, peeled and chopped

6 eggs

½ cup oil-packed sundried tomatoes, chopped, or ½ cup chopped cooked ham

½ cup crumbled feta cheese (or use Havarti, Swiss, or other cheese)

1 teaspoon dried Italian seasoning (or use ¼ teaspoon dried oregano and ¾ teaspoon dried basil)

¼ teaspoon salt

⅛ teaspoon pepper

Place the oven rack 4 to 5 inches from the heating element and preheat the broiler.

Microwave fresh spinach in a loosely covered bowl for approximately 3 minutes on high, or until it is slightly wilted. (For frozen spinach, place the open spinach box on a microwave-safe plate and microwave it for 4 minutes on high.)

While the spinach wilts, spray the bottom and sides of a heavy 12-inch ovenproof skillet with nonstick cooking spray. Heat 1 tablespoon of the oil in the skillet over medium-high heat and add the onion.

Cook it for 4 to 5 minutes until it is lightly browned.

While the onion cooks, beat the eggs thoroughly in a large bowl with a whisk. Add the sundried tomatoes or ham. Remove the spinach from the microwave, dry it thoroughly with paper towels, chop it roughly, and add it to the eggs, along with the cheese, Italian seasoning, salt, and pepper. Stir well.

Add the remaining 2 teaspoons of the olive oil to the skillet with the onions and tilt the pan to distribute the oil evenly. Pour the egg mixture into the skillet, evenly distributing the spinach and tomatoes with the back of a wooden spoon. Cook the frittata over medium heat without stirring it for about 7 minutes, or until only the surface is loose. Immediately put the skillet under the hot broiler and cook it for 2 more minutes, or until the surface is light brown. Before serving it, run a knife around the edge of the frittata to loosen it from the pan. Flip it onto a cutting board or leave it in the pan. Slice it into wedges and serve it hot.

These tostadas are fun to make with the kids. Your child may want to help you smash the filling on top of the broiled tortillas. For less adventurous eaters, try serving the tortillas with melted cheese only. Serve the tostadas with a Southwestern Bean Salad (see p. 298).

holy guacamole tostadas

Prep + Cook =
30 minutes

6 servings

Nutritional
Information per
serving:

Calories 330, Total
Fat 22g, 34%, Saturated Fat 7g, 35%,
Cholesterol 20mg,
7%, Sodium 500mg,
21%, Total Carbohydrate 26g, 9%, Dietary Fiber 6g, 24%,
Protein 10g, Sugar 1g

1 can (6 ounces) pitted, sliced ripe black olives, drained

2 ripe avocados, peeled and finely diced

1 small red bell pepper, finely chopped

⅓ cup chopped fresh cilantro

2 tablespoons finely chopped red onion

2 tablespoons fresh lime juice (about ½ lime)

6 soft-taco-sized flour or whole wheat tortillas

1 teaspoon vegetable oil

1⅓ cups shredded Monterey Jack or Cheddar cheese

Preheat the broiler. In a medium bowl, stir together the olives, avocado, pepper, cilantro, onion, and lime juice.

Put the tortillas on a large baking sheet and brush the tops with the oil. Broil the tortillas 3 to 4 inches from the heat until they are light golden, about 45 seconds. Flip the tortillas and repeat on the other side.

Sprinkle the tortillas evenly with cheese and broil them until the cheese is melted and bubbling, about 30 seconds.

Divide the olive-avocado mixture among the tortillas, spread the topping to the edges of the tortillas with the back of a spoon, and cut each tortilla into 4 wedges or fold it in half to serve.

{ **cantaloupe** Cantaloupe is one of the healthiest foods for adults and kids—and it tastes so good. Let the melon ripen on the counter until it smells slightly fragrant, then refrigerate it until you're ready to serve it.

best fish for people and the planet

The Six O'Clock Scramble menus usually include one fish recipe each week. I do this for several reasons. First, I think fish is a delicious dinner option, and my family enjoys it. Second, fish is a good source of protein without the high saturated-fat content that a lot of meat has. Finally, there is a lot of evidence that fish has other health benefits: Many fish contain omega-3 fatty acids, which is good brain food for children and adults. Some fish also contain other nutrients, such as calcium, vitamins A and D, and antioxidants.

As with many foods, eating fish may also have drawbacks. Some of the same oily fish that contain omega-3's can also contain harmful chemicals, such as mercury, dioxins, and PCBs. These are the unfortunate result of environmental pollution of the oceans. The FDA has issued warnings about limiting consumption of certain fish such as tuna and swordfish, especially for pregnant women and children. To learn more about mercury in seafood and how much tuna is safe for children and adults to eat, visit the Environmental Working Group's Web site, www.ewg.org.

Despite these downsides, leading nutrition experts recommend eating two portions of fish each week, believing that the health benefits outweigh the risks. In picking which fish to recommend, I put taste first. I only suggest fish recipes that my family enjoys. I also consult an excellent resource, the Seafood Selector, from Environmental Defense (www.environmentaldefense.org). The Seafood Selector helps me choose fish that are safest from the standpoint of human health and the environment. Among their best choices are catfish, crab, mahi-mahi, wild salmon, some shrimp, and tilapia, all fish that I think taste great. As consumers and parents, we have to weigh the advantages and the risks of foods and make the best choices that we can for our families. For me, that means including a variety of fish in our weekly dinners.

Using precooked sausage makes kabobs quick and easy, though you can also use marinated chicken or beef, or portobello mushrooms for a vegetarian alternative. If you don't want to use skewers, you can grill everything on a vegetable tray instead. You can also make this dish in the broiler with or without skewers. Serve the kabobs with corn on the cob and warm pita. Make an easy yogurt sauce to serve on the side: Combine plain yogurt, fresh mint, and a dash of honey.

grilled sausage kabobs with summer vegetables

Prep + Cook =
30 minutes

4 servings

Nutritional
Information per
serving:

Calories 200, Total
Fat 12g, 18%, Saturated Fat 3g, 15%,
Cholesterol 45mg,
15%, Sodium 910mg,
38%, Total Carbohydrate 9g, 3%, Dietary
Fiber 2g, 8%, Protein
16g, Sugar 3g

1 medium zucchini, cut on diagonal into ½-inch slices

1 medium yellow squash, cut on diagonal into ½-inch slices

1–2 tablespoons olive oil

½ teaspoon kosher salt

1 package (12 ounces) fully cooked gourmet chicken sausage (any flavor), cut into ½-inch slices

1 pint cherry tomatoes

1 teaspoon fresh oregano or ½ teaspoon dried

Spray or oil the grill and preheat it to high heat.

In a medium bowl, toss the zucchini and yellow squash with the oil and salt to coat. (If you are using portobello mushrooms instead of meat, add them now, too.)

Thread the sausage, zucchini, and squash onto about 6 metal skewers. Thread the cherry tomatoes onto 2 separate skewers. Grill the skewers with the sausage and squash for about 10 minutes on medium-high heat, turning them several times, until they are browned on all sides. For the last minute or two, add the tomatoes to the grill.

Carefully remove all the skewers from the grill and, using a hot glove and a fork, transfer the vegetables and sausage to a serving bowl. Toss them with the oregano and serve.

This combination makes for a colorful and delicious summer feast. Serve it with blue corn chips and salsa.

lime-garlic shrimp with black bean and corn salad

Prep + Cook =
30 minutes

6 servings

Nutritional
Information per
serving:

Calories 200, Total
Fat 3g, 5%, Saturated
Fat 0g, 0%, Choles-
terol 115mg, 38%,
Sodium 1020mg, 43%,
Total Carbohydrate
23g, 8%, Dietary
Fiber 7g, 28%, Pro-
tein 21g, Sugar 4g

for shrimp:

1 pound large shrimp, peeled and deveined

2 tablespoons lime juice (about ½ lime)

1 tablespoon minced garlic (about 6 cloves)

1 teaspoon kosher salt

1 tablespoon olive oil

¼ cup fresh chopped cilantro

sour cream for serving

for salad:

1 can (15 ounces) black beans, drained

1 can (14 ounces) unsweetened corn kernels, drained

1 red bell pepper, diced

1 teaspoon fresh lime juice

½ teaspoon salt

½ cup fresh chopped cilantro

In a large bowl, combine the shrimp, lime juice, garlic, and salt. Refrigerate it for 15 minutes while you prepare the salad.

To make the salad, mix all the ingredients together in a medium bowl. Refrigerate it until you're ready to serve dinner.

In a large nonstick skillet, heat the oil over medium-high heat. With a slotted spoon, remove the shrimp from the marinade, reserving the marinade. Add the shrimp to the skillet and cook them for 2–3 minutes until they begin to turn pink. Add the reserved marinade and continue cooking the shrimp for about 2 more minutes, until they are cooked through. Toss them with the fresh cilantro.

Serve the shrimp and salad with a dollop of sour cream. For extra flavor, blend or stir a little lime juice and cilantro into the sour cream first.

This is a fresh-tasting summer pasta. Serve it with a green salad with diced Gouda cheese, pistachios, and halved grapes.

rigatoni with asparagus and lemon

Prep + Cook =
30 minutes

8 servings

Nutritional
Information per
serving:

Calories 300, Total
Fat 7g, 11%, Satu-
rated Fat 3g, 15%,
Cholesterol 15mg,
5%, Sodium 210mg,
9%, Total Carbohy-
drate 47g, 16%, Di-
etary Fiber 3g, 12%,
Protein 13g, Sugar 3g

1 package (16 ounces) rigatoni pasta

1½–2 pounds asparagus

1 pint cherry tomatoes

1 tablespoon olive oil

1 tablespoon minced garlic (about 6 cloves)

¼ teaspoon salt

pepper to taste

1½ tablespoons lemon juice (about ½ lemon)

15 fresh basil leaves, chopped

5 fresh mint leaves, chopped

1 cup shredded or diced smoked Gouda or other smoky cheese (or use crisp bacon)

Cook the pasta according to the package directions.

Meanwhile, break the dry ends off the asparagus, discard them, and slice the asparagus spears on the diagonal into 1-inch pieces. Cut the cherry tomatoes in half.

When the noodles are about halfway cooked, heat the oil in a large skillet over medium-high heat. Add the asparagus, tomatoes, and garlic, and cook them for several minutes. Season the vegetables with salt and pepper to taste.

Scoop out about ½ cup of the cooking water from the pasta and set it aside. Drain the cooked noodles. Add the noodles, the reserved cooking water, lemon juice, salt, basil, and mint and toss gently. Transfer it to a large serving bowl (preferably a metal bowl to retain heat) and add the cheese. Toss the noodles and cheese to melt the cheese slightly. Serve it warm.

TIP: If you are making Celia's Honey Chicken tomorrow night, marinate the chicken tonight while the pasta is cooking.

This chicken is a favorite of our daughter, who loves eating drumsticks. The recipe also works well with chicken thighs. (Of course, it would work well with bone-in breasts, with or without skin, too.) Serve it with fried rice (see p. 106) or steamed rice and steamed broccoli. For a larger meal, combine this recipe with tomorrow night's eggplant stir-fry.

celia's honey chicken

Prep (5 minutes) +
Cook (30 minutes)
+ Marinate

6 servings

Nutritional
Information per
serving:

Calories 300, Total
Fat 7g, 10%, Saturated Fat 2g, 10%,
Cholesterol 160mg,
54%, Sodium 860mg,
36%, Total Carbohydrate 12g, 4%, Dietary Fiber 0g, 0%,
Protein 42g, Sugar
12g

12 chicken drumsticks, thighs, or any combination, with or without skin

½ cup honey

½ cup soy sauce

Place the chicken in a medium-sized baking dish with sides.

Put the honey in a large glass measuring cup and warm it for 20 seconds in the microwave on high. Add the soy sauce and stir it thoroughly.

Pour the honey-soy mixture over the chicken and turn the chicken to coat it. Marinate it in the refrigerator, covered, for at least 30 minutes or up to 24 hours, if time allows.

Preheat the oven to 375 degrees.

Bake the chicken at 375 degrees for about 30–40 minutes, basting and turning it occasionally, until it is cooked through. For browner skin, broil the chicken for the last few minutes.

I adapted this sweet and delicious recipe from our friend David Yang's superb recipe. Japanese eggplants are a delicacy—they cook a little more quickly and have a slightly sweeter flavor and softer texture than regular eggplants. Serve this dish over white or brown rice with steamed dumplings to complete the meal.

japanese eggplant and green beans in garlic sauce

Prep + Cook =
25 minutes

8 servings

Nutritional Information per serving:

Calories 110, Total Fat 9g, 14%, Saturated Fat 1.5g, 7%, Cholesterol 0mg, 0%, Sodium 270 mg, 11%, Total Carbohydrate 14g, 5%, Dietary Fiber 4g, 17%, Protein 3g, Sugar 6g

1½–2 cups dry white or brown rice

1 pound green beans

2–3 medium Japanese eggplants (about 1 pound total)

2 tablespoons rice wine

2 tablespoons rice vinegar

2 tablespoons soy sauce

1 tablespoon hoisin sauce or black bean sauce (available with Asian foods)

2 teaspoons sesame oil

1 teaspoon sugar

¼ teaspoon ginger powder

3 tablespoons peanut or vegetable oil

2 teaspoons minced garlic (about 4 cloves)

4 scallions, chopped

Cook the rice according to the package directions.

Meanwhile, trim the ends from the green beans and cut the beans into 1-inch pieces. Cut each eggplant into 4 long strips, and cut those strips into 2-inch pieces.

In a measuring cup or small bowl, mix together the rice wine, rice vinegar, soy sauce, hoisin or black bean sauce, sesame oil, sugar, and ginger.

In a large nonstick skillet, heat the peanut or vegetable oil over medium-high heat. Add the eggplant and green beans and cook them until they start to brown, about 5 minutes. Add the garlic and stir-fry the mixture for about 1 minute.

Reduce the heat to medium, add the sauce, stir the mixture, and cover the pan for 3 to 4 minutes until the ingredients blend and the vegetables soften. Add the scallions, increase the heat to medium-high, and stir-fry the vegetables for 1 minute. Serve them over the rice.

Your family will enjoy this simple lime marinade for chicken breasts, and the fresh salsa makes this a delicious summery meal. (This salsa would also be great on top of a firm white fish, such as sea bass or halibut.) If you don't want to grill the breasts, you can cook them over medium-high heat in a skillet instead. Serve the chicken with steamed sugar snap peas and warm tortillas.

grilled lime chicken with avocado salsa

Prep + Cook =
30 minutes

6 servings

Nutritional
Information per
serving:

Calories 210, Total
Fat 10g, 15%, Saturated Fat 1.5g, 8%,
Cholesterol 65mg,
22%, Sodium 870mg,
36%, Total Carbohydrate 5g, 2%, Dietary
Fiber 3g, 12%, Protein 27g, Sugar <1g

1½–2 pounds boneless, skinless chicken breasts

2 tablespoons lime juice (about ½ lime)

1 tablespoon olive oil

1 tablespoon kosher salt

Avocado Salsa

2 avocados, diced or mashed, or 1 package frozen vacuum-packed guacamole

1 tomato, diced

¼ red or yellow onion, finely diced (about ½ cup)

¼ teaspoon salt or more to taste

Place the chicken breasts in a flat dish with sides. Use a dish just large enough to hold them in a single layer. Add the lime juice, oil, and salt and flip the chicken several times to coat it well.

In a medium-sized serving bowl, combine the salsa ingredients (avocados through salt) and mix them thoroughly. (Add a teaspoon of cilantro and/or lime juice for some additional flavor.)

Preheat the grill to medium-high heat. Cook the chicken breasts for about 3 to 4 minutes per side until they start to brown on the outside and are no longer pink in the middle of the thickest part of the breast. Remove them from the heat and serve them whole or sliced into strips, topped with the avocado salsa.

When I worked in Washington, D.C., and had a few extra dollars, I would splurge on a smoked salmon sandwich from the Red Sage Café. These sandwiches are ideal for an outdoor summer concert. Serve them with a Greek Salad (see p. 297).

smoked salmon and dill sandwiches

Prep = 10 minutes

4 servings

Nutritional Information per serving:

Calories 250, Total Fat 4.5g, 7%, Saturated Fat 1.5g, 8%, Cholesterol 15mg, 5%, Sodium 1560mg, 65%, Total Carbohydrate 34g, 11%, Dietary Fiber 1g, 4%, Protein 17g, Sugar <1g

4 large pita pockets, bagels, or sandwich rolls

cream cheese to taste (about 2 tablespoons per sandwich)

2 teaspoons fresh or dried dill

4 teaspoons capers

6–8 ounces sliced smoked salmon (nova or lox)

Warm the pitas in the microwave oven for about 30 seconds on high power to soften them. With a bread knife, slice the pita pockets (or bagels or rolls, if you are using them) in half lengthwise. Spread a layer of cream cheese on the inside of each pita. Top each one with about ½ teaspoon of the dill, 1 teaspoon of the capers, and a layer of smoked salmon. Press the top half of the pita on top of the salmon and slice each sandwich in half crosswise for serving. Wrap them tightly in foil for a picnic.

crunch time Adding pita chips to a salad gives it a lovely Middle Eastern flavor. Just be sure to add them at the last minute so they don't get soggy.

This basic recipe for a flavorful tomato sauce originated with longtime family friend Karen Shapiro. It's a great one to modify based on your taste or your refrigerator's contents, and impressive enough to serve to visitors. Try adding chopped mushrooms, eggplant, zucchini, or whatever fresh ingredients you have on hand. Serve the ziti with bread and sliced summer peaches.

ziti with tomato and artichoke sauce

Prep + Cook =
30 minutes

8 servings

Nutritional
Information per
serving:

Calories 410, Total
Fat 7g, 11%, Saturated Fat 1g, 4%,
Cholesterol 0 mg,
0%, Sodium 250 mg,
10%, Total Carbohydrate 76g, 25%, Dietary Fiber 9g, 36%,
Protein 13g, Sugar
24g

2 tablespoons olive oil

1 large onion, chopped

1 tablespoon minced garlic (about 6 cloves)

1 jar (6 ounces) quartered and marinated artichoke hearts with their liquid

8 fresh tomatoes, diced (or use 2 15-ounce cans diced tomatoes, drained)

25 fresh basil leaves, chopped

10–12 pitted Greek or Spanish olives, chopped

⅓ cup red wine

1 package (16 ounces) ziti or other cut pasta

grated Parmesan cheese for serving

In a large skillet, heat the oil over medium-high heat. Add the onions and garlic and sauté them until the onions start to brown, about 5 minutes.

Add the artichoke hearts, tomatoes, basil, olives, and wine. Simmer the sauce gently for at least 15 minutes and up to 45 minutes.

Meanwhile, cook the pasta according to the package directions and drain it.

Toss the pasta with the sauce and serve it with the grated Parmesan cheese.

These ribs are fantastic! They get so flavorful and tender on the grill that your family will surely devour them. Serve them with soft dinner rolls and grilled pineapple rings.

grilled baby back ribs with pineapple glaze

Prep (10 minutes) + Cook (45–60 minutes)

4 servings

Nutritional Information per serving

Calories 390, Total Fat 17g, 26%, Saturated Fat 6g, 30%, Cholesterol 110mg, 37%, Sodium 860mg, 36%, Total Carbohydrate 7g, 2%, Dietary Fiber <1g, 4%, Protein 50g, Sugar 5g

- 1 teaspoon paprika
- 1 teaspoon salt
- 1 teaspoon chili powder
- 1 teaspoon cinnamon
- 1 teaspoon + 2 tablespoons brown sugar
- 2–3 pounds baby back pork ribs (1 or 2 racks)
- ¼ cup pineapple juice (use juice from a can of pineapple rings)
- ¼ cup ketchup
- 2 tablespoons Worcestershire sauce

In a small bowl, combine the paprika, salt, chili powder, cinnamon, and 1 teaspoon of the brown sugar. Lay the ribs flat in a dish with sides. Sprinkle the spice mixture evenly over both sides of the ribs and rub it into the meat with your fingers. You can cook the ribs right away or refrigerate them for up to 24 hours.

To make the glaze, combine the pineapple juice, ketchup, Worcestershire sauce and 2 tablespoons of the brown sugar in a small saucepan. Bring it to a boil and simmer it for about 5 minutes until it is slightly thickened. Set the sauce aside.

Grill the ribs, turning them after 10 minutes or so, for 20 minutes. Then, brush one side of the ribs with the glaze and continue to cook them, flipping and brushing them with sauce every 5 to 10 minutes, until the ribs are nicely browned and the meat cuts easily with a sharp knife, about 50 to 60 minutes total. If the ribs start to blacken, reduce the heat and move them off the direct heat.

If any glaze remains, bring it to a boil on the stovetop for a couple of minutes to eliminate any bacteria from the raw meat, and serve it on the side with the ribs.

Cut them into individual ribs to serve.

I still remember the great TV ads for V8 vegetable juice from the '70s: "Wow (hand slapped to forehead), I could have had a V8!" It turns out that V8 juice also makes a nice base for a sauce. If you can't find red snapper, use salmon or tilapia, but adjust the cooking time for their thicknesses. Serve the fish with kasha and bowties (buckwheat and bows, sold together in a box with rice mixes or kosher foods) and baked asparagus.

red snapper V8

Prep + Cook =
15 minutes

4 servings

Nutritional
Information per
serving:

Calories 180, Total
Fat 5g, 7%, Saturated
Fat 2g, 11%, Choles-
terol 60 mg, 20%,
Sodium 290 mg, 12%,
Total Carbohydrate
3g, 1%, Dietary Fiber
0g, 0%, Protein 30g,
Sugar 2g

- 1–2 red snapper fillets (about 1–1½ pounds total)
- ¼ teaspoon kosher salt
- paprika to taste
- 1 small can (8 ounces) V8 (vegetable) juice
- 1 teaspoon lemon juice (about ¼ lemon)
- 1 tablespoon butter

Preheat the oven to 375 degrees. Line a baking sheet with foil and spray the foil with nonstick cooking spray.

Put the fillets on the pan and sprinkle them with the salt and paprika. Bake them until the fillets are white and cooked through, about 15 to 20 minutes.

Meanwhile, in a small saucepan, bring the V8 juice to a boil. Simmer it for about 5 minutes. Turn off the heat and stir in the lemon juice and butter.

When the fish is cooked, remove it to a plate, top it with the sauce, and serve it hot.

Though I don't make steak often, this is my kids' absolute favorite meal. Serve it with grilled broccoli and Oven-Roasted Potatoes (See p. 300).

grilled steak with garlic and parmesan crust

Prep + Cook =
20 minutes

4 servings

Nutritional Information per serving:

Calories 340, Total Fat 15g, 23%, Saturated Fat 6g, 28%, Cholesterol 135 mg, 46%, Sodium 180 mg, 8%, Total Carbohydrate 1g, 0%, Dietary Fiber 0g, 0%, Protein 48g, Sugar 0g

2 pounds boneless New York strip or Delmonico steak (2 or 3 steaks)

1 tablespoon margarine or butter

¼ cup grated Parmesan cheese

½ teaspoon garlic powder

Preheat the grill to medium-high heat.

With the lid closed, grill the steaks on one side to the desired doneness (about 4 minutes for medium rare).

Flip the steaks and spread a light coating of margarine or butter on top of the cooked side of each steak. Sprinkle each generously with the Parmesan cheese and garlic powder. Cook the steaks to the desired doneness.

Remove the steaks to a plate or cutting board and slice them into strips for serving.

Most store-bought fish sticks are tasty but full of fat and additives. This healthy homemade version from Lisa Flaxman is almost as easy as heating commercially prepared fish sticks—and even more delicious. Serve the fish with green beans and couscous.

pan-fried fish sticks

Prep + Cook = 15 minutes

6 servings

Nutritional Information per serving:

Calories 260, Total Fat 7g, 11%, Saturated Fat 2.5g, 11%, Cholesterol 105 mg, 34%, Sodium 370 mg, 15%, Total Carbohydrate 14g, 5%, Dietary Fiber 0g, 0%, Protein 34g, Sugar 1g

1½–2 pounds white fish fillet (such as lemon sole or flounder)

1 cup bread crumbs

¼ cup grated Parmesan cheese

1 egg

2 tablespoons butter

2 tablespoons lemon juice (about ½ lemon)

Wash the fillets and pat them dry. Cut them into strips (optional).

In a shallow bowl, mix together the bread crumbs and Parmesan cheese. In another shallow bowl, beat the egg.

Dip each piece of fish in the egg and then roll it in the bread crumb mixture. Set the fish aside on a plate.

In a large nonstick skillet, melt 1 tablespoon of the butter over medium heat. Place the fish in the pan.

Cook one side of the fish until it is brown, 2 to 3 minutes. Pour 1 tablespoon of the lemon juice over the fish and cook it for 1 more minute. Carefully flip the fish and repeat the process for the second side, cooking it for 2 to 3 minutes, or until the fish flakes easily.

Saag Paneer is one of our favorite dishes at Indian restaurants. Traditionally, it is made with a soft cheese that is hard to find but has always reminded me of tofu, which I have used instead of the cheese. One of our kid-testers, six-year-old Eleanor Shapiro, liked this so much she had three helpings. Serve this over Basmati rice with warm pita bread and extra yogurt.

indian spinach curry (saag paneer)

Prep + Cook =
30 minutes

6 servings

Nutritional
Information per
serving:

Calories 180, Total
Fat 9g, 14%, Saturated Fat 3.5g, 18%,
Cholesterol 15mg,
5%, Sodium 510mg,
21%, Total Carbohydrate 16g, 5%, Dietary Fiber 4g, 16%,
Protein 10g, Sugar 9g

1 tablespoon vegetable oil

2 tablespoons butter

1 yellow onion, finely chopped

1 tablespoon minced garlic, about 6 garlic cloves

1 tablespoon minced fresh ginger, or ½ teaspoon ground ginger

1 teaspoon salt

2 teaspoons curry powder

1 teaspoon garam masala (an Indian spice blend)

2 packages (10 ounces each) frozen chopped spinach

1 cup water

1 cup low-fat plain yogurt

1 package (12 ounce) extra-firm silken tofu, drained and cut into ½-inch cubes

Heat the oil and butter in a large heavy-duty skillet over medium-high heat. Add the onion, garlic, and ginger and sauté them for 5 to 7 minutes until the onion begins to brown. Add the salt, curry powder, and garam masala and stir through for 1 minute.

While the onion is browning, put the spinach in a microwave-safe dish and partially thaw it for several minutes on the highest setting. Add the spinach and its liquid plus 1 cup of water to the pan with the onions and break up the spinach with a spatula as it continues to thaw. Reduce the heat to medium and simmer it with the lid off the pan, stirring occasionally, until almost all the liquid has evaporated, about 10 minutes.

Stir in the yogurt and then gently stir in the tofu. Cover the pan and heat it through for about 3 minutes.

Serve it over rice with a dollop of yogurt, if desired.

In summer, gardens are bursting with fresh basil, so now is the perfect time to make a batch of pesto. If you have enough basil, make a double recipe and freeze half. Serve it with Italian-Style Cauliflower (see p. 298).

penne with presto pesto

Prep + Cook =
20 minutes

6 servings

Nutritional
Information per
serving:

Calories 510, Total
Fat 24g, 37%, Satu-
rated Fat 4g, 20%,
Cholesterol 5mg, 2%,
Sodium 110mg, 5%,
Total Carbohydrate
59g, 20%, Dietary
Fiber 3g, 12%, Pro-
tein 13g, Sugar 2g

- 1 package (16 ounces) penne pasta
- 2 cups fresh basil leaves, tightly packed
- 1 teaspoon minced garlic (about 2 cloves)
- 3 tablespoons pine nuts
- ½ cup olive oil
- ½ cup grated Parmesan cheese (or more for desired consistency)
- 1 large tomato, diced (optional)

Cook the pasta according to the package directions and drain it.

Meanwhile, place the basil, garlic, 2 tablespoons of the pine nuts, the oil, and the Parmesan cheese in a food processor or blender and coarsely chop it. Lightly toast the remaining 1 tablespoon of the pine nuts.

Toss the pesto with the warm penne (you may not need to use all the sauce, depending on your tasks). Top it with the tomatoes and the toasted pine nuts.

TIP: Leftover pesto is delicious on crackers or over steamed green beans.

These baked drumsticks are the closest I've come to fried chicken without actually deep-frying. The trick is cooking them as long as necessary to get the skin really well browned. You can substitute thighs or wings for the drumsticks, but I don't recommend white meat, as the inside may get dried out before the outside is crispy. Serve the chicken with baked potatoes and carrot chips with ranch dressing.

crispy baked drumsticks

Prep (15 minutes) +
Cook (50 minutes)

6 servings

Nutritional
Information per
serving:

Calories 270, Total
Fat 9g, 14%, Saturated Fat 2.5g, 13%,
Cholesterol 80mg,
27%, Sodium 210mg,
9%, Total Carbohydrate 16g, 5%, Dietary Fiber 1g, 5%,
Protein 28g, Sugar 1g

¾ **cup cornmeal**

¼ **cup flour**

¼ **cup grated Parmesan cheese**

½ **teaspoon salt**

1 **teaspoon Italian seasoning (such as dried basil and oregano or thyme)**

¼ **teaspoon garlic powder**

½ **cup low-fat milk**

12 **chicken legs (or a combination of legs and thighs), skinned if desired**

2 **tablespoons butter, melted**

Preheat the oven to 400 degrees. Spray a baking sheet with nonstick cooking spray. If possible, put a baking rack on top of the sheet to elevate the chicken, and spray that, too. If you don't use a rack, flip the chicken halfway through baking so both sides brown.

In a shallow bowl, combine the dry ingredients. Pour the milk into another shallow bowl. Dip the chicken in the milk and let the excess drip off. Coat the chicken with the cornmeal mixture. Brush or drizzle the chicken with the butter, and spray the tops of the chicken lightly with nonstick cooking spray.

Bake the chicken for at least 50 minutes until the skin is golden brown.

make fruits and vegetables a daily habit

Registered dietitian Susan Mayer reminded me of an important nutritional goal for adults and children: eating five to nine servings of fruit or vegetables a day. We came up with some suggestions to help you achieve this goal.

Keep your home stocked with fruit and vegetables. When you do the weekly shopping, buy lots of fruit and vegetables. Frozen and canned vegetables are fine, as long as you avoid varieties with lots of added sugar or salt. Stock up on what's on sale or in season.

Make fruits and vegetables accessible. Kids enjoy reaching into the fruit or vegetable drawer to help themselves to an afternoon snack. (Don't forget to teach your kids the importance of washing fruit thoroughly before eating it.) A bowl of ripe fruit or plate of cut veggies and dip on the table is also enticing.

Get kids involved in nutrition. Solomon and Celia have recently mastered peeling carrots, and their carrot consumption has skyrocketed with their newfound skill! They also like to blend their own smoothie concoctions (under my supervision), with fresh or frozen fruit, yogurt, and honey. It's a great activity for play dates.

Grab and go. My family loves cantaloupe, so I often buy two each week when they're in season. When they're ripe, I cut the melons into bite-sized pieces and store them in the fridge for quick access. Try to include at least a serving of fruit in school lunches, and bring fruit in the car for healthy snacks on the go.

You may already be eating five-a-day. Here's what counts as a serving: 1 medium-sized fruit; 6 ounces of 100 percent juice (have only one of these a day); ½ cup fresh, frozen, or canned fruit or vegetables; 1 cup of raw leafy greens; ½ cup peas or beans; or ¼ cup dried fruit.

Of course, include fruit and vegetables in your family dinners. Serve them as part of the main dish and/or as side dishes each night.

These enchiladas, from subscriber Gina Kaufman, are easier to make than traditional enchiladas because you layer them like a casserole rather than rolling them. I don't usually used canned soup in recipes, but it gives these enchiladas such a rich flavor without lots of fat. Serve them with diced honeydew melon.

chicken enchilada casserole

Prep (20 minutes) + Cook (25–30 minutes)

10 servings

Nutritional Information per serving:

Calories 260, Total Fat 7g, 11%, Saturated Fat 3.5g, 18%, Cholesterol 35mg, 12%, Sodium 510mg, 21%, Total Carbohydrate 34g, 11%, Dietary Fiber 3g, 12%, Protein 17g, Sugar 2g

2 cans (10¾ ounces each) low-sodium cream of chicken soup

1 cup (8 ounces) fat-free sour cream

1 can (4 ounces) chopped green chilies or ½ cup salsa verde (green salsa)

2 cups reduced-fat shredded Cheddar cheese

1 bunch scallions, chopped (about 1 cup)

1½ cups cooked chicken, cubed (I use a rotisserie chicken from the supermarket)

18 corn tortillas

Preheat the oven to 350 degrees. Coat a 9 × 13-inch baking dish with nonstick cooking spray.

In a medium bowl, combine the soup, sour cream, and chilies.

In a separate medium bowl, combine the cheese, scallions, and chicken.

Spread about 3 tablespoons of the soup mixture in the bottom of the pan. Cover it with 6 of the tortillas, overlapping them slightly if necessary, and a third of the chicken mixture. Continue layering: soup mixture, tortillas, chicken mixture; soup mixture, tortillas, chicken mixture; ending with soup mixture.

Bake the casserole for 25 to 30 minutes, uncovered, until it is bubbly. To serve it, allow it to cool slightly, then use a serrated knife to cut it into squares.

When our power went out after a big storm, my friend Lisa Flaxman took me in for lunch and served this delicious French salad (her version of Salad Nicoise), which I dubbed salad Licoise. Younger kids can enjoy the components of the salad separately with or without dressing. Serve it with a baguette and French Brie.

salad licoise

Prep + Cook = 30 minutes

4 servings

Nutritional Information per serving:

Calories 370, Total Fat 25g, 38%, Saturated Fat 5g, 25%, Cholesterol 125mg, 42%, Sodium 810mg, 34%, Total Carbohydrate 21g, 7%, Dietary Fiber 6g, 24%, Protein 17g, Sugar 5g

- 4 new potatoes
- 2 hard-boiled eggs, sliced
- 1 tablespoon lemon juice (about ¼ lemon)
- 1 tablespoon Dijon mustard
- 4 tablespoons olive oil
- ¼ teaspoon salt, or to taste
- 1 bag (6–9 ounces) baby spinach or salad greens
- 2 ripe tomatoes, diced
- 1 cup sweet peas, chopped (or use thawed frozen peas)
- ¼ cup kalamata or other flavorful black pitted olives
- 1 can (6 ounces) chunk light tuna
- ¼ cup pistachios or slivered almonds
- ¼ cup crumbled blue cheese

Boil the potatoes for about 15 minutes in salted water until they are fork tender. (If the eggs need to be cooked, do that now too).

To make the dressing, whisk together the lemon juice, mustard, oil, and salt until they are emulsified (well blended and thickened). Allow the potatoes to cool for a few minutes, then cut them into wedges and toss them with 1 tablespoon of the dressing.

On serving plates, neatly assemble the salads, starting with the greens, and then adding layers of the other ingredients. (For younger kids, you may want to keep everything separate on their plates and leave off the dressing.) Spread the potatoes around the edges. Drizzle the remaining dressing over the salads before serving.

TIP: To make hard-boiled eggs, immerse the eggs in cool water in a pan just large enough to hold them in one layer. Bring the water to a low boil, and cook the eggs at a very low boil, uncovered, for 12 minutes. Run the eggs under cold water, then peel and slice them. Hard-boiled eggs can be kept in the refrigerator for up to a week, so consider making extras for snacks or school lunches if you or your kids enjoy them.

This crustless spinach quiche from my mother-in-law, Barbara Gold-farb, couldn't be much simpler. For dinner, serve it with a French baguette and baked sweet potatoes (see p. 300).

popeye pie

Prep (15 minutes) + Cook (45 minutes)

4 servings

Nutritional Information per serving:

Calories 290, Total Fat 22g, 34%, Saturated Fat 6g, 30%, Cholesterol 180mg, 60%, Sodium 410mg, 17%, Total Carbohydrate 15g, 5%, Dietary Fiber 3g, 12%, Protein 11g, Sugar 6g

3 eggs, beaten

½ cup milk (any kind)

¾ cup light mayonnaise

2 tablespoons flour

1 package (10 ounces) frozen chopped spinach, defrosted and squeezed dry

½ cup Swiss cheese, cut into ¼-inch cubes (or use your favorite hard cheese)

½ cup chopped scallions (about 4 scallions)

Preheat the oven to 375 degrees. Spray a 9-inch pie dish or an 8-inch square baking dish with nonstick cooking spray. In a large bowl, combine all the ingredients and mix them well. Pour them into the baking dish and bake it for 45 minutes until it is light brown and puffy. Serve it hot or warm.

My friend Debbie Lehrich introduced me to this creative way to wrap up a quick and healthy weeknight meal. Our family had fun making our own wraps at the table. The fillings and sauces are infinitely variable based on what's in your fridge or your imagination. For a crunchier option, use the lettuce leaves as the wrappers rather than the tortillas. Serve them with vanilla yogurt topped with granola.

crunchy rainbow wraps

Prep = 20 minutes

6 servings

Nutritional Information per serving:

Calories 180, Total Fat 7g, 11%, Saturated Fat 3g, 15%, Cholesterol 10mg, 3%, Sodium 240mg, 10%, Total Carbohydrate 23g, 8%, Dietary Fiber 3g, 12%, Protein 4g, Sugar 3g

- 4 ounces veggie cream cheese (other sauce options: Boursin cheese, hoisin sauce, blue cheese dressing)
- 6 large flour or whole wheat tortillas
- 6 leaves iceberg lettuce
- 1 cup shredded carrots
- 1 cup shredded red cabbage
- ¼ red onion, finely diced
- 1 avocado, sliced or smashed
- ½ cup crumbled blue cheese (or use shredded Monterey Jack)

Spread a thin layer of cream cheese (or other sauce) on each tortilla and top it with a lettuce leaf.

Divide the veggies and cheese among the tortillas and roll them up.

Cut each wrap in half diagonally to expose the rainbow within.

cry now, smile later When chopping onions, chop as much extra onion as you can manage. Then simply use what you need and freeze the rest. Save on tears and time.

These slightly tangy and sweet noodles appeal to adults and kids. Serve it with Lemony-Garlic Spinach (see p. 298).

chinese barbecue noodles

Prep + Cook =
20 minutes

8 servings

Nutritional
Information per
serving:

Calories 300, Total
Fat 4.5g, 7%, Satu-
rated Fat 0g, 0%,
Cholesterol 0mg, 0%,
Sodium 700mg, 29%,
Total Carbohydrate
54g, 18%, Dietary
Fiber 2g, 8%, Protein
11g, Sugar 11g

- **16 ounces Chinese wide lo mein noodles (sold with international foods) or fettuccine**
- **½ cup ketchup**
- **4 tablespoons soy sauce**
- **4 tablespoons lime juice (about 1 lime)**
- **4 tablespoons brown sugar**
- **2 teaspoons rice vinegar**
- **3 teaspoons sesame oil**
- **½ red onion, slivered**
- **1½ cups grated carrots**
- **½–1 pound cooked tofu or chicken (optional)**
- **½ cup fresh cilantro**

Cook the noodles according to the package directions until they are al dente. Drain and rinse them.

Meanwhile, to make the sauce, in a large measuring cup, whisk together the ketchup, soy sauce, lime juice, brown sugar and rice vinegar and 2 teaspoons of the sesame oil.

In a large nonstick skillet, heat the remaining 1 teaspoon of the sesame oil over medium heat. Add the onion and carrots and stir-fry them for several minutes until they are slightly softened. Add the cooked noodles, sauce, tofu or chicken (optional), and cilantro. Toss the ingredients together until they are heated through.

My sister, Sheba, and I teamed up to invent this simple sweet and savory marinade for a quick weeknight meal, which has become a Scramble subscriber favorite. The chicken comes out moist and delicious, and the apricots add an elegant flair. Serve it with couscous and steamed asparagus.

baked apricot chicken

Prep (10 minutes) +
Cook (20–25
minutes)

4 servings

Nutritional
Information per
serving:

Calories 270, Total
Fat 4g, 6%, Saturated Fat 1g, 5% Cholesterol 100mg, 33%,
Sodium 470mg, 20%,
Total Carbohydrate
17g, 6%, Dietary
Fiber 0g, 0%, Protein
41g, Sugar 15g

- 1½ pounds boneless, skinless chicken breasts
- ½ cup apricot jam
- 2–3 tablespoons lemon juice (about ½ lemon)
- 2 tablespoons soy sauce
- 1 teaspoon minced garlic (about 2 cloves)
- 2 tablespoons Dijon mustard
- 1 tablespoon olive oil
- 6 dried apricots, coarsely chopped

Preheat the oven to 350 degrees. Lay the chicken breasts flat in an oven-safe dish with sides.

In the measuring cup you used to measure the apricot jam, mix together all the remaining ingredients except the dried apricots. Pour the mixture over the chicken breasts. Top them with the dried apricots.

Marinate the chicken in the refrigerator, covered, for up to 24 hours, or bake it immediately for 20 to 25 minutes until it is just cooked through.

I had the chance to watch a young visitor from Milan make this authentic Italian pasta. It was so simple that you can easily re-create it. It goes well with a spinach salad with chopped hearts of palm, pecans, and dried cranberries.

tortellini tossed with fresh mozzarella

Prep + Cook =
20 minutes

8 servings

Nutritional
Information per
serving:

Calories 290, Total
Fat 10g, 15%, Saturated Fat 5g, 25%,
Cholesterol 50mg,
17%, Sodium 530mg,
22%, Total Carbohydrates 34g, 11%, Dietary Fiber 2g, 8%,
Protein 15g, Sugar 6g

- 1 pound (16 ounces) tortellini filled with pesto or cheese
- 1 tablespoon olive oil
- ½ yellow onion, chopped
- 1 teaspoon minced garlic (about 2 cloves)
- 1 can (28 ounces) whole or diced tomatoes with their juice
- 1 tablespoon dried basil or ½ cup fresh, chopped
- ¼ teaspoon crushed red pepper (optional)
- ¼ teaspoon pepper
- ½ tablespoon sugar
- ½ pound fresh mozzarella, diced

Cook the tortellini according to the package directions.

In a large heavy-duty skillet, heat the oil over medium heat. Add the onion and garlic and sauté them for 5 minutes, stirring them occasionally. Add the tomatoes, basil, red pepper (optional), pepper, and sugar and simmer it until the pasta is ready.

When the tortellini is done, drain it and put it in a large bowl. Toss it with the sauce. When the pasta has cooled slightly, add the mozzarella and toss it again. (This prevents the mozzarella from melting too much and getting stringy.)

TIP: Fresh mozzarella can often be found in the deli department of supermarkets or with fancier cheeses.

This is a delicious and flavorful one-pot meal suggested by Scramble newsletter subscriber Vicki Taylor. It's very healthy and satisfying for all ages. Serve it with diced mango.

thai rice pot

Prep (20 minutes) +
Cook (20 minutes)

6 servings

Nutritional
Information per
serving:

Calories 280; Total
Fat 18g, 28%, Satu-
rated Fat 6g, 30%,
Cholesterol 55mg,
18%, Sodium 680mg,
28%, Total Carbohy-
drate 12g, 4%, Di-
etary Fiber 2g, 8%,
Protein 17g, Sugar 3g

- 2 teaspoons peanut or vegetable oil
- 2 bell peppers (preferably different colors), cut into ¼-inch strips
- 8 ounces sliced shiitake or conventional mushrooms
- 1 pound lean ground pork, turkey, or vegetarian ground "meat"
- ¾ cup dry white rice
- 1 can (15 ounces) chicken or vegetable broth plus ½ cup water
  (see the Tip below)
- 3 tablespoons soy sauce
- ¾ teaspoon salt
- ¼ teaspoon pepper
- 4 scallions, chopped
- 1 cup shredded carrots
- ¼ cup chopped cilantro
- 2 tablespoons fresh lime juice (about ½ lime)

In a medium skillet, heat 1 teaspoon of the oil over medium-high heat. Add the peppers and mushrooms and cook them, stirring them occasionally, until they are softened, about 5 minutes.

In a stockpot with a tight-fitting lid, heat 1 teaspoon of the remaining oil over medium heat. Add the meat and brown it. Spoon off the fat, if there is any, and add the peppers and mushrooms, rice, broth and water, soy sauce, salt, and pepper. Bring it to a boil, reduce the heat, and cover the pot. Simmer it without removing the lid until the rice is fully cooked, 15 to 20 minutes (depending on your rice's package directions).

Stir in the scallions, carrots, cilantro, and lime juice and serve it.

TIP: If you're using shiitake mushrooms, you can buy them dried and soak them in 2 cups of warm water for about 10 minutes. That water can then be added to the pot in place of some of the water (use the same total amount of liquid the directions call for) for extra flavor.

This is a delicious marinade for almost any meat or fish, so try it with salmon or chicken if you prefer. I like using flank steak because its lower in fat and costs less, but it does need to marinate for a while to be tender. Serve this dish with white or brown rice and steamed edamame (Japanese soybeans) or lima beans.

ginger-soy flank steak

Prep + Cook = 25 minutes + Marinate

6 servings

Nutritional Information per serving:

Calories 220, Total Fat 12g, 18%, Saturated Fat 4g, 20%, Cholesterol 55mg, 18%, Sodium 600mg, 25%, Total Carbohydrate 2g, 1%, Dietary Fiber 0g, 0%, Protein 24g, Sugar 0g

1½–2 pounds flank steak
1 tablespoon minced garlic (about 6 cloves)
1 tablespoon minced ginger
3 scallions, finely sliced
2 tablespoons peanut oil
3 tablespoons soy sauce
2 teaspoons rice vinegar

Put the flank steak in a flat dish with sides. Use a dish just large enough to hold the steak in a single layer.

In a small bowl, whisk together the remaining ingredients. Pour this sauce over the steak. Flip the steak a few times to coat it with the sauce. Refrigerate the steak for at least 30 minutes and up to 24 hours.

Preheat the grill to medium-high heat, or preheat the broiler for 10 to 15 minutes. Transfer the flank steak to the grill or a broiler pan. Grill or broil it for 4 to 6 minutes per side until it is browned on the outside and no longer very pink in the middle. Slice the meat on the diagonal (try to go against the grain of the steak so it won't be stringy) and serve it.

healthy dessert idea Many fruits taste candy-sweet when served frozen. Try freezing ripe, cut and peeled bananas, grapes, blueberries, pineapple, sliced mangoes, and strawberries. Don't forget to wash and dry the berries and grapes before freezing them.

Our friend Kristen Donoghue invented this fabulous dinner salad. Her husband, Jon Hacker, said he never thought of salad as a satisfying dinner until he had this one. If any members of your family don't like salad, you can leave some chicken and corn plain (defrost extra corn) for them to eat separately. Serve it with warm pita—the salad is also good stuffed inside a pita pocket. Make sure to dress the salad lightly, as the warm chicken and slightly melted cheese provide lots of flavor.

warm chicken salad with mixed greens

Prep + Cook =
30 minutes

6 servings

Nutritional Information per serving:

Calories 260, Total Fat 10g, 15%, Saturated Fat 2.5g, 13%, Cholesterol 50mg, 17%, Sodium 750mg, 31%, Total Carbohydrate 22g, 7%, Dietary Fiber 3g, 12%, Protein 23g, Sugar 11g

- 1–1½ pounds chicken tenderloins
- 1 cup (or to taste) balsamic vinaigrette (Newman's Own or Newman's Own Light is a great choice)
- ½ cup dried cherries or cranberries
- ½ cup slivered almonds
- 1 bag (8 ounces) gourmet salad mix
- 10 fresh basil or mint leaves (optional)
- ½ cup crumbled Gorgonzola cheese
- 1 cup frozen corn kernels

In a resealable plastic bag, marinate the chicken tenderloins in about ¾ cup of the dressing for at least 10 minutes or overnight.

Preheat the toaster oven or traditional oven to 400 degrees. Bake the chicken in the marinade for 10 to 15 minutes, until it is no longer pink in the middle.

While the chicken is baking, assemble all the remaining ingredients except the corn in a large salad bowl, with the Gorgonzola cheese on top. When the chicken is almost cooked through, warm the corn kernels in the microwave for 1 to 2 minutes, then add them to the salad.

Slice the cooked chicken and add it to the salad. Top the salad with about ¼ cup of the salad dressing and toss it thoroughly. Taste it and add more dressing if needed.

This recipe makes moist and slightly sweet burgers. Serve them with ketchup or duck sauce and Chinese mustard, with or without buns. These go well with Baked Potato Chips (see p. 300).

asian turkey burgers

Prep + Cook =
20 minutes

6 servings

Nutritional
Information per
serving:

Calories 140, Total
Fat 7g, 11%, Satu-
rated Fat 2g, 10%,
Cholesterol 60mg,
20%, Sodium 400mg,
17%, Total Carbohy-
drate 4g, 1% Dietary
Fiber 0g, 0%, Protein
14g, Sugar 3g

1 pound ground turkey

½ teaspoon ground ginger

¼ red bell pepper, finely chopped

2 scallions, finely chopped

2 tablespoons soy sauce

1 tablespoon honey

1 teaspoon sesame oil

6 whole wheat buns (optional)

In a large bowl, mix all the ingredients thoroughly. Pat the mixture gently into 6 burgers.

Cook the burgers in a large nonstick skillet over medium heat, flipping them occasionally, until they are browned and cooked through, about 10 minutes. Lower the heat and cover the pan if the outsides of the burgers get too well done before the insides cook through.

This pasta tastes light and delicious and is simple to prepare. It's the kind of dish I could eat over and over and never get tired of. For a stronger flavor, add chopped olives or capers. Serve it with sautéed Swiss chard with Parmesan cheese (see p. 298).

farfalle with feta, pine nuts, and tomatoes

Prep + Cook =
25 minutes

6 servings

Nutritional
Information per
serving:

Calories 350, Total
Fat 13g, 20%, Satu-
rated Fat 3.5g, 18%,
Cholesterol 10mg,
3%, Sodium 340mg,
14%, Total Carbohy-
drate 46g, 15%, Di-
etary Fiber 2g, 8%,
Protein 11g, Sugar 2g

- **1 package (16 ounces) farfalle or other short pasta**
- **¼ cup olive oil**
- **3 tablespoons pine nuts**
- **1 tablespoon minced garlic (about 6 cloves)**
- **½ teaspoon dried oregano**
- **½ teaspoon salt**
- **½ teaspoon pepper**
- **4 large plum tomatoes or 2 large regular tomatoes, diced**
- **1 cup crumbled feta cheese**

Cook the pasta according to the package directions.

When the pasta goes into the water to cook, heat the oil in a skillet over medium heat. Add the pine nuts and garlic and cook them, stirring, until the pine nuts are lightly browned, about 5 minutes. Add the oregano, salt, and pepper and stir it well. Add the tomatoes and cook the sauce for about 3 minutes until it is heated through and the tomatoes are slightly softened.

Drain the pasta and transfer it to a large metal bowl. Toss it with the sauce combination. Top it with the feta cheese. Cover it with plastic wrap and let it stand for about 5 minutes so the flavors meld. Serve the pasta warm.

{ **aw, nuts!** To keep nuts tasting fresh, store them in the freezer. Because of their high oil content, they don't freeze, and they'll stay fresh this way for many months.

Tilapia is a great fish for a weeknight meal. It is thin, so it cooks quickly, and it's about half the price of many other varieties of fresh fish. Tilapia's mild flavor is kid-friendly, too. In fact, our son sometimes calls it chicken. Serve it with quick-cooking couscous, which can be ready in five minutes, and corn kernels for a speedy meal.

quick tilapia with lemon, garlic, and capers

Prep + Cook = 10 minutes

4 servings

Nutritional Information per serving:

Calories 200, Total Fat 8g, 12%, Saturated Fat 0g, 0%, Cholesterol 95mg, 32%, Sodium 150mg, 6%, Total Carbohydrate 4g, 1%, Dietary Fiber 0g, 0%, Protein 28g, Sugar 0g

- **1–2 tablespoons olive oil**
- **1 teaspoon minced garlic (about 2 cloves)**
- **4 tilapia fillets (about 1–1½ pounds)**
- **salt and pepper to taste**
- **2–3 tablespoons lemon juice (about ¾ lemon)**
- **1 tablespoon capers, drained (or use 2 tablespoons chopped green olives)**

In a large nonstick frying pan, heat the oil over medium heat. Add the garlic and cook it for 1 minute. Add the tilapia fillets and season them with a little salt and pepper. Cook them for about 3 to 4 minutes, depending on the thickness of the fillets, until the bottoms start to brown.

Flip the fillets, pour lemon juice over them, and season the second side with salt and pepper. Top the fish with the capers. Cook it for another 3 to 4 minutes. When the tilapia is white throughout and flakes easily with a fork, remove it to a plate and serve it hot.

{ **factory lemon:** I love shortcuts, but here's one I do not recommend: Don't substitute lemon concentrate for fresh lemon juice. Its flavor comes nowhere near the real thing.

This summer soup is pretty to look at and good to eat. You can set some of the ingredients aside and keep them separate if you're not sure your kids will eat the soup. Serve it with a loaf of whole grain bread.

light summer minestrone

Prep + Cook =
30 minutes

8 servings

Nutritional
Information per
serving:

Calories 230, Total
Fat 5g, 8%, Saturated
Fat 1g, 6%, Choles-
terol 30mg, 9%,
Sodium 660mg, 28%,
Total Carbohydrate
38g, 13%, Dietary
Fiber 6g, 24%, Pro-
tein 10g, Sugar 7g

- 1 tablespoon olive oil
- 1 large onion, diced
- 2 large carrots or 10–15 baby carrots, diced
- 2 cans (15 ounces each) chicken or vegetable broth
- 2 soup cans water
- 1½ cups uncooked thin egg noodles
- 1 medium yellow squash (about ½ pound), diced (or use zucchini)
- ¾ cup frozen peas
- 1 can (15 ounces) cannellini or pinto beans, drained
- 1 can (15 ounces) diced tomatoes or 2 cups fresh tomatoes (about 2 tomatoes)
- 10 fresh basil leaves
- salt and pepper to taste
- grated Parmesan cheese for serving

In a large saucepan, heat the oil over medium-high heat. Add the onion and sauté it for a few minutes while you chop the carrots.

Add the carrots, broth, and water. Cover the pan and bring it to a boil.

Add the noodles and simmer them for about 5 minutes. Add the squash, peas, beans, and tomatoes and return the soup to a simmer. Cook it for a few more minutes until the squash is tender.

Stir in the basil and season the soup with salt and pepper to taste.

Serve the soup topped with Parmesan cheese.

TIP: If you are making the Peanut Beef (or Chicken or Tofu) tomorrow night, you can marinate the meat or tofu while the soup is cooking tonight.

I wanted to re-create a Thai satay (marinated meat on a stick) but realized that putting all those little pieces of meat on sticks could easily burn 20 minutes of prime dinner-prep time. Instead I made beef satay without the sticks. If you want, you can thread the strips of meat onto skewers or wooden sticks for a nicer presentation. If you prefer, you can use the same marinade to make chicken or extra-firm tofu with peanut sauce instead, and you can even add some chopped carrots or peppers to the marinade. Serve this dish with steamed rice with peas.

peanut beef (or chicken or tofu)

Prep + Cook = 25 minutes + Marinate

8 servings

Nutritional Information per serving:

Calories 350, Total Fat 22g, 34%, Saturated Fat 7g, 37%, Cholesterol 75mg, 26%, Sodium 630mg, 26%, Total Carbohydrate 9g, 3%, Dietary Fiber 1g, 4%, Protein 29g, Sugar 6g

2 pounds boneless beef steak, such as top round (or use boneless, skinless chicken breasts or tofu)

½ cup peanut butter (preferably natural)

2 tablespoons lemon juice (about ½ lemon)

2 tablespoons honey

4 tablespoons soy sauce

1 tablespoon peeled and chopped fresh ginger

2 teaspoons chopped garlic (about 4 cloves)

Cut the beef into ½-inch-thick slices.

In a blender or food processor, combine all the remaining ingredients. In a plastic bag or a flat dish, combine the beef with the sauce from the blender and mix them to coat the meat thoroughly. Marinate the meat, covered and refrigerated, for at least 30 minutes or overnight, if possible.

Preheat the broiler and put the rack about 3 inches from the heat source. On a foil-lined baking sheet, broil the meat for about 4 minutes per side until it is browned and cooked through. (Alternatively, you can grill the meat.)

can we feed our children safer produce?

Our kids love fruit, and they eat a lot of it—especially in the summer. I have often wondered if I should buy more organic produce to reduce the amount of pesticides they consume with all that healthy fruit. The market where I usually shop doesn't carry organic produce, so buying organic means making a special trip, and often paying higher prices.

If you also struggle with this decision, a report from the nonprofit Environmental Working Group can help educate you about which fruits and vegetables have the highest pesticide levels (these tend to be those with edible skins) so may therefore be worth buying organic, and which have the lowest pesticide contamination, so can more safely be purchased conventionally. Unfortunately, some of my family's favorites are on the Worst list.

Best: The 12 Least Contaminated

Asparagus	Avocados	Bananas
Broccoli	Cauliflower	Corn
Kiwis	Mangoes	Onions
Papayas	Pineapples	Peas

Worst: The 12 Most Contaminated (Even after washing!)

Apples	Bell Peppers	Celery
Cherries	Imported Grapes	Nectarines
Peaches	Pears	Potatoes
Raspberries	Spinach	Strawberries

Does this mean our kids shouldn't be eating the fruit on the second list? Definitely not! Five-a-day remains an important goal. As the EWG report says, "The best option is to eat a varied diet, wash all produce, and choose organic when possible to reduce exposure to potentially harmful chemicals." Peeling fruits with edible skins also reduces their pesticide levels.

I think it's important to keep this issue in perspective. Contaminants are ubiquitous—they're in our air, water, and food, and there is little we can do to avoid them (though I think we should be educating ourselves and our children about how to reduce them). As my ninety-two-year-old grandfather, who has never knowingly purchased organic produce, says, "Everything in moderation."

My friend Jessica Honigberg shared this quick and delicious recipe for the classic Italian pasta with me. You can serve it with breadsticks and a spinach salad with chopped walnuts, dried cranberries, and Gorgonzola cheese. Use a good red wine in the sauce and enjoy the rest with dinner.

spaghetti with meat sauce

Prep + Cook =
25 minutes

8 servings

Nutritional
Information per
serving:

Calories 400, Total
Fat 12g, 18%, Satu-
rated Fat 4g, 20%,
Cholesterol 40mg,
13%, Sodium 530mg,
22%, Total Carbohy-
drate 49g, 16%, Di-
etary Fiber 2g, 8%,
Protein 19g, Sugar 7g

1 package (16 ounces) spaghetti

1 tablespoon olive oil

1 small onion, chopped

3 cloves minced garlic, (about 1½ teaspoons)

1 pound ground beef (or ground chicken, turkey, or vegetarian ground "meat")

2 cans (15 ounces each) diced tomatoes with Italian seasoning

2 tablespoons tomato paste or ½ cup red pasta sauce

¼ cup red wine

1 tablespoon sugar

½ teaspoon salt

¼ teaspoon pepper

grated Parmesan cheese for serving

Cook the spaghetti according to the package directions and drain it.

Meanwhile, in a large saucepan, heat the oil over medium heat. Add the onion and garlic and sauté them until they are softened, about 5 minutes. Add the meat, stirring it frequently until it is browned. Add the diced tomatoes, tomato paste or sauce, red wine, and sugar. Simmer the sauce for 10 minutes until it is slightly thickened. Add the salt and pepper.

In a large bowl (preferably metal, because it retains the heat), combine the spaghetti and sauce and cover it with plastic wrap until you're ready to serve dinner, so the spaghetti absorbs some of the juices.

Serve the spaghetti topped with Parmesan cheese.

TIP: To make your own seasoned tomatoes, add 1 teaspoon dried basil and ½ teaspoon dried oregano to 2 cans of plain diced tomatoes.

Andrew's college friend John Stanley is crazy about this vegetable pie and insists it is one of the greatest dinners of all time! Serve it with cornbread and a fruit salad.

baked zucchini pie

Prep (20 minutes) +
Cook (30 minutes)

8 servings

Nutritional
Information per
serving:

Calories 200, Total
Fat 12g, 18%, Satu-
rated Fat 4.5g, 23%,
Cholesterol 65mg,
22%, Sodium 520mg,
22%, Total Carbohy-
drate 11g, 4%, Di-
etary Fiber <1g, 4%,
Protein 11g, Sugar 1g

1 tablespoon butter

2 large zucchinis, thinly sliced (about 4–5 cups)

½ large onion, chopped

1 teaspoon minced garlic (about 2 cloves)

½ teaspoon salt

½ teaspoon pepper

½ teaspoon dried basil

½ teaspoon dried oregano

1 tablespoon Dijon mustard

1 prepared 9-inch pie crust, thawed if frozen

2 eggs

2 cups shredded part-skim mozzarella cheese

In a large skillet, melt the butter over medium heat. Add the zucchini, onion and garlic and sauté them until they are soft, about 10 minutes. Add the salt, pepper, basil, and oregano.

Meanwhile, preheat the oven to 375 degrees and spread the mustard over the bottom of the pie crust.

In a large bowl, combine the eggs, cheese, and zucchini mixture. Pour this mixture into the pie crust and spread it evenly.

Bake the pie for 30 minutes until it is lightly browned. Allow it to cool for 5 minutes, cut it into wedges, and serve it hot.

Use your favorite herbs to create a fresh-tasting sauce for grilled fish. Serve the salmon with wild mushroom risotto (to reduce sodium, I discard about a third of the seasoning packet) and steamed broccoli sprinkled with fresh lemon juice and pepper.

grilled salmon with herb pesto

Prep + Cook = 25 minutes

4 servings

Nutritional Information per serving:

Calories 240, Total Fat 15g, 23%, Saturated Fat 2g, 10%, Cholesterol 60mg, 20%, Sodium 50mg, 2%, Total Carbohydrate 2g, 1%, Dietary Fiber 2g, 8%, Protein 23g, Sugar 2g

- 1–1½ pounds salmon fillet (preferably wild Alaskan salmon)
- 2 tablespoons + 1 teaspoon vegetable oil
- salt and pepper to taste
- ¼ cup fresh herbs, including chives, basil, and cilantro (any combination)
- 1 tablespoon water
- 2 tablespoons fresh lemon juice (about ½ lemon)
- 1 tablespoon pine nuts (optional)
- 1 teaspoon honey

Preheat the grill to medium-high heat. Brush both sides of the salmon with 1 teaspoon of the oil and season the fish with salt and pepper to taste.

In a blender or food processor, puree the herbs, 2 tablespoons of vegetable oil, water, lemon juice, pine nuts, and honey. Transfer the mixture to a small serving bowl.

Grill the salmon for about 5 minutes per side until it flakes easily and is no longer dark pink in the middle. Serve it topped with the herb pesto.

safer salmon Whenever possible, opt for wild Alaskan salmon (also called Chinook, chum, coho, pink, or sockeye). These varieties are not as heavily overfished and don't contain such dangerous levels of environmental contaminants as other varieties.

This smooth, creamy soup tastes like a fresh version of the classic Campbell's Tomato Soup I loved as a child. This wonderful and simple recipe was suggested by Scramble newsletter editor Kathryn Spindel. She suggests serving the soup with grilled cheese sandwiches or strips of toast for a perfect weeknight dinner. We also like it with crackers crumbled on top.

creamy tomato soup

Prep + Cook = 25 minutes

8 servings

Nutritional Information per serving:

Calories 150, Total Fat 7g, 11%, Saturated Fat 4g, 20%, Cholesterol 20mg, 7%, Sodium 630mg, 26%, Total Carbohydrate 17g, 6%, Dietary Fiber 2g, 8%, Protein 6g, Sugar 10g

4 tablespoons butter

½ cup chopped onion

3 tablespoons flour

4 cups low-fat milk

1 bay leaf

1½ teaspoons sugar

1¼ teaspoon salt

½ teaspoon baking soda

3 cups fresh tomatoes or 1 can (28 ounces) crushed tomatoes with their liquid

In a stockpot, melt the butter over medium heat.

Add the onion and stir it occasionally until it is softened but not browned, about 3 minutes. Add the flour and continue to stir it for 1 to 2 minutes.

Add the milk, bay leaf, sugar, and salt. Turn the heat up slightly. Continue to cook the mixture, stirring it occasionally, until it is slightly thickened, about 10 minutes.

Stir the baking soda into the tomatoes. Add the tomatoes to the stockpot. Bring the soup to a low boil. Remove it from the heat and remove the bay leaf.

Puree the soup using a blender or food processor, or right in the pot with an immersion (hand) blender.

TIP: Try serving the soup in mugs for the kids.

This dish is a cinch to put together and is a nice alternative to burritos. If your family likes more meat, add a layer or two of cooked ground beef or turkey to the stacks. Serve it with guacamole, salsa, sour cream, and tortilla chips for a Mexican feast.

terrific tortilla tower

Prep (10 minutes) +
Cook (15 minutes)

8 servings

Nutritional
Information per
serving:

Calories 270, Total
Fat 10g, 15%, Satu-
rated Fat 5g, 24%,
Cholesterol 20 mg,
7%, Sodium 660 mg,
27%, Total Carbohy-
drate 34g, 11%, Di-
etary Fiber 5g, 18%,
Protein 12g, Sugar 5g

1 can (15 ounces) pinto beans, drained

1 can (15 ounces) unsweetened corn kernels, drained

1 can (14 ounces) Mexican-style diced tomatoes, drained, or 1½ cups mild salsa

5 soft-taco-sized flour or whole wheat tortillas

1½ cups shredded Cheddar cheese

Preheat the oven to 425 degrees. Spray a 10-inch round cake pan with nonstick cooking spray.

In a medium bowl, mix together the beans, corn, and tomatoes or salsa.

Make the tortilla tower by alternating layers. Start with 1 tortilla (lay it flat at the bottom of the pan), topped with a big scoop of the bean mixture, then a large handful of Cheddar cheese. Continue stacking until all the ingredients are used, ending with the cheese.

Bake the tower, covered with foil, for 10 minutes. Remove the cover and bake it for 5 more minutes. To serve it, allow it to cool for a few minutes, then cut it into wedges.

{ **cutting corn** To cut the kernels off an ear of corn, cut off the stem of the corn and stand the cob on its flat end in a wide rimmed bowl (to catch the kernels). Using a serrated or paring knife, slice the kernels off from the top to bottom.

While it's not quite as easy as the kind in a box with the bright orange powder, you'll know exactly what's in it, and this mac 'n' cheese tastes good enough for the whole family to enjoy. For a lower-fat version, use reduced-fat milk and cheese. Serve it with steamed broccoli tossed with Parmesan cheese.

baked macaroni and cheese

Prep (30 minutes) + Cook (25 minutes)

8 servings

Nutritional Information per serving:

Calories 300, Total Fat 13g, 20%, Saturated Fat 8g, 40%, Cholesterol 40mg, 13%, Sodium 400mg, 17%, Total Carbohydrate 32g, 11%, Dietary Fiber 1g, 4%, Protein 14g, Sugar 5g

- 8 ounces elbow macaroni
- 2 tablespoons butter
- 2 tablespoons flour
- 2 cups low-fat milk
- ½ onion, minced
- ¼ teaspoon paprika
- ½ teaspoon dry mustard
- ½ teaspoon salt
- 2 cups shredded Cheddar cheese
- ½ cup bread crumbs (optional)

In a medium or large saucepan, cook the macaroni according to the package directions. Preheat the oven to 375 degrees. Spray a ½- to 2-quart casserole dish with nonstick cooking spray.

When the water boils, add the macaroni and cook it for 5 minutes.

While the macaroni cooks, melt the butter in a large saucepan over medium heat. Whisk in the flour, then gradually add the milk while stirring the sauce. Mix in the onion, paprika, mustard, and salt and bring it to a low boil. Turn off the heat and stir in 1 ¾ cups of the cheese until the sauce is smooth.

Drain the macaroni, add it to the cheese sauce, and toss it to coat it thoroughly. Pour it into the casserole dish and top it with the remaining cheese and the bread crumbs (optional).

Bake the macaroni, uncovered, for 25 minutes until it is hot throughout and slightly browned.

If your kids don't like sauce on their chicken, remove some of the chicken before adding the lime juice and salsa to the pan. Make this meal complete by serving the chicken with Southwestern Bean Salad (see p. 298).

fiesta chicken and rice

Prep + Cook =
25 minutes

8 servings

Nutritional
Information per
serving:

Calories 290, Total
Fat 6g, 9%, Saturated
Fat 2.5g, 13%, Choles-
terol 60mg, 20%,
Sodium 850mg, 35%,
Total Carbohydrate
31g, 10%, Dietary
Fiber 0g, 0%, Protein
25g, Sugar 2g

1 package (10 ounces) yellow (saffron) rice

1 teaspoon cumin

½ teaspoon garlic powder

½ teaspoon salt

4 boneless, skinless chicken breasts (1 ½–2 pounds)

1 tablespoon olive oil

2 tablespoons lime juice (about ½ lime)

1 jar (12–16 ounces) mild chunky salsa

¾ cup shredded Cheddar cheese

Cook the rice according to the package directions. Meanwhile, in a small bowl, combine the cumin, garlic powder, and salt. Sprinkle and rub the mixture evenly over the chicken breasts. Cut the chicken into ½-inch-wide strips.

In a large skillet, heat the oil over medium heat. Add the chicken and cook it for about 4 minutes per side, flipping it once, until it is no longer pink in the center. If the outside is cooking more quickly than the inside, cover the pan for a few minutes.

Sprinkle the lime juice over the chicken and pour the salsa over everything. Stir it gently until it is warmed through. Sprinkle the chicken and salsa with the cheese and serve it over the rice.

For those who are willing to try veggie burgers, or those who are already fans of them, Boca burgers are the closest relative I've found to an actual hamburger, but much healthier—and they taste great. Our kids like these better than fast-food burgers. If you prefer, use traditional burgers for this recipe. Serve them with Baked French Fries (see p. 300) and ketchup.

boca burgers with mushrooms, onions, and cheddar

Prep + Cook =
25 minutes

4 servings

Nutritional
Information per
serving:

Calories 350, Total Fat 15g, 24%, Saturated Fat 5g, 26%, Cholesterol 20 mg, 6%, Sodium 330 mg, 14%, Total Carbohydrate 29g, 10%, Dietary Fiber 3g, 12%, Protein 18g, Sugar 8g

- 1 teaspoon plus 1 tablespoon olive oil
- 4 Boca burgers (or use any kind of burger)
- 1 onion, halved (from top to bottom) and cut into thin slices
- 8 ounces sliced mushrooms
- 4 slices Cheddar cheese (about 2 ounces)
- 4 English muffins or whole wheat buns
- ketchup or barbecue sauce for serving

In a large nonstick skillet, heat 1 teaspoon of the oil over medium heat. Add the burgers and cook them, flipping them every couple of minutes, until they are browned and heated through, about 8 minutes. (For meat burgers, cook them for about 5 minutes per side until they are no longer pink in the middle.)

While the burgers are cooking, heat the remaining 1 tablespoon of the oil in a medium skillet over medium-high heat. Add the onions and mushrooms, and cook them, stirring them occasionally, until they are softened and the onions are slightly browned, about 5 to 8 minutes.

When the burgers are cooked through, top them with the sliced cheese and cover the pan for a minute until the cheese melts. Put the burgers on English muffins or buns, dress them with ketchup or barbecue sauce, and top the burgers with the onions and mushrooms.

This grilled fish has a wonderful smoky flavor. If you can't find trout at your market, substitute salmon or another small whole fish. Serve it with breadsticks and Green Beans Almondine (see p. 298).

grilled trout with garlic and rosemary

Prep + Cook =
30 minutes

4 servings

Nutritional
Information per
serving:

Calories 230, Total
Fat 11g, 17%, Satu-
rated Fat 2.5g, 13%,
Cholesterol 85mg,
28%, Sodium 200mg,
8%, Total Carbohy-
drate <1g, 0%, Di-
etary Fiber 0g, 0%,
Protein 30g, Sugar 0g

4 whole trout (about 2 pounds total), cleaned and boned (have the fish market do this)

1 tablespoon olive oil

2 teaspoons minced garlic (about 4 cloves)

¼ teaspoon salt

4 sprigs fresh rosemary

lemon wedges for serving

Preheat the grill to medium-high. Rinse the trout inside and out and pat it dry.

With a pastry brush or your fingers, brush the oil all over the inside and outside surfaces of the fish. Distribute the garlic evenly inside each trout. Shake a little salt over the inside and outside surfaces of the fish. Put one sprig of rosemary inside each fish. Close the fish.

Grill the fish for 3 to 4 minutes per side until the flesh is white and flakes easily in the thickest part.

Remove the rosemary and serve the fish with lemon wedges.

TIP: If you prefer to cook the trout in the oven rather than on the grill, preheat the oven to 400 degrees and bake the fish for 25 minutes in a baking dish coated with nonstick cooking spray.

This is my favorite vegetarian chili. It's sweet, chunky, and just a little spicy. If your kids won't eat these foods mixed together, remove a couple of spoonfuls of the beans and corn and set some extra carrots aside for them. Serve the chili alone or over rice or noodles, with extra carrots with ranch dressing on the side. You may also like the chili topped with shredded Cheddar cheese.

veggie chili

Prep + Cook =
30 minutes

8 servings

Nutritional
Information per
serving:

Calories 230, Total
Fat 3g, 5%, Saturated
Fat 0g, 0%, Choles-
terol 0mg, 0%,
Sodium 1100mg, 46%,
Total Carbohydrate
41g, 14%, Dietary
Fiber 12g, 48%, Pro-
tein 10g, Sugar 13g

1 tablespoon olive oil

1 medium onion, diced

1 red bell pepper, diced

1 cup diced baby carrots (about 20 baby carrots)

1 can (15 ounces) red kidney beans with their liquid (preferably unsweetened)

1 can (15 ounces) black beans with their liquid

1 cup mild salsa

1 can (28 ounces) crushed tomatoes

1 tablespoon chili powder

1 can (15 ounces) unsweetened corn kernels, drained

low-fat plain yogurt for serving

In a large heavy saucepan or skillet, heat the oil over medium heat. Add the onions and peppers and sauté them until the onions start to brown, about 5 minutes.

Add the carrots, beans with their liquid, salsa, crushed tomatoes, and chili powder to the pot. Bring the chili to a boil, lower the heat, and simmer it, uncovered, for 20 minutes or up to 40 minutes, if time allows. About 10 minutes before serving, add the corn.

Serve the chili in bowls or over rice, topped with a dollop of yogurt.

the good stuff The quality of the salsa can make all the difference in a meal. Try a few varieties to learn your family's favorite, then stock up. Our favorite is Jardine's.

Taco night is popular at our house because we all get to make our own the way we like them. Crunchy or soft, they're irresistible. If you like more spice, season your meat with chili powder. Many families like to use their own favorite fillings, such as diced tomatoes or avocado. Serve the tacos with guacamole and sliced mango on the side.

make-your-own tacos

Prep + Cook =
15 minutes

8 servings

Nutritional
Information per
serving:

Calories 320, Total
Fat 18g, 27%, Satu-
rated Fat 7g, 37%,
Cholesterol 40 mg,
14%, Sodium 260 mg,
11%, Total Carbohy-
drate 21g, 7%, Di-
etary Fiber 2g, 10%,
Protein 21g, Sugar 1g

1 pound ground beef, turkey, or chicken (or use 1 can black beans, drained)

salt to taste

¼ head iceberg lettuce, chopped

shredded Cheddar cheese

1 jar (12 ounces) salsa

1 tomato, diced (optional)

½ cup sour cream (optional)

1 box taco shells or 1 package soft-taco-sized flour or whole wheat tortillas

If you are using the taco shells, heat them on a baking sheet in a 350 degree pre-heated oven for about 5 minutes, watching them carefully so they don't burn.

In a medium skillet, brown the meat and add salt to taste. Make an assembly line with all the ingredients, or bring them to the table in bowls so family members can assemble their own tacos.

We love the texture of these Italian potato dumplings, and I've received great feedback on this recipe. If you can't find the tricolor variety, use regular white gnocchi instead. Serve it with a loaf of bread and a Carrot and Apple Salad (see p. 298).

gnocchi with artichokes and sundried tomatoes

Prep + Cook =
20 minutes

6 servings

Nutritional Information per serving:

Calories 330, Total Fat 14g, 22%, Saturated Fat 3.5g, 18%, Cholesterol 25mg, 8%, Sodium 550mg, 23%, Total Carbohydrate 41g, 14%, Dietary Fiber 6g, 24%, Protein 11g, Sugar 2g

1 package (16 ounces) tricolor gnocchi (sold with pastas)

¼ cup olive oil

¼ teaspoon red pepper flakes (optional)

1 teaspoon minced garlic (about 2 cloves)

½ cup marinated sundried tomatoes, drained and cut into strips

1 can (14 ounces) artichoke hearts, drained and quartered

4 fresh sage or basil leaves, slivered

½ cup grated or diced Gouda cheese (or use grated Parmesan cheese)

Cook the gnocchi according to the package directions.

Meanwhile, in a large skillet, heat the oil over medium heat. Add the red pepper flakes (optional) and garlic and cook them for 1 minute. Add the tomatoes and artichokes and sauté them over medium-low heat for 5 to 10 minutes.

Drain the gnocchi and add it to the skillet, along with the sage or basil leaves. Stir the mixture until it is heated through. Transfer the gnocchi to a serving bowl and top it with the cheese. Stir everything together and serve it hot.

For a sweet twist on grilled tuna, try this pineapple marinade. If you use the pineapple juice from a can of pineapple rings, the kids can have the pineapple as a side dish with the tuna. Or, for a fancy flourish, top the tuna with grilled pineapple rings. Serve the fish with green beans sautéed with a little olive oil and garlic.

tuna steaks in pineapple-ginger marinade

Prep + Cook = 15 minutes + Marinate

4 servings

Nutritional Information per serving:

Calories 220, Total Fat 9g, 14%, Saturated Fat 2g, 9%, Cholesterol 45 mg, 14%, Sodium 550 mg, 23%, Total Carbohydrate 5g, 2%, Dietary Fiber 0g, 0%, Protein 28g, Sugar 4g

- ½ cup pineapple juice
- 2 tablespoons soy sauce
- ½ teaspoon ginger powder or 1 teaspoon fresh minced ginger
- 1 tablespoon olive oil
- 1–1½ pounds thick tuna steaks or mahimahi

In a large measuring cup, mix together the pineapple juice, soy sauce, ginger, and oil.

In a dish with sides (use a dish just large enough to hold the tuna in a single layer), marinate the tuna in the pineapple juice mixture for at least 30 minutes and up to 12 hours. Be sure to refrigerate the tuna while it marinates.

Preheat the grill to high heat, or heat a nonstick skillet to medium-high heat. Cook the tuna steaks for about 2 minutes per side for rare, or up to 4 minutes per side for well done.

While the tuna cooks, pour the remaining marinade into a small saucepan, bring it to a boil, and cook it for several minutes until it is slightly reduced. Serve the tuna with the sauce spooned over it.

When I took this salad to the Summer Serenade concert at the National Zoo, five-year-old Sam Masling begged me for the recipe! The kids and adults at the picnic agreed that this dish is a hit. To make your meal complete, serve it with a roast chicken from the supermarket or pita wedges with hummus. This is an ideal recipe for picnics or potlucks because it is good cold or warm.

indonesian curry rice salad

Prep + Cook =
25 minutes

4 servings

Nutritional Information per serving:

Calories 290, Total Fat 16g, 25%, Saturated Fat 2g, 10%, Cholesterol 0mg, 0%, Sodium 560mg, 23%, Total Carbohydrate 31g, 10%, Dietary Fiber 6g, 22%, Protein 6g, Sugar 12g

- 1 box (7 ounces) rice pilaf, any flavor
- 1 teaspoon curry powder
- ½ teaspoon salt
- ½ cup slivered almonds (or use cashews), lightly toasted
- ½ cup dried cranberries
- 2 stalks celery, diced
- 1 can (5 ounces) diced water chestnuts
- ¼ cup orange juice
- 2 tablespoons soy sauce
- 2 tablespoons peanut oil

Prepare the rice pilaf according to the package directions, discarding the flavor packet and adding the curry powder and salt instead.

While the rice is cooking, put the nuts, cranberries, celery, and water chestnuts in a medium bowl.

In a measuring cup, mix together the orange juice, soy sauce, and peanut oil.

When the rice is done, add it to the bowl with the nuts and vegetables, and pour the sauce over everything. Mix it thoroughly and chill the salad until you're ready to serve it.

TIP: To toast the nuts, use the broiling pan in the toaster oven and set the toaster to the lightest setting. When the toaster pops, remove the nuts and add them to the salad. Nuts cook quickly and burn easily, so watch them closely.

You can substitute similar amounts of your favorite vegetables for those in this recipe, but these work nicely. Spinach, mushrooms, or asparagus also works well in this basic and flavorful frittata, which is also great for brunch. Use twelve egg whites instead of the eggs for a meal lower in calories and cholesterol. Serve it with a green salad and corn muffins.

frittata with onion, peppers, and zucchini

Prep + Cook =
30 minutes

6 servings

Nutritional
Information per
serving:

Calories 200, Total
Fat 12g, 18%, Satu-
rated Fat 4g, 20%,
Cholesterol 360mg,
120%, Sodium 170mg,
7%, Total Carbohy-
drate 6g, 2%, Dietary
Fiber 1g, 4%, Protein
16g, Sugar 3g

1 tablespoon olive oil

1 tablespoon butter

1 red onion, halved and thinly sliced

1 zucchini, cut into thin rounds

1 red bell pepper, diced

10 large eggs, lightly beaten

1 cup grated Swiss, Gruyere, or Fontina cheese

salt and pepper to taste

2 teaspoons dried or fresh rosemary

Preheat the oven to 400 degrees.

In a 12-inch oven-proof nonstick skillet, heat the oil and butter over medium-high heat. Cook the onions until they are nicely browned, about 10 minutes. Add the zucchini and bell pepper and stir the vegetables while they cook for 3 to 4 minutes.

In a large bowl, whisk together the eggs, cheese, salt, and pepper. Pour the eggs over the veggies. Remove the skillet from the heat and gently shake it to distribute the eggs evenly. Sprinkle the top with rosemary.

Bake the frittata for 10 to 12 minutes, uncovered, until the eggs set. Remove it from the oven (you can invert the frittata onto a plate or cutting board if you want to), cut it into wedges, and serve it warm.

This is a delicious savory marinade for steaks or chicken. If your kids like plain food, you can keep one steak out of the marinade and rub it with kosher salt instead before grilling. In general, the more expensive the steak, the more tender it will be. Serve the steak with green beans tossed with pesto sauce (see p. 298).

grilled steak with rosemary and dijon

Prep + Cook =
30 minutes

6 servings

Nutritional
Information per
serving:
Calories 430, Total
Fat 24g, 37%, Saturated Fat 7g, 36%,
Cholesterol 105 mg,
36%, Sodium 570 mg,
24%, Total Carbohydrate 1g, 0%, Dietary
Fiber 0g, 0%, Protein
49g, Sugar 0g

- ¼ cup Dijon mustard
- 2 tablespoons olive oil
- 1 teaspoon kosher salt
- 1 tablespoon fresh or dried rosemary leaves
- 2–3 boneless steaks (3 pounds total), at least 1-inch thick

Preheat the grill to high heat. (These steaks can also be prepared in a nonstick skillet over medium-high heat on the stovetop.)

In a large flat dish with sides, mix together the mustard, oil, salt, and rosemary.

Lay the steaks flat in the dish and coat both sides with the marinade.

When the grill is very hot, grill the steaks for 4 to 6 minutes per side, depending on the desired doneness. For the first minute of grilling on each side, leave the top of the grill open, and then close it until you are ready to flip the steaks.

Slice the steak in strips to serve it.

TIP: If you plan to make the Barbecue Chicken with Yogurt Marinade tomorrow, get a head start by marinating it tonight.

This is a great dinner to set up in the morning, so all you have to do is grill the chicken when dinnertime rolls around. Serve it with grilled broccoli spears (see p. 299).

barbecue chicken with yogurt marinade

Prep + Cook =
25 minutes +
Marinate

5 servings

Nutritional
Information per
serving:

Calories 230, Total Fat 4.5g, 7%, Saturated Fat 1g, 5%, Cholesterol 80mg, 27%, Sodium 490mg, 20%. Total Carbohydrate 10g, 3%, Dietary Fiber 0g, 0%, Protein 36g, Sugar 9g

1½ cups (12 ounces) low-fat plain yogurt

1 tablespoon olive oil

2 tablespoons fresh lemon juice (about ½ lemon)

1 teaspoon minced garlic (about 2 cloves)

¾ teaspoon dried thyme or 2¼ teaspoons fresh

½ teaspoon dried tarragon or mint or 1½ teaspoons fresh, chopped

¾ teaspoon salt

1 tablespoon honey

1½–2 pounds boneless, skinless chicken breasts

In a large measuring cup, make the marinade by combining the yogurt, oil, lemon juice, garlic, herbs, and salt. Remove about ½ cup of the mixture to a small serving bowl and stir the honey into it. Set this mixture aside to serve with the cooked chicken.

Cut ½-inch-deep slits in the top and bottom of each chicken breast. Lay the chicken breasts in a flat dish with sides (use a dish just large enough to hold them in a single layer), and top them with the marinade. Flip the chicken several times to coat it with the sauce. Cover the dish and refrigerate it for at least 2 hours and up to 24 hours.

Preheat the grill to medium-high heat. Remove the chicken from the marinade to a plate, shaking off the excess yogurt mixture and discarding it along with the rest of the marinade from the dish.

Grill the chicken over medium-high heat, with the grill closed, until the juices run clear and the meat is no longer pink in the center, about 5 to 8 minutes per side. (Alternatively, you can cook the breasts on the stovetop in a nonstick skillet over medium heat.)

Cut the cooked chicken into strips and serve it with the reserved sauce.

TIP: If the inside of the chicken is still pink and the outside is getting too browned, finish cooking the meat in the microwave for 1 or 2 minutes.

This family-pleaser was suggested by Scramble newsletter subscriber Kelly O'Rourke. Our daughter, Celia, called it "better than plain pasta"—high praise in her book. Serve it with sliced watermelon and a baguette.

broiled zucchini pasta with cheese

Prep + Cook =
25 minutes

6 servings

Nutritional
Information per
serving:

Calories 340, Total
Fat 7g, 11%, Satu-
rated Fat 3g, 15%,
Cholesterol 10mg,
3%, Sodium 230mg,
10%, Total Carbohy-
drate 47g, 16%, Di-
etary Fiber 2g, 8%,
Protein 16g, Sugar 4g

12 ounces ziti or other short pasta (you can make the whole 16-ounce package and leave some plain)

1 tablespoon olive oil

1 large zucchini, halved and thinly sliced

1½ teaspoons chopped garlic (about 3 cloves)

1 can (15 ounces) diced tomatoes with their liquid

½ cup white wine

1½ teaspoons dried basil

1 cup shredded mozzarella cheese

½ cup shredded Cheddar cheese

Preheat the broiler.

Cook the pasta according to the package directions.

While the pasta is cooking, heat the oil in a large ovenproof skillet over medium heat. Add the zucchini and garlic and cook them for 3 minutes. Add the tomatoes and their liquid, wine, and basil. Simmer the sauce, stirring it occasionally, until the pasta is done, about 10 to 15 minutes.

Drain the pasta well and add it to the skillet with the tomatoes and zucchini. Cover the mixture with the cheeses and put the skillet under the broiler for 3 to 4 minutes until the top is browned (but not burned!).

Large, firm portobello mushroom caps make a great natural crust for many interesting fillings. They also are the perfect size for individual pizzas. (If you can't find large portobello mushroom caps in your area, you can use a prepared pizza crust for this recipe.) The fillings can be varied according to your family's tastes. You can get creative with olives, peppers, chopped tomatoes, and different cheeses. Serve them with a loaf of bread and a green salad with pine nuts and diced strawberries.

portobello mushroom pizzas

Prep + Cook =
15 minutes

6 servings

Nutritional Information per serving:

Calories 250, Total Fat 14g, 21%, Saturated Fat 4.5g, 21%, Cholesterol 15 mg, 5%, Sodium 350 mg, 15%, Total Carbohydrate 11g, 4%, Dietary Fiber 3g, 13%, Protein 10g, Sugar 6g

3 tablespoons olive oil

¼ teaspoon salt

6 large whole portobello mushroom caps

3 tablespoons pesto sauce (store-bought or homemade: see p. 214)

2 tablespoons crumbled feta cheese

2–3 tablespoons red pasta sauce

¼ cup shredded mozzarella cheese

6 leaves fresh basil, chopped

Preheat the oven to 450 degrees. Line a large baking sheet with foil. In a small bowl, combine the oil and salt.

With a damp paper towel, wipe the outsides of the mushroom caps to remove any dirt. With a serrated spoon, scoop out the stem of each mushroom and set the stems aside on a cutting board. Scrape off the black gills from the insides of the mushroom caps and discard the gills. Finely chop the mushroom stems.

With a pastry brush, brush all the surfaces of the mushroom caps with the oil. Put the caps on the baking sheet.

For pesto feta pizzas: Spread about 1 tablespoon of pesto sauce inside each mushroom cap. Fill the caps with chopped stems, chopped basil, and feta cheese.

For mozzarella pizzas: Spread 1 tablespoon of pasta sauce inside each mushroom cap. Top it with chopped mushroom stems (optional), basil, and mozzarella cheese.

Bake the pizzas for 5 to 8 minutes until the cheese melts and the mushrooms are thoroughly heated.

TIP: These also cook very quickly in a toaster oven and make a fun appetizer for parties.

This amazingly simple dish, a popular recipe from our 1998 cookbook, tastes fresh and fruity and is a colorful addition to a plate. If your kids are picky eaters, set aside some cooked shrimp or chicken before adding the remaining ingredients. Serve this dish with yellow rice and steamed green beans.

mango-salsa shrimp or chicken

Prep + Cook =
25 minutes

6 Servings

Nutritional
Information per
serving:

Calories 170, Total
Fat 5g, 7%, Saturated
Fat 1g, 5%, Choles-
terol 70mg, 24%,
Sodium 65mg, 3%,
Total Carbohydrate
4g, 1%, Dietary Fiber
0g, 0%, Protein 27g,
Sugar 4g

1 tablespoon vegetable oil

1 pound shrimp, peeled and deveined, or 3–4 boneless, skinless chicken breast halves, cut into bite-sized pieces

1 jar (12–15 ounces) mild chunky salsa

1 ripe mango, peeled and diced

¼ cup fresh cilantro, chopped

In a large nonstick skillet, heat the oil over medium heat. Add the shrimp or chicken. Sauté the shrimp, stirring them often, until they turn pink, about 3 minutes. (Sauté the chicken for about 5 to 7 minutes until it is no longer pink inside.)

Add the remaining ingredients. Cook the mixture over medium heat until it is heated through.

simple side dishes

One of my tricks for whipping together a complete dinner is sticking with easy side dishes. While I can put together a tasty main dish each night without too much sweat, I find it hard to fuss over side dishes, too, so I keep them very simple. That way, they can be prepared while the pasta is cooking, the soup is simmering, or the casserole is baking. Here are my suggestions for making easy side dishes all week long.

Buy a few extra vegetables and lettuce for a salad on your weekly grocery trips. The veggies can easily be steamed, microwaved, or roasted while dinner cooks.

Keep some flavored (or plain) rice mixes and couscous preparations on hand to serve alongside meats or stews.

In the freezer, keep several side dishes ready, such as Asian dumplings and egg rolls, frozen vegetables, and vacuum-packed guacamole to serve with chips. Look for low-salt and low-fat versions of all these prepared side dishes.

Finally, keep your pantry stocked with cornmeal and biscuit mix for quick and easy muffins, breads, and biscuits. When you shop, buy some pita, bread sticks, or other breads to serve with dinner. You might even consider using a bread machine.

Salads

Try topping a green salad or spinach salad with interesting combinations of fresh and dried fruits, cheeses, vegetables, and nuts. Here are a few of my favorite toppings for salads:

diced oranges, walnuts, and goat cheese
diced avocado, oranges, and grated Parmesan cheese
feta cheese, chopped tomatoes, and diced cucumbers
walnuts, diced red bell peppers, and blue cheese
goat cheese, pecans, and sliced pears
shredded carrots, diced red bell peppers, and diced avocado
dried cranberries and pine nuts
grated carrots and red cabbage
diced apples, Gorgonzola cheese, and slivered almonds

Cucumber Salad: Peel and chop 3 cucumbers and combine them with 1/4 cup crumbled feta cheese, 15 or so chopped fresh mint leaves, and 1 teaspoon honey.

Greek Salad: Combine chopped tomato, cucumber, and feta cheese and drizzle it with olive oil and red wine vinegar. Add pita chips for extra crunch.

Waldorf Salad: Combine 2 diced apples, 4 diced celery stalks, and a handful of walnuts. Toss it with about 2 teaspoons mayonnaise and 1 tablespoon pineapple juice

Tropical Fruit Salad: Combine diced kiwi, mango, and banana.

Ambrosia Fruit Salad: Toss cut fruit of your choice with 2 tablespoons yogurt, 1 teaspoon fresh lemon juice, and 1 tablespoon honey.

Carrot and Apple Salad: Toss shredded carrots and shredded apples with 1 tablespoon each of orange juice and fresh lemon juice.

Coleslaw: Combine 1 bag coleslaw mix (or grate one head cabbage and a couple of carrots) with ½ cup light mayonnaise, ¼ cup low-fat sour cream, ¼ cup reduced-fat milk, ¼ cup white vinegar, 1 tablespoon sugar, and ½ teaspoon salt. Refrigerate the slaw until you are ready to serve it.

Japanese Salad: Combine edamame (shelled soybeans), chopped avocado, 2 tablespoons balsamic vinegar, and 2 tablespoons olive oil.

Italian Salad: Layer sliced tomatoes, sliced fresh mozzarella, and whole basil leaves and drizzle the salad with balsamic vinegar.

Southwestern Bean Salad: Combine 1 can (15 ounces) black beans, drained and rinsed, 1 can (14 ounces) corn kernels, 1 diced red pepper, 1 teaspoon fresh lime juice, ½ teaspoon salt, and ½ cup fresh cilantro. Refrigerate the salad until you are ready to serve it.

Guacamole: Mash 2 avocados with the juice of half a lemon or lime and salt and garlic powder to taste. Serve this with tortilla chips.

Steamed and Sautéed Vegetables

Lemony-Garlic Spinach: In a skillet, sauté 1 teaspoon minced garlic in 1 tablespoon olive oil for 30 seconds (don't burn it!). Add 1 bag (9 ounces) fresh baby spinach. Stir it, cover the pan, and steam it for 3 to 5 minutes or until it is limp, but don't overcook it. Sprinkle it with 1 tablespoon fresh lemon juice.

Italian-Style Cauliflower: Cut a head of cauliflower into florets and steam them until they are very soft, 15 to 20 minutes. Toss the cauliflower with 2 tablespoons butter, 1 tablespoon grated Parmesan cheese, 2 tablespoons bread crumbs, and 1 tablespoon chopped parsley.

Swiss Chard: Wash the Swiss chard thoroughly and trim the ends. Chop the leaves and stems. Heat 1 tablespoon olive oil over medium heat in a large nonstick skillet and add 1 teaspoon minced garlic. When the garlic starts to brown, add the Swiss chard and ¼ cup water, reduce the heat to low, cover the pan, and cook it for about 10 minutes. Remove the cover, raise the heat to medium-low, and cook it until it is very tender, about 10 more minutes. Top it with a little salt and grated Parmesan cheese.

Artichokes: To steam artichokes, put them thorny side down in boiling water for about 30 to 40 minutes, depending on the size of the artichokes. Cover the pot and maintain a low boil until the artichokes are tender.

Green Beans, Broccoli, or Asparagus: Toss 1 pound of steamed vegetables with any of the following mixtures:

Almondine: ¼ cup sliced almonds that have been sautéed in butter or margarine
Sesame-soy-ginger sauce: 1 teaspoon sesame oil, 1½ teaspoons soy sauce, 1 teaspoon fresh minced ginger or a few shakes of ginger powder, 1 teaspoon sesame seeds, and 1 teaspoon sugar. (Serve hot or cold.)
Parmesan: 1 tablespoon butter, margarine, or olive oil and 1 tablespoon grated Parmesan cheese
Pesto: 1–2 tablespoons pesto sauce and toasted pine nuts
Goat cheese: 3 tablespoons goat cheese, 1

tablespoon lemon juice, and salt and pepper to taste

Lemon-pepper: 1 tablespoon lemon juice and ⅛ teaspoon pepper

Teriyaki: 2 tablespoons teriyaki sauce and 1 tablespoon toasted sesame seeds

Asparagus with yogurt and dill: Top steamed asparagus with plain yogurt mixed with fresh dill

Sesame stir-fry: Heat 1 tablespoon sesame oil in a wok or frying pan over medium-high heat. Lightly brown 2 teaspoons minced garlic. Add 1 pound green beans, broccoli, or asparagus and ⅛ cup water. Cover the pan and cook the vegetables for 2 to 4 minutes. Add 1 tablespoon soy sauce and stir-fry the veggies for 1 minute.

Roasted Vegetables

Baby Carrots, Asparagus, or Green Beans: Toss 1 pound of vegetables with 1–2 tablespoons olive oil, ½ teaspoon kosher salt, and ¼ teaspoon pepper. Roast them in the oven at 450 degrees until they are slightly browned, 10 to 20 minutes. To the asparagus and green beans, add 1 tablespoon fresh lemon juice with the olive oil, if desired.

Grilled Vegetables and Bread

Zucchini: Cut the zucchini (or yellow squash) into quarters, lengthwise, and then cut the strips into several smaller strips. Toss the strips in a bowl with about 1 tablespoon olive oil and salt and pepper to taste. Place the coated zucchini on a vegetable tray or sturdy piece of aluminum foil. Grill it for 10 to 20 minutes until it reaches the desired tenderness.

Sweet Potatoes: Cut a large sweet potato into ¼-inch slices. In a bowl, toss the sweet potato slices with 1 teaspoon olive oil, 1 teaspoon honey, a few shakes of salt, and a couple shakes of balsamic vinegar. Wrap the potatoes tightly in foil and grill them for 20 to 30 minutes. (These take much longer to cook than steaks or fish, so place them on the grill while it is warming up.) Rotate the foil packet on the grill several times while they are cooking. The potatoes come out soft and browned.

Asparagus or Broccoli Spears: Use a vegetable tray or foil to keep the vegetables from falling through the grates. Toss the spears with a little olive oil or butter and grated Parmesan cheese once they are cooked (about 10 to 15 minutes).

Corn on the Cob: Clean 4 ears of corn and lay them on a large sheet of aluminum foil. Melt 1 tablespoon butter and drizzle or brush it on the corn. Season the corn with salt. Tightly wrap the corn in a single layer in the foil and grill it for 10 to 15 minutes.

Grilled Bread: Cut a loaf of Italian bread into 1-inch slices. Mix together olive oil (about ¼ cup or more), 1 teaspoon kosher salt, and about 1 tablespoon chopped fresh rosemary leaves. With a pastry brush, lightly coat about 8 slices of the bread with the mixture. Place the slices on the heated grill for 1 to 2 minutes per side until lightly browned.

Grains

Festive Wild Rice: Toss cooked wild rice with toasted pecans, dried cranberries, and a splash of vinaigrette dressing.

Spaetzle or Gnocchi Parmesan: Spaetzle is a German dumpling prepared like pasta. If your supermarket doesn't carry spaetzle, substitute Italian dumplings (gnocchi). Toss cooked spaetzle or gnocchi with 1 tablespoon butter, a splash of milk, and some grated Parmesan cheese.

Bulgur Wheat: Cook it in chicken broth and toss it with a handful of chopped grapes.

Rice and Peas: Mix cooked white or brown rice with cooked frozen peas and 1 tablespoon soy sauce.

Asian Rice Pilaf: Cook a box of rice pilaf according to the package directions, but don't use the flavor packet. To the cooked pilaf, add half of a diced red bell pepper, ½ cup diced carrots, 2 diced scallions, and 1 tablespoon each of sesame oil, soy sauce, and teriyaki sauce. Chill the pilaf for 2 hours before serving, if time allows.

Potatoes

Use 1 large or 2 small potatoes per person. Unless specific potatoes are called for, you can use any variety. Scrub them and remove the eyes, then prepare them one of the following ways:

Oven-Roasted: Slice the potatoes into wedges and parboil them (place them in boiling water for 2 to 3 minutes and then drain them). Toss them with 1 to 2 tablespoons olive or vegetable oil, 1 teaspoon oregano, and salt and pepper to taste. Bake them at 450 degrees on a baking sheet, turning them every 10 minutes, until crispy brown, about 20 to 30 minutes total. (Alternatively, skip parboiling and roast the potatoes for an extra 10 to 15 minutes.) For crispier potatoes, put them under the broiler for the final 2 or 3 minutes.

Baked Potato Chips: Thinly slice your favorite variety of potatoes (unpeeled) and toss the slices with 2 tablespoons peanut or vegetable oil, ½ teaspoon salt, and a pinch of rosemary. Spread the potatoes in a single layer in a lightly oiled pan and bake them at 450 degrees until they are crispy, about 20 minutes.

Hash Browns: Cut the potatoes into 1-inch cubes and boil or microwave them until they are soft. Sauté 1 diced onion and 1 teaspoon minced garlic (about 2 cloves) in 1 to 2 tablespoons butter until the onion is soft and translucent. Add the potatoes and sauté them for about 5 minutes. Add salt and pepper to taste. Serve the hash browns hot with ketchup or salsa.

Sweet Potato Fries: Scrub 2 or 3 medium sweet potatoes and slice them lengthwise, making long thin strips. Place them in a roasting pan, toss them with 1 to 2 tablespoons vegetable or peanut oil, and roast them in the oven at 450 degrees, turning them every 10 minutes until they are done, about 20 minutes. They become soft, not crispy.

Baked Sweet Potatoes: Poke several holes in the potatoes and wrap them in aluminum foil. Bake them on the oven rack for 1 hour (or more if time allows) at 400 degrees until they're syrupy sweet. If you're in a hurry, you can microwave them, without foil, for 10 to 15 minutes until soft, turning them every 5 minutes.

Creamy Mashed: Cut up the potatoes and boil them until they are tender, 15 to 20 minutes. Drain them and, in the same pot, mash them with a fork. Add enough milk to make them creamy, 2 to 3 tablespoons butter or margarine (to taste), and 2 to 3 tablespoons sour cream (to taste). Reheat the potatoes and add salt, pepper, and/or lightly sautéed garlic if desired.

Baked French Fries: Cut 3 or 4 Yukon Gold potatoes into strips. Boil them for 3 minutes, drain and dry them, then toss them with 2 tablespoons peanut oil and salt to taste. Roast them at 450 degrees for 15 minutes, then broil them for 5 to 10 minutes, turning them once, until they are brown and slightly crisp.

beyond cheerios

ideas for feeding babies and toddlers

As they near the end of the first year, babies can begin to eat what the family eats, as long as your doctor okays it. Unfortunately, after their first bowls of rice cereal and between nursings or bottles, we all run out of ideas for feeding our hungry babies.

Babies' tolerance for baby food is limited. It's not long before they are pushing the spoon away, wanting to eat finger foods and to establish some independence. When they are little, their minds are wide open and their taste preferences yet undecided, so it's the perfect time to encourage experimentation. We were surprised when our babies liked tofu, hummus, and lentils!

When your leftovers won't do, here are some snack and meal ideas for babies and young children that are both tasty and nutritious. Always test the food with your tongue to make sure it's not too hot!

WARNING: Not all foods are appropriate for all babies and children. Check with your doctor before introducing new foods, and take a CPR class to ensure your child's safety in the event of a choking incident or allergic reaction.

Cereals and Grains

pizza bagels (toasted bagels topped with tomato sauce and mozzarella cheese and toasted or broiled)

oatmeal with milk and a touch of brown sugar

crackers with hummus, avocado, or veggie cream cheese

toast with applesauce or apple butter

cream of wheat

mini muffins

wheat toast with butter

sweet potatoes or white potato cubes (boiled or microwaved until they are soft)

pancakes cut in shapes with cookie cutters

rice and peas

Pasta

pasta or cheese tortellini with tomato sauce

pasta with cottage cheese, peas, and cannellini beans

ramen noodles (cooked without the salty flavor packet)

pasta with butter

cooked couscous mixed with shredded Cheddar cheese (kids may enjoy mixing this themselves)

Fruits and Vegetables

fresh fruit in season, cut into small pieces
(grapes, strawberries, cantaloupe,
blueberries, melon, oranges, bananas, etc.)

steamed broccoli or green beans

applesauce

peas

chopped tomatoes

avocados (fed to the child with a spoon)

raisins and other dried fruit

fruit smoothies (blend fruit with yogurt, milk,
or juice)

ice pops (freeze juice blended with fruit)

canned pineapple

sliced apples dipped in honey

Proteins

baked beans or canned black beans, alone or
mixed with canned corn

ground turkey, chicken, or beef made into
little meatballs

shredded cheese or cheese cubes

celery filled with or dipped in peanut butter or
cream cheese

fried eggs cut into animal shapes

hard-boiled eggs

grilled peanut butter and butter sandwiches

peanut butter spread on tortillas and warmed
in the microwave

grilled turkey and cheese sandwiches

pine nuts, alone or mixed with dried
cranberries

vegetarian hamburgers

grilled cheese sandwiches (with tomato or
avocado)

tuna and melted cheese on an English muffin
or toast

cooked chicken dipped in a sauce of ketchup
and mayonnaise

yogurt mixed with dried fruit or cereal

mashed peanut butter and banana, alone or in
sandwiches

peanut butter or cheddar cheese and apple
sandwiches

shish kabobs of cubed chicken or hot dogs
with pineapple on toothpicks (beware of
kids biting the ends!)

eggs scrambled with cottage cheese and plain
yogurt

school and day-care snacks and lunches

send kids packing with healthy food they'll eat

Packing snacks and lunches for school or day care gives parents some element of control over their kids' diets—it's an opportunity for us to ensure that our children get some healthy food into their bodies each day. Children are usually hungry enough at lunchtime to eat what's in their lunch boxes (especially if we avoid the temptation to give them too much food). If food remains in the lunch box when they come home, you may be overpacking, or you may need to discuss some new lunch options with your kids.

Some parents tell me they feel like they are running out of ideas for what to pack for their kids' lunches. While some creativity is called for, many kids are happy eating virtually the same thing day after day. The routine may even be comforting, especially for younger children. But when the jelly sandwich goes uneaten or the turkey slices come back home a couple of days in a row, I ask the kids to suggest new items to pack.

Before school starts each fall, I make a list with Solomon and Celia of what they would like for lunches. I explain the need to have some dairy, fruit, protein, and grains each day, and they come up with some interesting options. Perhaps, before school starts, your kids can help you create a list of healthy foods that they will look forward to eating. Also, let them pick out their own lunch boxes and a variety of different-sized reusable food containers that they think are great.

Giving kids input into the process like this makes them more likely to eat what you pack. In fact, kids as young as six can start to help pack lunches themselves to save you time and keep them interested.

Like most things, packing lunches is easier if you plan ahead. Dedicate an area in the kitchen for nonperishable lunch fixings and a shelf in the fridge for perishable items, so you'll be able to grab and go in the morning. Save leftover cooked chicken, steak, or even pasta (or make extra) to cut into bite-sized pieces for lunches. Don't forget to include a dip, or use leftover packages of condiments from your last carry-out meal.

Freeze some lunch-box items, like yogurt in tubes and drinks in cartons. These will keep the other items cool during the day and will defrost by lunchtime just enough to provide a cold treat. Put a paper towel in the bottom of the lunch box to catch drips and minimize odors—it can double as a napkin if needed (yeah, right!).

Occasionally, just for fun, include a note, sticker, or word game in the lunch box as a special treat.

Pick at least one item from each category below for a nutritious, balanced lunch or snack to nourish and energize your kids during the day:

Grains

pasta mixed (when hot) with grated Parmesan cheese, butter, and a splash of milk

tortellini

soup (like alphabet or chicken noodle) in a thermos

rice and peas

cheese sandwiches

peeled cucumber and mayo or cheese sandwiches

peanut butter (or soy nut butter) and jelly, honey, banana, or apple sandwiches

pita bread with cream cheese or hummus

bagels with cream cheese or butter

tortilla wraps filled with cheese, peanut butter, or luncheon meats and secured with plastic wrap

dry cereal

popcorn

pretzels

tortilla chips and salsa

goldfish or cheese crackers

wheat crackers

healthy granola bars

Protein and Dairy

yogurt, in a cup or tube

cheese cubes or string cheese

black beans and corn kernels mixed together

peanuts, pine nuts, almonds, or other nuts

cottage cheese, plain or with pineapple or raisins mixed in

cheese and tomato sandwiches

tofu cubes marinated with teriyaki or soy sauce

tuna salad and crackers

sliced turkey, rolled and secured with plastic wrap

turkey and cheese roll-ups, secured with plastic wrap

hard-boiled eggs

garbanzo beans

sunflower or pumpkin seeds

cooked chicken or steak

homemade trail mix

Fruits and Vegetables

raisins, dried cranberries, or other dried fruit

apple slices for dipping in peanut butter or honey

applesauce

grapes, strawberries, pineapple chunks, cut melon, bananas, mango, blueberries, plums, peaches, sliced kiwi, orange wedges—or any other fruit you can think of

black olives (mild variety)

pickles

cherry tomatoes

baby carrots, peeled and sliced cucumber, red pepper strips, or steamed broccoli with dip (try hummus, peanut butter or ranch dressing)

celery filled with peanut butter or cream cheese

sliced apples and cheddar cheese

Recipe Index by Category

Super Scrambles: Dinner in 20 Minutes or Less

Best for Potlucks/Picnics

Great for the Grill

One-Pot/Pan Meals

Casseroles

index

Aviva Goldfarb is the author and publisher of *The Six O'Clock Scramble* (www.thescramble.com), a newsletter of easy, healthy, and delicious dinner recipes with a grocery list e-mailed to subscribers each week. A freelance writer and mother of two, she is also coauthor, with Lisa Flaxman, of the family cookbook *Peanut Butter Stew and Couscous, Too: Quick, Healthy, Delicious Meals that Grown-Ups and Kids Love.* Numerous TV and radio programs and magazines have featured her recipes and articles. She lives with her family in Chevy Chase, Maryland. When not huddling over pots in her test kitchen, she can be reached at aviva@thescramble.com.

To learn more about the Six O'Clock Scramble's easy dinner recipes, to send feedback on recipes, or suggest new recipes, or to subscribe to the Six O'Clock Scramble e-mail newsletter, please visit www.thescramble.com.

The Six O'Clock Scramble Online
Free 2-Week Trial Subscription

Six o'clock looms, and dinner has to be on the table pronto—the kids don't care if you've just come home from work exhausted and out of ideas or you spent the afternoon ferrying them from school to play date to tae kwon do practice. The Scramble to the rescue! Each week's worth of recipes is utterly organized, easy to prepare, and designed to please both adult tastes and finicky children's palates. Inventive, flavorful, and healthy are Aviva Goldfarb's watchwords. Her Scramble recipes include:

- Five flavorful and healthy tried-and-true dinner recipes e-mailed to you each week, with side dish suggestions

- Recipes that can be prepared in 30 minutes or less, perfect for busy parents

- Weekly menus so parents need only grocery-shop once a week

- Vegetarian main course options each week

- Meals that kids can help prepare

- Complete nutritional information for each recipe

"Creative, healthy, unprocessed and kid-friendly without being adult-alienating . . . a whole new kind of happy meal."
—*O, the Oprah Magazine*

Get Your FREE Two-Week Trial Subscription Today. You will receive two weekly newsletters with recipes for the week, plus grocery lists, to help you get dinner on the table each night.

www.thescramble.com/cookbook/freetrial

Offer good through 12/31/06.